PENGUIN BUSINESS
EFFECTIVE PEOPLE

T.V. Rao is one of the father figures of human resource development (HRD) in India. He is a teacher, author, researcher, social entrepreneur and institution builder. Born in rural India, he was brought up by his mother and grandparents. He received his BSc from Andhra Loyola College; BEd from Regional College of Education, Mysuru; MA in psychology from Osmania University; and PhD from Sardar Patel University. He is associated with pioneering the departments of psychology at the Andhra and Udaipur universities and the education and training department at the National Institute of Health Administration and Education, New Delhi.

Dr Rao joined Indian Institute of Management Ahmedabad in 1973 and taught until 1994 as a full-time professor and as a visiting/adjunct professor until 2014. He was also a member of the IIMA Society and was on the board of governors of the institute. He co-founded the National HRD Network and the Academy of HRD, both renowned institutions in the field. He has authored over sixty books, including *Managers Who Make a Difference*. He has received several awards such as the HR Professional of the Year 2019 from the Asia Pacific Federation of HRM, lifetime achievement award from the Indian Academy of Management and Ravi Matthai National Fellowship Award from the Association of Indian Management Schools. He is currently chairman, TVRLS, a research-based consulting services firm.

PRAISE FOR THE BOOK

'*Effective People* is an insightful exploration into the lives of individuals who have made a significant impact in their respective fields. Drawing from a wealth of personal experience and extensive research, Rao delves into what constitutes effectiveness and how various personalities harness their talents to influence and improve the lives of others. This book offers not just narratives, but a blueprint for readers to cultivate their own effectiveness. It's an essential read for anyone looking to understand the nuanced dynamics of impactful leadership and personal growth'—Marshall Goldsmith, *Thinkers50* #1 executive coach and *New York Times* bestselling author of *The Earned Life*, *Triggers* and *What Got You Here Won't Get You There*

'T.V. Rao introduces a simple but powerful performance metric for measuring effective people—anyone who lifts up the lives of others. *Effective People* presents compelling research and storytelling that leaders in any profession can read to identify and nurture talent'—Satya Nadella, CEO, Microsoft

'A valuable guide on how a person can expand his or her sphere of influence to make a positive and lasting contribution to society'—N.R. Narayana Murthy, co-founder, Infosys

'Prof. T.V. Rao, who taught me at IIMA, searches into the meaning of effectiveness with his usual diligence'—Harsha Bhogle, Indian cricket commentator and journalist

'A truly inspirational book . . . will benefit individuals who want to become effective and change their lives in a positive way'—K.K. Nohria, former chairman and MD, Crompton Greaves, and president, All India Management Association

'This is a must-read for those who want to be educational entrepreneurs'—Prof. M.R. Rao, former dean, Indian School of Business, and former director, Indian Institute of Management Bangalore

EFFECTIVE PEOPLE

Discover, Apply and Multiply Talent for IMPACT

T.V. RAO

PENGUIN
BUSINESS

An imprint of Penguin Random House

PENGUIN BUSINESS

USA | Canada | UK | Ireland | Australia
New Zealand | India | South Africa | China | Singapore

Penguin Business is an imprint of the Penguin Random House group of companies
whose addresses can be found at global.penguinrandomhouse.com

Published by Penguin Random House India Pvt. Ltd
4th Floor, Capital Tower 1, MG Road,
Gurugram 122 002, Haryana, India

Penguin
Random House
India

Published by Random House India in 2015
Published in Penguin Business by Penguin Random House India 2024

10 9 8 7 6 5 4 3 2 1

ISBN 9788184005837

Typeset in Adobe Garamond Pro by Manipal Digital Systems, Manipal
Printed at Repro India Limited

www.penguin.co.in

MIX
Paper from
responsible sources
FSC® C047271

This is a legitimate digitally printed version of the book and therefore might not
have certain extra finishing on the cover.

To the youth of India,
may they discover their talents and become more effective

Contents

Self-Assessment Tools in This Book   ix

Preface   xi

1. Introduction   1

2. Doctors   19

3. Film Actors   49

4. Civil Servants   69

5. Educational Entrepreneurs   99

6. Professors   129

7. Social Workers   157

8. Other Professions   185

9. Discover Your Inner Talent   221

10. Stretch Your Talent   238

11. Values Are the Core Drivers   266

12. Be Compassionate   287

13. Live with Purpose   302

14. Reach Out to Many   326

15. Take Initiative: Build Institutions   346

16. Be Integrative Not Divisive   371

Epilogue   389

Suggested Reading   393

Acknowledgements   395

Notes   397

Self-Assessment Tools in This Book

1. Self-Assessment Tool for Doctors:
   How Effective Are You, Doctor? 45–48
2. How Effective Are You as an Actor? 66–68
3. Assessing the Effectiveness of Civil Servants 95–98
4. Effective Educational Entrepreneurs 125–28
5. Self-Assessment Tool for Professors:
   How Effective Are You as a Professor? 154–56
6. Self-Assessment Tool: How Effective Are
   You as a Social Worker? 182–84
7. Checklist for Effective Scientists and Others in
   National Institutions of Research and Action 209–12
8. How Effective Are You as a Student? 217–18
9. How Effective Are You in Your First Job? 218–19
10. The Personal Effectiveness Questionnaire 260–63
11. How Value Driven Are You? 283–85
12. The Compassion Questionnaire: How
    Compassionate Are You? 300–01
13. Exercise: How to Cultivate Goal Setting and
    Purposeful Living 321–25

14. Self-Assessment Test on Personal Effectiveness   338–39
15. Some Questions for Prospective
    Institution Builders   369–70
16. Are You Divisive or Integrative? Assess Yourself   384–87

Preface

An Update on Effective Persons, Very Effective Persons and Super Effective Persons Covered in the Book

This book has made an impact since its publication nine years ago. The stories covered in this new edition were first discussed in recent seminars and conferences at colleges and universities and the author was encouraged to disseminate the same for the benefit of the younger generation, to help them become more effective from their early years. To encourage the youth to appreciate thinking effectively, a short section has been added in Chapter 8, on youth in education and early careers.

A quick review of some of the effective people covered in this book, a decade after it was first written, indicates that almost all of them continue on their journey to serve others. All the film actors continued their impact on society in many ways, including the films they chose to highlight social issues and also through their philanthropic activities. Their work is very much in the public domain. In the civil services for example, Inderjit Khanna has documented his professional journey—his book *Flashes Before My Eyes: The Civil Service and More*, with a foreword by Amitabh Bachchan, is being circulated among civil servants and those aspiring to be civil servants. Kaza Gandhi expanded his Truth Labs and is serving in different territories. Vinod Rai continues to share his insights, thoughts and experiences and impact people through his books such as *Not Just an Accountant* and *Not Just a Nightwatchman*. D.R. Mehta continues as a full-time honorary volunteer and under his leadership, the Bhagwan Mahaveer Viklang Sahayata Samiti (BMVSS) emerged as the largest organization for the handicapped in the world, providing artificial limbs and calipers and other aids and appliances benefiting more than 1 million people so far. E. Sreedharan, Kiran Bedi and others continue to share their expertise in various forums. Educational entrepreneurs like Manjula Shroff, Sridhar Rajagopalan, Sharat Chandra, Amitabh Shah and Dr Ashok Agarwal continue to expand their institutions, and some of their work has resulted in new initiatives given the opportunities available. K.K. Nair, after many years of impacting and building Ahmedabad Management Association (AMA), retired and offers his advisory services to NGOs and others. Mukesh Patel expanded the Japanese Studies Centre at AMA and has even developed a Japanese garden in Ahmedabad to spread good lessons from Japan to India. Among the professors, Anil Gupta, Jagdeep Chhokar, Trilochan Sastry, Shantha Sinha, Kiran Seth, P.N. Khadwalla, Kavil Ramachandran continue to impact society through their active work, publications and work on Indian social issues. Social workers Gagan Sethi, Jadav Payeng (who was honoured with Padma Shri and received an honorary doctorate from Assam Agricultural University and Kaziranga University for his contributions), Ayyappa Masagi (Water Literacy Foundation), Narayanan Krishnan (Akshaya Trust), Laxmi Gautam, Balaji Sampath, Virendra Singh and Shanthi Ranganathan have continued their social and philanthropic work impacting many people. Among doctors, Dr Devi D. Shetty expanded his work across the country, chairs the board of Indian Institute of Management Bangalore (IIMB) and frequently shares his thoughts on medical education. Doctors played a significant role during the pandemic. They are expanding their expertise and operations and moving ahead to use AI and other technological developments for healthcare. It looks from this account that once you are set to be an effective person, there is no looking back. *The author only cautions that moral values and ethics should never be compromised as they could bring down all the great work done by any effective person.*

How to Use This Book

For the purposes of this book, anyone who uses his or her talent to help others and makes a difference is an effective person. If a person employs her/his talent to reach out to a large number of people and takes this up as a mission, then we may call them not merely an effective person (EP) but a very effective person (VEP) or super effective person (SEP).

This book is an attempt to enhance the effectiveness of all people in different professions or areas of specialization, irrespective of their background. Effective people make an impact by their service offered through use of their talent (knowledge, attitudes, skills, etc.) and actions. Very effective people extend their impact through various mechanisms by impacting large numbers. It could be developing others to spread their talent or skills, or by writing books, using media and other sources. Super effective people are those who ensure continued impact even after they become older by establishing institutions that can carry on their work.

The following are some suggestions by the author on how to use this book:

The book has short, inspirational case studies followed by a discussion of qualities and activities that make the people effective in their respective context. This is followed by a series of self-assessment tools in the form of questions or prompts that will help you become more effective or move from an EP to VEP or SEP. These exercises could also form discussion agenda in team meetings, professional gatherings or classroom discussions.

For the medical profession: First, try to be a good doctor. This can be done by showing full devotion to your patients when they come to see you. Your focus should be on the patient and his/her issues and not on the fee you collect. You may standardize your fee or work out your earnings, as it is important equally to survive after having spent so much of your resources to complete your studies and equip yourself with professional skills. If you heal your patients and leave them healthy and happy, money will flow on its own. So strive to make yourself an effective doctor in any specialization you have decided. This is your first phase. In the second phase, you should use your skill set, knowledge and qualities to benefit a much larger number of people. This is made possible by inviting a large number of people to study with you (as interns, observers, etc.), teaching in a college, converting your knowledge into videos and films or writing manuals, books, etc. For example, Dr B.M. Hegde gives many talks, shares them on YouTube and remains popular and impactful. Sharing does not diminish your popularity but enhances it. If you have graduated from this stage, you are ready to be a super effective doctor. Here, you should explore the possibility of establishing an institution. The stories given in Chapter 2 of this book may provide insights for taking this step. Aim at establishing an institution that spreads your knowledge and wisdom and trains others even after you exit this world. Do this, not with an intention to increase your name or fame, but with an intention to make your talent, knowledge or wisdom available to others. Even if you don't build an institution, collaborating with others, writing books, making films, videos, etc. and making them available for a larger number of people makes you an SEP.

For civil service: If you are planning to enter civil service (any of the central or state services) this book is likely to give an idea of the lives of people who are totally service-driven. The stories may inspire you. Some of the civil servants I described in this book, like Inderjit Khanna and Vinod Rai and many others, have published impactful books in recent times. If you're already in civil service, this book may be just a beginning. There are many things you need to be clear about. If you are aspiring to be a civil servant or if you are already one and would like to be effective and leave a mark in society, you will get a list of qualities in the chapter on civil servants. The stories of over a dozen civil servants are covered in this chapter. There are many others from IAS, IPS and other services who have already made a mark and their stories are being written. Why not be one of them in future?

For social workers and CSR promoters: CSR and social service activities have become a backbone for developing communities, weaker sections and nations. All development agents will find the stories of different categories of social workers discussed in this book inspiring. Every big accomplishment that benefits a large number of people in society starts small and grows in time. How small initiatives grow into larger social change movements is presented in the various stories of social workers. Students of social work and other social sciences will find special meaning and can draw inspiration from these stories. All of them started small, and the qualities described in this book and self-tests may help you become a more effective social worker or CSR agent.

For industry: While this book does not focus on the corporate sector or other industries separately, in recent times education, health, science, CSR activities and even spiritual bodies have become like industry and have a lot of lessons to offer to businesses. For example, bodies like Isha Foundation, Chinmaya Mission Schools, other educational institutions and hospitals follow many principles of management and leadership and offer lessons for business. Businesses can be great promoters of education, health, social work, etc. Human resource leaders, finance managers, CEOs, CXOs, young and old employees can learn lot from the stories here and draw inspiration to be effective in their respective jobs. The corporate sector needs more effective people who are committed to their work and carry it out like effective employees. Use this to inspire managers in classrooms and draw lessons for effective management of people.

For students: This book is intended to communicate to students how great things get achieved with a small beginning. This will allow them to search for their inner talent from their school and college days and begin to cultivate their strengths. The qualities of effective people drawn from various professions is highlighted in this book. By reading, internalizing, introspecting and indulging in these activities, students can learn to use, cultivate and multiply their talent. The chapter on students and youth gives a lot of insights about how to start being an effective person from your early years, beginning with school, college or the start of your career.

For teachers: We have millions of teachers in our country. Everyone is in the business of preparing young minds for the future and building the nation. In reading these stories we expect young minds to cultivate hard work, perseverance, clarity of thought, compassion, honesty, integrity, etc. Teachers can become instruments for helping youth imbibe the values of being effective and very effective people. They may use the case studies given here to coach and inspire young people. They can also create their own case studies from their neighbourhood. They can get students to write stories and undertake projects that have been enriching learning experiences.

For educational entrepreneurs: Some unusual models of designing educational institutions are offered in this book. The educational entrepreneurs who have chosen a path less travelled have made a lot of difference in the lives of others. Read the chapter on teachers and education entrepreneurs to lay the foundation for success by applying your own innovative thinking. Convert your personal experiences, failures and inadequacies around to give birth to new innovative ventures and change the world.

For coaches: This book will help you understand the various facets and qualities of all good professionals. In your coaching session you may like to encourage your clients to read this book, read the stories of effective and very effective people and help them write their own stories to be more effective than before. This is intended to be good source book for any profession. I hope this encourages you to speak and write about more effective people in our own profession.

For any other profession: You will discover some qualities and behaviours that apply to people across all professions Chapter 8 onwards. Read one chapter a day through the week or one a week across a couple of months and start discussion groups about them. List the qualities you encounter, pick one quality every week and prepare action plans for developing them in yourself, your team or in your profession.

This book is recommended especially for aspiring youth and young professionals from medicine, civil services, education, management, social work, banking, social sciences and other professions as well as social and educational entrepreneurs.

The book gives many tests and self-assessment tools at the end. The objective of this book is to expand the scope of the impact you are making or are likely to make and to inspire you to set goals for being more effective than you are at present. This book defines effectiveness as self-discovery and application. First, you need to discover what you're good at. Once you have settled on your inner strengths and found people who are likely to benefit from your talent, the next step is to keep making that available to a larger number of people. You need to have various tools for such expansion and impact. It could grow from small to medium and big. It could be from a self-starter to a big employer.

Read each chapter or the chapter relevant to your profession from the first eight. Chapters 1 to 8 are relevant to all professions. Take the relevant self-tests, then read the next seven chapters (9 to 15). Take the self-tests where possible and reflect about your scores.

Identify your strengths and make an action plan for discovering your strengths. You may like to test yourself in activities you have not engaged in so far. Trying new things and seeing how much you enjoy them may be a good way of self-discovery. Once you discover what you're good at, the next step is to articulate your strong points and prepare action plans to multiply them. The next few chapters will give you insights on how to stretch yourself, how to disseminate and multiply your strengths, and finally how to periodically review and renew yourself to transform into an effective, very effective and super effective person.

Best wishes for making yourself a great contributor to society.

T.V. Rao

Stories Covered Prominently in This Book

Doctors
Mukesh Chawla, Ramakant Panda, Deepak Chopra, Devi Prasad Shetty, Sudhanshu Bhattacharya, Ashok Raj Gopal, M.G. Bhat, M.C. Modi, Naresh Trehan, Pratap Reddy.

Film Actors
Anupam Kher, Kangana Ranaut, Amitabh Bachchan, Aamir Khan, Shah Rukh Khan.

Civil Servants
Inderjit Khanna, Anil Bordia, N. Vittal, E. Sreedharan, Kiran Bedi, K.P. Ch. Gandhi, J. Jayaprakash Narayan, D.J. Padyan, Abhayanand, B.N. Yugandhar, K.R. Venugopal.

Educational Entrepreneurs
Kiran Bir Sethi, Manjula Shroff, K.K. Nair, Sridhar Rajagopalan, Sharat Chandra, Ashok Agarwal, Amitabh Shah, Mukesh Patel.

Professors
Samuel Paul, Anil Gupta, Shanta Sinha, Kiran Seth, P.N. Khadwalla, Kavil Ramachandran, M.S. Pillai, Abdul Kalam, C.K. Prahalad, Vijay Govindarajan.

Social Workers
Shanti Ranganathan, Gagan Sethi, Thomas Raja, Ayyappa Masagi, Narayanan Krishnan, Laxmi Gautam, Balaji Sampath, Uttam Teron, Rajani Paranjape, Virendra Singh.

Bankers, Scientists and Nation Builders
R.K. Talwar, K.V. Kamath, Anil Khandelwal, Homi Bhabha, Salim Ali, Verghese Kurien, C.N.R. Rao, Abdul Kalam.

Youth

Shreyas Harish, Divya Raghavendra Rao, Akarsh Sharma.

Others

Udai Pareek, Ravi Matthai, Mukesh Patel, G.V. Prasad, Rahul Dravid, Sarath Babu, Prayag Mehta, Mother Teresa, Mahatma Gandhi, Ela Bhatt, Bhushan Punani, A. Mutuganathan, G. Venkataswamy, Vijay Mahajan, Sanjiv Bikhchandani, Dilip Banerjee, Renu Singh, Narayan Murthy, Kiran Mazumdar-Shaw, Aruna Roy, Renu Singh (Samadhan), Ramoji Rao, K. Balachander, S.P. Balasubramanyam, Mallika Sarabhai, Kandaswamy Bharatan, Rajinikanth and many more from the field of sports, music and dance.

1 Introduction

Rev. Fr Douglas Gordon was the principal of Andhra Loyola College, Vijayawada, in the late fifties and early sixties. I graduated from the college (1961–65) with mathematics, physics and chemistry as my subjects. A tall and handsome priest of Irish origin, Fr Gordon had a very striking and pious personality. For some reason he was very fond of me—maybe it was because he knew I was being brought up by my mother and grandparents (my father ran away, along with his riches, even before I was born). Or maybe he thought I was too young to be in college—I was only fourteen when I joined the college to do my Pre-university course and eighteen when I graduated. Even though a year and a half was added to my registered age (a common practice in those days), I am sure he saw through that. Fr Gordon did not speak Telugu and I always had difficulty following his accented English but I had no trouble recognizing his affection. I graduated with decent marks, a second class, and wanted to do my master's in chemistry. As soon as the results were out, he sent me a postcard asking me to see him. I travelled sixteen kilometres from my village to meet my principal. I landed at his place and was shown details of an announcement from the Regional College of Education, Mysore (RCEM) for a one-year BEd programme with a stipend of Rs 75 a month. This programme was started in collaboration with the Ohio

State University by the *National Council of Educational Research and Training* (NCERT). Fr Gordon said, 'You apply for this and if you get admission, study for a year. I will appoint you as a demonstrator in the chemistry laboratory when you return having completed the programme and while you are here you can apply for an MSc in chemistry as you are too young to do MSc now.' I filled in the application and was later called for selection tests and an interview and got admitted in RCEM. I was again the youngest of the lot as almost all the rest of them who came there were already working as teachers and some of them were postgraduates.

Dr Prafullachandra N. Dave is a professor who came to RCEM that year. He had recently returned from St. Louis, USA, after studying there for a few years. We had many teachers who were educated abroad. Dr Dave taught us the paper on psychological foundations of education. He would get rats into the class and teach us how these animals could search and find food in a maze. He would also give us many psychological tests. I used to listen attentively and learn a lot and would constantly top in the psychology class. Once another professor, Dandapani, gave a test to our class and was amazed at my performance in that subject. I finished my one-year BEd and topped the RCEM science stream. When the results were declared I went to the college to collect my mark sheet and met Dr Dave. He asked me about my plans. I told him that there were already people from my neighbouring village coming to ask if I would teach in their school but that I would prefer to join Loyola College as a demonstrator in chemistry and apply for an MSc a year later. Dr Dave said that I should not be wasting my time and life in chemistry as I had a special aptitude for psychology. He suggested that I do my master's in psychology. In those days you needed to be a graduate in psychology even to apply for an MA in that subject. I told Dr Dave that no one would take me for an

MA because I didn't have a bachelor's degree in psychology. Dr Dave said he knew a psychology professor at Osmania University in Hyderabad and as RCEM is an experimental college with an unusual syllabus he might agree to treat it as an equivalent to a BA in psychology. He wrote a personal letter and told me to give it to the professor in Hyderabad.

Dr E.G. Parameswaran, EGP, a Tamilian, was then heading the department of psychology in Osmania University. He was a student of the famous psychologist G.D. Boaz from Madras and was specially brought in to start the psychology department. This department in those days functioned separately from the philosophy department. EGP looked more like a college student than a head of department. He admitted me without hesitation after reading Dr Dave's letter. In the psychology department we were like a family and often visited EGP at his home, played with his children and with the children of other professors like Goverdhan Reddy, Tara Manohar Rao and Yadgiri Reddy. Shalini Bhogle, popular sports commentator Harsha Bhogle's mother, was our senior at the university. I topped the university and even created a new record in those days. EGP was a great teacher who continues to inspire. Back then, he was offered positions by the Indian Institute of Management (IIM) Ahmedabad and Calcutta but he preferred to stay in Osmania and teach. He felt the IIMs were too commercial and not meant for good teachers who liked to get closely involved in their students' lives. He encouraged me to apply for a PhD in the US and particularly to work with Dr Udai Pareek who was at that time in the University of North Carolina. While I was corresponding with Dr Pareek and others to try for an admission in the US, the Andhra University (AU) was on the verge of opening a department of psychology and parapsychology and was looking for lecturers. EGP suggested that I join AU to develop the department until I got a PhD admission; he wrote a letter of recommendation to Dr Ramakrishna Rao, RKR, who was heading psychology in AU at that time.

RKR offered me an assistant lectureship on an ad hoc basis without hesitation and said that he would get it regularized once the appointments were announced. He decided to pay me from his parapsychology fund until I was regularized. Parapsychology dealt with paranormal phenomena like telepathy and clairvoyance. RKR was the president of the International Parapsychological Association and was working very closely with the famous parapsychologist, J.B. Rhine. I registered for my PhD to work on dreams at AU with RKR as my guide. RKR even got special equipment shipped in from Germany to study dreams using tachistoscopic exposure of certain stimuli. He gave me all the freedom to design and start psychology MA courses in AU. Within six months of joining AU I came to know that Dr Udai Pareek was returning to India to work in Delhi. I decided to go to Delhi and work with Dr Pareek as I had my share of discomfort with parapsychology in which AU was beginning to specialize. Only a few months later I joined Dr Pareek at the National Institute of Health Administration and Education (NIHAE) in Delhi to work on an Indian Council of Medical Research (ICMR) project on the impact of teacher behaviour on student mental health.

Dr Udai Pareek, a social scientist, institution builder, author, researcher and a great human being turned, in later years, into a friend, philosopher and guide. A few months after he recruited me to work with him as an assistant research officer, we found that NIHAE was planning to recruit an assistant professor of education and training—someone with teaching experience of three years and a BEd degree. I did not qualify in terms of experience, but Dr Pareek thought that I am well suited for the post. Perhaps he was impressed with my hard work or the unusual combination of BSc, BEd and MA psychology. The selection committee of the ministry of health at that time was chaired by the celebrated Dr V. Ramalingaswamy. Dr Pareek drove to his residence and handed over my biodata enabling me to be considered as a contact candidate—a provision available in those days for appointments in government for those who did not exactly meet criteria but were considered suitable by the selection committee. I was selected and appointed as assistant professor of education and training in 1969 by NIHAE. Udai took me to co-author some of the books he was writing and initiated me into a lot of activities he had undertaken. We partnered on many books and worked together in Delhi, Udaipur and Ahmedabad, Indonesia and back in Jaipur as long as he lived until 2010.

Ravi Matthai, whom I met in 1973—a year after he stepped down as director of IIMA—had shown interest in wanting to work with education and other sectors to professionalize their management. I was writing a book along with Udai on 'A Status Study of Behavioural Science Research in Population' to be published by Tata McGraw-Hill and sponsored by the Family Planning Foundation (of the Tatas). Udai joined IIMA as a professor in early 1972 and I joined him in Ahmedabad to complete the book in the summer of 1973. On Udai's suggestion, I expressed my interest in joining IIMA as they were planning to start work in education systems with Ravi Matthai as the focal point. Ninety per cent of the faculty at IIMA at that time had PhDs from abroad. I did my PhD from Sardar Patel University for which I worked in NIHAE as a part-time student. I didn't think IIMA would be interested in an Indian PhD. I met Ravi, and Samuel Paul and Dwijendra Tripati, Director and Dean respectively of IIMA at that time. Our discussion largely concerned my doctoral thesis which was on medical education. I jokingly say in my thesis that I have proved that medical colleges spoil medical students. I still remember the intense discussion we had on college climate and how it affects student values. I suppose it was Ravi Matthai and Samuel Paul who took the decision to take me in. My work with Ravi and Udai has provided me very rich experiences and I feel that they have made a major contribution as mentors in many of my accomplishments. I was offered a place in 1973 and in December that year began my long sojourn with IIMA.

As far as I am concerned, IIMA has been a great platform to learn, write, teach, research, manage, influence and also earn. We started the first Human Resources Development (HRD) department in 1974–75 in Larsen & Toubro (L&T) and created history in HRD. This was the result of a consulting project undertaken through IIMA. We started many courses and made HRD popular. We started a course in laboratory in entrepreneurship and laid a path for subsequent developments of entrepreneurs in IIMA. I started the National HRD Network, a successful professional body across the world, in 1985 and invented a methodology for developing leaders which became popular as 360 Degree Feedback in the US. I mention some of these accomplishments in a subsequent chapter.

Now the conundrum is—in this rich life that I have led and among the various remarkable people that I have known—who is an effective person? As far as I am concerned all the characters I have described: Fr D. Gordon, Dr Dave, Dr EGP, Dr RKR, Dr Udai Pareek, Dr Paul and Ravi Matthai are all effective people as each one of them made a difference in my life. So I would like to propose a definition: 'Those who make a difference in the lives of others are effective people.' By this definition, any, and every one of us who makes a difference in lifting up the lives of others may be an effective person. Then the question arises—how many among us are effective people? There may be many, how does it matter? Do we lose our speciality if there are many?

Points in Life

Consider the line below:

A_____B

How many parts is the line above divided into in the line below?

A_____P_____B

Normally our response is two—AP and PB. I had a classmate in my BEd days; he would pose this problem and say, 'Your answer is wrong. It is divided into three parts—AP, P itself and PB.' Many of us don't realize the significance of 'P', the point. Life is full of such points. Each point gives a different direction in life. Fr Gordon calling me for the RCEM application; Dr Dave's letter to EGP; EGP admitting me by going out of his way to reinterpret the rules; RKR procuring for me the special equipment to work on my PhD; EGP putting me in touch with Udai Pareek; Udai Pareek driving down to meet Dr Ramalingaswamy to recommend me as a contact candidate; Samuel Paul agreeing to interview me; Ravi Matthai starting the education group and getting me involved; Udai Pareek asking me to join him for the L&T project; and so on are all points in my life that changed the direction of the line. If a point helps you to discover or apply yourself further—or benefits you or others—then the point is a significant point and the person who has created that point is an agent of change, consciously or unconsciously. There are some people who are constantly and consistently fostering change in the lives of others; so much so that it often seems as though they live for the benefit of others. There are many around us and we need to recognize them.

They are effective people. Fr Gordon continued to help many people who came in touch with him until he died in the late nineties. EGP continued to work with students of Osmania University and later with the Academy of HRD and many other institutions he was associated with until he died a few years ago. Dr Dave retired as a professor and continued to guide people until he died a few years ago. Same with Udai Pareek and Ravi Matthai. Samuel Paul set up an institute for public affairs and established a scorecard methodology.

The points that they make are not limited to one person's life but many lives. These are undoubtedly effective people.

Why are they not well known? It is not necessary for all effective people to be famous. There are many people who make a difference in the lives of others but only those directly affected by their goodwill remember them. It is not uncommon for some of them to go unnoticed altogether. How many of the people who made a difference in our lives get remembered or acknowledged?

Who Is an Effective Person?

My search for effective people began with a definition of an effective person. I have defined an effective person as follows:

'Anyone who discovers inner talent, uses it to make a difference in the lives of other people in a way that benefits them can be considered an effective person. We are all born talented and in different settings. However, some master their circumstances and manage them through their inner talent. These people may be teachers, social workers, doctors, nurses, lawyers, entrepreneurs, civil servants, development workers, businessmen, managers, chartered accountants, scientists, actors, or self-employed, etc.'

This book attempts to draw lessons from the lives of such effective people from various fields.

I started my search three years ago when I signed a contract with Random House to write this book. I have written a sizeable number of specialized and functional books—whether on health management for doctors, or on education managers, institution builders, entrepreneurs and those wanting to be entrepreneurs, managers, HR professionals, trainers, NGOs and so on. The closest I have come to writing a general book is my last one for IIMA, and the first in the IIMA business series—*Managers Who Make a Difference*. IIMA wanted me to write such a book for those who could not afford to go through IIMA courses. I have also written one for line managers when I documented the life stories of 100 managers in action based on their 360 Feedback scores.

Naturally when I got down to writing this book, I wanted to do a search for the so-called effective people. I have done the following in this pursuit:

- Started discussions on the concept of effective people with my professional friends and colleagues;
- Put up announcements on social media, like Twitter, Facebook, LinkedIn and the like;
- Put summer trainees on the job to list out and make case studies of effective people;
- Used my own experiences to identify those whom I considered effective people;
- Considered the names of effective people from the lists on the net (Google, Wikipedia, etc.) from various professions;
- Took the help of friends and publishers;
- Searched literature from books like those written by Rashmi Bansal, Srinivas Pandit, Professor S.N. Chary, Deenanath Harapanahalli, Centre for Social Initiative and Management (CSIM), etc. and reviewed various documents.

None of these yielded satisfactory results. I found that most people are indifferent to the concept of effective people. I think the reason is that most Indians don't want to acknowledge anyone else other than themselves as an effective person.

Recently a business magazine called *Business Manager* approached me for my help to bring out an annual issue of the magazine devoted to 'Legends in HR and OD'. The editor came and discussed the issue with me. I encouraged the idea to feature the legends in HR. I put forward the following criteria:

- The person should be a senior citizen above the age of sixty (although I don't believe age has anything to do with it. I was, to my embarrassment, given the distinction of 'legend' when I was about forty-six);
- The person should be an academic, preferably with a PhD;
- Should have written one or more books;
- Should have academic papers; and
- Should have influenced others through books, articles and lectures.

I helped the editor identify a few. However, I wondered if I was biased and decided to cast the net wider. I called a few of my friends including those whose names I had given as recommendations. The response I got was appalling. Hardly any of them mentioned more than a couple of names; while without any help I could give twenty such names in a few minutes to the editor. I wonder why Indians are not forthcoming in acknowledging the greatness of others. There seems to be a great hesitation in acknowledging the contributions of the deserving. Perhaps it arises out of one's own insecurities and also perhaps as a result of low self-respect. If we don't respect ourselves we can't respect others. For this book, when I failed to find enough suggestions, I decided to bank on my own experiences.

I started my career in 1968. In my time, I have worked in fifteen institutions for short or long periods of time in various capacities—the longest being IIMA. Others include: Andhra University; NIHAE; University of Udaipur; XLRI; Harvard University; East-West Center, Honolulu; Institute of Development Studies, Sussex; PUSDIKLAT, Indonesia; MARA Institute of Technology, etc. I surveyed over fifteen other institutions—engineering colleges, polytechnics, the effectiveness of a project called 'IMPACT' by the Swiss Agency for Development and Cooperation; visited at least a dozen other institutions like the other IIMs, NIEPA, IIHMR, NID, EDI, PDPU, etc. and evaluated several of them; worked with about 300 organizations for short-term to long-term assignments; worked with international agencies like UNESCO, FAO, USAID, Commonwealth Secretariat, EZE Germany, UNIDO, UNFPA, UNESCO, ICOMP; worked for various durations as a consultant in more than ten countries (Thailand, Malaysia, Indonesia, Philippines, Sri Lanka, Oman, Nigeria, Egypt, UK, Canada, USA, Mexico, Bangladesh) besides India with different corporations; and taught over several thousands of executives at IIMA and later at T.V. Rao Learning Systems (TVRLS); profiled and interacted with another 10,000 or more top-level managers through 360 Degree Feedback; and networked with several thousands of HR staff for NHRDN and AHRD. I had to work with doctors starting with NIHAE and ending with the World Bank project on population management in Uttar Pradesh (1974–76); lawyers when my house was illegally taken away by goons; with civil servants. I worked closely with the ministry of education and later with the HRD and I&B ministry; the academy at Mussouri (IAS), Shimla (audit) and Nagpur (NADT) and Hyderabad (NPA); the Administrative Reforms Commission. I also worked in the banking sector for the Khandelwal committee report. Thus, drawing on my own rich experience of the last fifty years, I felt confident that I should be able to identify who fitted into the criteria for an effective person that I had stated earlier.

In the civil services, I had the privilege of working with education devotee Anil Bordia who was subsequently honoured with a Padma Bhushan, Inderjit Khanna who always maintained the importance of value-based civil service, N. Vittal who is known for his innovative practices and professionalism in turning around various organizations, and in recent times with D.J. Pandian who had the courage to introduce incentive systems in government. These are excellent examples of effective people. I had my own classmate and friend Dr Kaza Gandhi who established Truth Labs and Mr Ramana Murthy, IPS, who made sure justice was served when some people fraudulently tried to take away my house in Hyderabad. Then there's a good friend, Nityanandam, an IPS officer and former home commissioner of Gujarat, who set up a consultancy firm on security services after his retirement, and lives in an ordinary flat like any other citizen, and Jayanthi Ravi who went through my 360 Degree Feedback and is known for her innovations and change.

Among the lawyers, I found there are many who take up cudgels for the goons and also those who charge a high fee to protect the right people. But there are some like my own classmate who retired as a high court judge and is known to be a stickler for truth—Munnangi Venkateswara Reddy.

Among professors, there is no dearth of contenders. At IIMA itself I have had the privilege of working with and observing over 100 professors and many more staff members. Add to this those from institutions like XLRI, NIEPA, IIHMR, IIMK, etc. which I have been associated with, and I have a large sample of teachers. Besides this, my work with Lawrence School, Sanawar, Doon School, Dehra Doon and the Indian Public Schools Conference have put me in touch with many educationists. The EZE project of renewal in NGOs has also put me in touch with several of these organizations and I was fortunate to visit in 1975 itself the Social Work and Research Centre (SWRC) at Tilonia where Bunker Roy and Aruna Roy were working. Being the president of the Indian Society for Applied Behavioural Science (ISABS) has put me in touch with many other people trying to be effective by improving their personal and interpersonal processes. Teaching as a professor and performing various administrative roles at IIMA and as chairman of the postgraduate programme in management, as well as doctoral programmes has helped me to know more intimately students who have later become significant managers and leaders in society. For managers, my entire tenure at IIMA and subsequently my work on 360 with TVRLS has given me thousands of contacts. My book *100 Managers in Action* is an outcome of this. In addition, I have visited and interacted with many popular figures and award winners like Shantha Sinha, Aruna Roy, Dr Verghese Kurien, Dr Amrita Patel, Dr Anil Gupta, C.K. Prahalad, Narayana Murthy, Suresh Krishna, K.K. Nohria and so on.

With all this background I felt fully equipped to be selective in choosing and analysing effective people. In addition, being a thinking and application-oriented psychologist, I felt confident to be in a position to write about effective people. *My aim is to write a book that can help many more people to become effective.* I hope the stories, analysis and the suggestions to cultivate the qualities will help the reader to participate in the journey of being their most effective selves.

I began to seek answers to questions like the following:

- Who is an effective doctor, lawyer or CA?
- Who is an effective manager?
- Who is an effective CEO?
- Who is an effective social worker?

- Who is an effective actor?
- Who is an effective teacher?
- Are Padma awardees effective people?
- Are you an effective person? Am I an effective person?
- Who is an effective businessman?
- To what extent is the fee or remuneration received for service offered an indicator of effectiveness (doctors, consultants, actors, lawyers, etc.)
- What is the role of contributions made by an individual to intellectual capital building as an indicator of effectiveness?

I decided to expand the scope of this book by including anyone who makes a difference in the lives of others as an effective person. Effective people can come from any profession or background. They could be farmers, labourers, chaiwallahs, rickshaw pullers, shopkeepers and any ordinary citizen. However, if I start including all categories it will extend to millions and I have to adhere to the limit of space. I decided to curtail my search to those categories on which something is yet to be written. I came to the conclusion from my search that the following categories of people make a significant difference in the lives of others and hence should be covered:

- Doctors
- Actors
- Professors
- Educationists
- Social Workers
- Civil Servants

(I wanted to include lawyers and chartered accountants but my contacts are limited and my search has yielded only a few and some of them are covered as social workers or reformers.)

My effort was to search and document their stories and find out answers to the questions raised here: Their work and impact, background or life history where relevant, their philosophy and characteristics that got them to be effective, if their effectiveness can be further quantified, and the lessons that can be learnt from them. Many of these were interviewed by the author and in a few cases by summer trainees from Xavier University (XIMB).

We found that while some of the interviewees were very eager to respond to our questions, others preferred to give their time to some activity not related to those who write books.

How to Use this Book

For the purposes of this book 'anyone who uses his or her talent to help others and makes a difference is an effective person'. The only criterion is that the other person should feel that the candidate made a difference in their life and contributed to the same. It is not enough for a candidate to claim how many they helped. For example, by nature all doctors who are doing their job well are effective people. Any person who does their duty well by virtue of their preparation can be called an effective person. Because all professions are meant to help others—at least the professions we have listed above.

Any person in a helping profession carrying out their job or professional work *competently* using the competencies and *following the value systems of the profession* can be considered an effective person (EP). I assume that all doctors, professors, civil servants, social workers, educationists and actors are in helping professions. Even acting as a profession is meant to provide education, entertainment and preservation of values and culture. Service becomes the first indicator, especially service provided by doing one's job competently with a motive to serve. When money overtakes service, or when professional values are violated, then the person can't be considered effective by our definition. To an extent, the money earned or wealth accumulated is an indicator of the number of people served while adhering to professional values and doing service; the effectiveness may be considered high if the earning is more.

Some people may try to help a large number of people and take up helping as their profession and life goal. If a person extends their talent to reach out to a large number of people and *takes this up as a mission* then we may call them not merely an effective person (EP) but a very effective person (VEP).

Some people have taken the extension of their talent and service to others through their profession or area of specialization as a mission and *build institutions*. The institutions they build provide continued and lasting service to others. Through these institutions, not only do *they devote their life* to the service, *they extend their talent and make it available beyond their lifetime* as well. *Thus those who build other people and lasting institutions to continue their work are super effective persons (SEP).* Super effective people transcend their time and life through building systems, processes and institutions that spread their message beyond their life and their work. They institutionalize their service, have super-ordinate goals and hence can be called as super effective people.

So we have three levels of effective people: EPs, VEPs and SEPs. I would have liked to call VEP as HEP (highly effective people) but I will respect the brand name established by Stephen M. Covey.

Any doctor or professor or civil servant who does their job well and serves people and makes a difference in their lives is an effective doctor, professor, civil servant, etc. When a doctor, professor or civil servant takes up a mission approach and tries to extend the service to make a difference to a large number of people beyond the call of their role or duty, then the person is very effective.

All these people use their talent and make it available to others and make a difference in their lives.

If you do it just as a part of the minimum requirements of your profession then you are an EP. All the scores of managers, doctors, engineers, CAs, lawyers and social workers who do their job well and stay true to their profession following the values are all EPs. They do their jobs successfully and do not violate the value code of the profession. Violation of values definitely takes the person out of this list. Who decide this, you ask? First the person themselves, then the profession and the public at large.

At the onset this book presents the stories of select people from each of the above categories and attempts to build common characters between the EPs, VEPs and SEPs.

The first seven chapters deal with stories from each profession and the next eight chapters pertain to the qualities of the three categories of effective people and how they can be cultivated to move from one level of effectiveness to another.

Our search and analysis have indicated eight sets of qualities that are necessary and characterize EPs, VEPs and SEPs. The following chapters (9 to 16) give details. While the first five chapters (9 to 13) are essential for EPs, VEPs and SEPs, the next three deal with how one can move from being an EP to a VEP and finally to a SEP.

They think *differently*: They explore and discover their inner talent. They aim at serving people other than themselves (Chapter 9).

They *stretch their talent* by creating new circumstances and settings for themselves. They discover more and become self-aware and self-managing (Chapter 10).

They are value driven. They *live their values* and promote them among others. Character, integrity and honesty are their core values (Chapter 11).

They are *compassionate*. They exhibit and cultivate empathy (Chapter 12).

They have long-term goals and *live with purpose* or work with a mission (Chapter 13).

They *reach out to many* (Chapter 14).

They take *initiative and build institutions*—one or many (Chapter 15).

They are nation builders: They *integrate and do not divide* (Chapter 16).

2 Doctors

Dr Mukesh Chawla, MD, FRCP (UK), DNB had a clinic in Bandra, Mumbai. He was a gastroenterologist. I was paying him a friendly visit some time in the year 2001. It was about 6.45 p.m. He asked me to wait, pointing me to the sofa outside the examination room of his clinic. He was seeing a patient and at 7.30 p.m. the patient left and I thought Dr Chawla would call me in. He came out, apologized and said he had another couple of patients to see before he could be with me. As he called the next person in I started to grow impatient. It was 8.15 p.m. when another patient was summoned in. It was only at 9 p.m. that he finally came out—very apologetic about the delay. I was surprised to observe him take so much time with each patient; I was accustomed to visiting doctors who would spend five minutes, or less, on a patient. Brushing aside my disappointment at having had to wait for so long, I instead thought about his patients and how lucky they were! I heard many more stories about Dr Mukesh Chawla from his patients and fellow doctors fifteen years later, when he died at a young age of a genetic heart ailment in June 2015.

The Medical Council of India (MCI) prescribes a code of ethics for all doctors. The code includes the following:

1. A physician shall uphold the dignity and honour of his profession.

2. The prime object of the medical profession is to render service to humanity; reward or financial gain is a subordinate consideration.

3. Whosoever chooses his profession, assumes the obligation to conduct himself in accordance with its ideals.

4. A physician should be an upright man, instructed in the art of healings. He shall keep himself pure in character and be diligent in caring for the sick; he should be modest, sober, patient, prompt in discharging his duty without anxiety; conducting himself with propriety in his profession and in all the actions of his life.

5. The physician, engaged in the practice of medicine shall give priority to the interests of patients. The personal financial interests of a physician should not conflict with the medical interests of patients.

6. Utmost punctuality should be observed by a physician in making themselves available for consultations.

In recent times the medical council has also indicated that accepting gifts and incentives from pharmaceutical companies is against the code of ethics.

While a good number of doctors follow the code or at least attempt to do so, it is difficult to ascertain whether a doctor gives sufficient time to a patient or not. Giving sufficient time to each patient is an important yardstick for effectiveness of doctors. Some patients complain that their doctor gives the same medicine to all patients irrespective of their ailment. The perception may exist because some of the doctors don't communicate adequately about the medicines prescribed while others go to great lengths to mention the drug being given and the side effects if any, etc.

Some of the qualities ascribed to Dr Mukesh by his fellow doctors and patients after he died recently in Pune are:

- 'He is extremely meticulous in case history documentation and follow up. If he has done the case history—we know it will be thorough!'
- 'He spends a lot of time with patients till their queries have been fully addressed or history is understood. Also very patient with them.'
- 'Goes beyond his specialization. Acts not just as the gastroenterologist but also a mini psychiatrist or family/ personal counsellor.'
- 'Connects with patients and other colleagues/doctors or technical staff as a human/friend/guide.'
- 'Actively follows up on personal actions or discussions he had with them and pushes them to act. Is persuasive.'
- 'Hands-on in terms of training staff, in choosing the right equipment/instruments for the department.'

Dr Mukesh set up the gastro department in Guru Nanak Hospital, Bandra, in 1996, and Fortis, Mulund, in 2002 (when it was Wockhardt hospitals), in Mumbai from scratch including a well-trained and motivated support team that has been sustained since. He showed active leadership in setting up a first of its kind medical consultants' association in Guru Nanak Hospital and was willing to take up posts of responsibility. He enjoyed giving technical lectures at gastroenterology conferences. He was on the lookout to acquire fresh knowledge and learning in allied fields like medicine and health care.

Some other observations from doctors and patients:

- 'Active and trustworthy team member who accepted people openly once convinced of being on the same wavelength and clinical thoroughness.'
- 'Highly ethical, absolutely not into any kind of cut practice (getting a referral fee from other doctors)—giving or

receiving; willing to lose patients or money as long as he did not have to resort to cuts.'

- 'Helpful to all those who reached out to him—gave freely of himself without expecting anything in return. Treated underprivileged people free of charge many a times.'
- 'Kind to staff; presented support staff with sweets on every Diwali and Christmas without fail.'
- 'Kind and approachable at all times. Even on holidays and outside work timings he always answered his mobile and called back patients or doctors.'
- 'If a doctor referred some patient to him, he would call back after seeing the patient to update the doctor concerned with his diagnosis and treatment approach. Kept the doctor in the loop—something most others forget to do.'
- 'Sought professional excellence and was intolerant of substandard work, equipment or processes. Dutiful and very conscientious at all times—did not spare any effort.'
- 'Organized and structured. Lots of daily checklists even on personal matters or personal phone calls.'
- 'An embodiment of loving kindness.'

These comments of fellow medical practitioners, patients and staff form a kind of 360 Degree Feedback.

By all standards, of MCI or otherwise, Dr Mukesh is an effective doctor. He used his talent for others, treated his patients well and had all the qualities of a good doctor.

Effective and Famous Doctors in India

Generally, an effective doctor would be somebody who can successfully cure a patient. However, at times, even if a doctor is unsuccessful in curing a disease fully, there are other standards which determine a doctor's effectiveness: the way the doctor attends, explains and communicates to the patient. All efficient doctors may not be effective. Effectiveness is normally associated with the result or cure and at times administering the cure within a short period. While we all know that doctors are fallible human beings, some great doctors are equated with God because of their work and ethics. Mukesh was one such doctor—devoted to his profession while maintaining all ethical standards of the job. I know of a dentist who never spends more than a couple of minutes with each patient. When you visit such doctors, you do not return satisfied. There's another dentist who takes on two to three patients at a time, gets them to sit on separate dental chairs and attends to all three by rotation. Serving two to three patients at a time makes the patient feel uncomfortable and neglected and they perceive the doctor as business-minded rather than a caring person. Then there is one dentist whose charges are so exorbitantly high that people feel that he is charging them for his next vacation abroad but people go to him as he is considered very effective.

The MCI does not prescribe what fee doctors should charge and, in fact, encourages doctors to charge as they deem fit. Some doctors start charging high fees as they become effective and famous, which is quite okay, but some others charge exorbitant rates to be perceived as effective. It does not always work.

There are 9.36 lakh doctors in India according to a survey conducted at the end of 2014. There are 7,56,937 registered midwives and 16,73,338 nurses. India has six doctors and thirteen nurses, adding to a total of nineteen health workers for every 10,000 people as against the twenty-five per 10,000 prescribed by the WHO.[1]

Regarded as a life-giver rather than a life-saver job, the profession of a doctor enjoys the utmost respect and recognition in all countries across the globe. In my search for effective doctors in India, I have come across the following names repeatedly mentioned by different sources.

Dr Ramakant Panda is the vice chairman, managing director and chief consultant for cardiovascular thoracic surgery in the Asian Heart Institute, Mumbai. Dr Panda, who has performed over *18,000 cardiac surgeries* including over *1000 redo bypass surgeries and over 3000 high-risk surgeries,* is considered to be the best heart surgeon in India. He has specialized in coronary artery bypass grafting using only arterial grafts, beating heart surgery, redo bypass surgery, valve repair and complex aneurysms. He is one of the safest heart surgeons in the world with a 99.6 per cent success rate in bypass surgery. Dr Panda is credited and recognized among his peers as the first in the country to introduce the concept of 'Total Arterial Revascularization', as well as being one of the pioneers of 'off-pump' bypass surgery, redo bypass surgery and high-risk surgery. Under his leadership, the Asian Heart Institute has established itself as the best heart hospital in India in 2011 and 2012, as well as the highest accredited hospital with JCI, ISO and NIAHO accreditations. He has been honoured with the Padma Bhushan and has also been conferred with the degree of doctorate in science (Honorius Causa) from Utkal University, Orissa. He was awarded the prestigious Rashtriya Samman for being one of the highest taxpayers during the assessment years 1994–95 to 1998–99 by the Central Board of Taxes, Government of India. He set up the Sarla Madan Charitable Trust in Orissa, the Asian Heart Charitable Trust and has helped hundreds of economically handicapped patients.[2]

Doctors Listed in Another Website Include the Following:[3]

Deepak Chopra is a renowned global personality who was born in India and later on emigrated to America. Apart from being a physician, he writes extensively on Ayurveda and spirituality.

He is also the founder of the Chopra Foundation and is a public speaker. He has penned more than fifty-seven books.

Dr Devi Prasad Shetty is a cardiac surgeon by profession and is called the Henry Ford of the heart surgery business for bringing change to the 'hearts' of India. He is the founder of the world's largest and cheapest heart care institute called Narayana Hrudayalaya in Bangalore.

Dr Naresh Trehan, the CEO and managing director of Medanta—the Medicity, is one of the leading cardiologists of the country. He holds the credit for being a personal surgeon to the President of India and has received numerous awards for his contributions in the field of healthcare.

Dwarkanath Kotnis is a legendary Indian physician, who dedicated his entire life working as a battlefront doctor in China.[4]

The Super Doctors[5]

Ketan Tanna and Abantika Ghosh coined the term Super Doctors.[6] The site says that, 'We do not claim that we have covered every deserving name. The idea is to give a peep into the mystical world of these medicine men and discover their arcane views about life.' Some of the doctors who are listed as Super Doctors due to their popularity and fee charged include:

DR SUDHANSU BHATTACHARYYA, cardiac surgeon
This doctor charges a very high fee per operation. Around twenty-five people await their turn every night. A heart operation by this doctor costs in lakhs. 'I charge depending on the economic capability of the patient. For me, asking for what I deserve is a necessity.' Till a few years ago, he conducted up to six operations a day. Now, he does not go above three. For two years in the nineties, he was the highest tax-paying doctor in India for which he was awarded a certificate by the

government. He accepts fees only by cheque. His client list includes former Maharashtra governor Dr P.C. Alexander, film producer Rakesh Roshan and renowned cardiac surgeon Dr B.K. Goyal. Bhattacharyya travels by J-class Mercedes and takes two annual foreign vacations. 'I don't consider myself any less than the best doctors in the US or anywhere else. I see no reason why I should not charge what I deserve.' A few years ago, armed men attacked him. They slashed his arms, leaving behind deep scars. 'I don't know who was behind the attack, my rivals or some aggrieved patient.' His doctor wife, a retired gynaecologist with KEM hospital, worked for free. 'In my life, my wife is the 50 per cent which does charity and I am the 50 per cent which charges,' the doctor says.

DR S. NATARAJAN, eye surgeon
Less than twenty years ago, a forty-one-year-old Dr S. Natarajan used to earn Rs 4200 in the Bombay Hospital. Now the eye surgeon owns a modern four-storied eye hospital in central Mumbai called Aditya Jyot that is estimated to be worth over several crores. His monthly income is in the region of Rs 45 lakhs. Former Maharashtra chief minister Sushil Kumar Shinde and state home minister R.R. Patil are among his patients. As the doctor hurries around giving final touches to a live eye surgery demonstration using suture-less technology, his three assistants from different corners of the country say that they are privileged to work with the 'best retina doctor in India'. A product of the famous Shankar Netralaya in Chennai, the doctor says that for him money is a tool to chart out different frontiers in the development of his skills.

DR ASHOK RAJ GOPAL, orthopaedic surgeon
The fifty-four-year-old doctor at Fortis Hospital Delhi, is highly paid. 'I travel all over the world doing surgeries. I have

done extensive operations in Australia, Malaysia, Spain, China, France—you name it,' he says.

Sometime in the eighties, during his formative years in a Delhi hospital, he actually paid the medical bills of the first thirty patients ('about Rs 4,000–5,000 per head') who let him perform arthroscopy on them.

Arthroscopy is a system of orthopaedic examination with a pencil-sized instrument. Now, there are patients who are willing to wait just to be operated by him. Theatre person Salima Raza, who underwent bilateral knee replacement rates him very highly, 'I will give him 11 out of 10.'

As a surgeon who has treated at least two Presidents of India—Dr A.P.J. Abdul Kalam and K.R. Narayanan—Gopal is a high-society figure.

DR M.G. BHAT, general surgeon
In Bangalore, patients wait, sometimes for more than twenty days, for an appointment with fifty-eight-year-old general surgeon and laparoscopy expert Dr M.G. Bhat. Though associated with the Manipal Hospital, he currently practises at the upmarket Wockhardt. When not at the hospitals, Bhat runs his own clinic at the very corporate Prestige Towers, Residency Road.

He says that he does not run after money or prestige but admits in the same breath, 'I live my life luxuriously. Unlike my peers I don't hoard money. Money is for spending, not hoarding.' Bhat travels abroad about four times a year, but he ensures that he never takes favours from any pharma company.

Who Is an Effective Doctor?

Using MCI criteria and my many discussions with people, I arrive at the following criteria for a doctor to be called effective:

- A doctor who cures the disease of the patients that come to him.
- One for whom many patients line up.
- One who charges for his skills and not on the basis of the patient's clout.
- One who charges according to the financial ability of a patient.
- One who does a lot of charity work.
- One who listens to the patient carefully.
- One who communicates well and puts the patient at ease.
- One who diagnoses and treats well.
- One who does not prescribe more medicines than required.
- One who balances short-term and long-term benefits to the patient.
- One who follows the ethics and values of the profession.

Among the effective doctors there are different levels at which they function:

Level 1: Effective Doctors (EDs or EPs)

They seem to have the following characteristics:

1. They treat the patients well; they listen patiently, give accurate diagnosis and appropriate medicines.
2. Maintain ethical standards, follow MCI meticulously.
3. Show sensitivity to those who can't afford to pay (may refer to others or may work out appropriate strategies).

Dr Mukesh Chawla, Devi Shetty, Naresh Trehan, Ramakant Panda and many others mentioned earlier fit into this category. Those who are not competent in their profession, don't follow professional ethics and are primarily income-centric are not effective doctors. There are perhaps many among the doctors in general who don't pass through our designed criteria.

Level 2: Very Effective Doctors (VEDs/VEPs)

They are characterized by the criteria above and in addition:

1. They are charitable. They think, plan and help many people.
2. Spread their knowledge and skills by sharing experiences with others, attending seminars and conferences, writing and disseminating through public lectures, etc.
3. Help patients financially if needed by giving concessions, etc.
4. Treat many patients and propagate and educate prevention.

Level 3: Super Effective Doctors (SEDs/SEPs)

In addition to the criteria of EDs and VEDs, these doctors are mission driven and attempt to reach out to larger numbers by setting up systems, processes and institutions. They leave behind a legacy which continues their mission. They:

1. Spread their skill, values and attitudes, and build institutions.
2. Share their knowledge and skills with other interested doctors and paramedical staff.
3. Serve many patients through an institutional base.
4. They develop successors to continue their work so that it transcends their own lifetime.
5. They are visionaries and are driven by their mission.

We give below a few case studies of doctors who can be considered VEPs or SEPs.

DR MURUGAPPA CHANNAVEERAPPA MODI (1916–2005)[7]

M.C. Modi is a legendary figure and a doctor worth writing about for the rarity of such people. He was an ophthalmologist. Born of humble parentage—a Kannadiga from Bijapur district—Modi threw away a lucrative career in private practice after attending Gandhiji's historic prayer meeting in Bombay on 8 August 1942 where the Quit India resolution was passed. Modi was widely known as Kannu Kotta Annu ('the brother who gifted us sight') in rural Karnataka. Helen Keller described him as 'a light piercing the darkness in selfless service' at a felicitation in New York. Newspapers all across south India referred to him as the 'Cataract King'. His organization of marathon eye camps for the cataract-blind came to be known as 'assembly line surgery'.

As a medical student, Modi pledged that he would devote his life to free eye care. But while working at KBHB Eye Hospital, Mumbai, he discovered that cataract patients were coming to him after selling away their cows, jewellery, even houses. It is then that he conceived of the touring eye hospital. Thus the first eye camp was organized at Pattan, close to Gandhiji's place of birth in Gujarat and some philanthropists arranged the venue, medicine and food for the patients. There was no looking back after that.

For Modi, after the first camp, combating cataracts and restoring vision to the blind became his all-consuming passion. Free eye camps in towns and villages were organized with the help of local donors and philanthropists, and choultries, marriage halls and community centres were opened up for the purpose. Patients were laid out on eight tables in a row and Dr Modi would move from table to table lifting the opaque veil from the patient's eye lens with the flick of the knife. By the time he reached the eighth table, a new patient would be in the place of the first. Thus he was able to treat a large number of patients in a day.

Even while travelling in a train he would go up and down the coaches to examine the eyes of passengers. Once he and his wife were travelling by train and Modi completely forgot about her. Having habitually examined the eyes of all the afflicted passengers, he felt his work was over and got off at the wrong station leaving his wife in the train.

His crusade against humanity's greatest scourge kept Modi from being a family man. His wife Leela and son Amarnath who lived in Dharwar saw him sometimes only twice a year and that too if an eye camp was being organized in that area. In fact, Modi had no idea how his wife and son managed—Amarnath's school fees were actually paid by the doctor's friends. 'I serve the poor. God takes care of all the other arrangements,' Modi would say modestly.

Modi started working at feverish pace as pressure grew and more and more camps started up.

Later he preferred Davangere to his native Bijapur because of its central location in Karnataka and finally opted to set up home and headquarters in Bangalore following persistent requests from the then chief minister K. Hanumanthaiah who declared him a state guest wherever he went in the state.

Shy, unassuming, Modi led a spartan life, relishing vegetarian food, black tea, *elneer* (coconut water) and papaya. Personal well-being could never be a concern for him—selfless service was all that mattered. Honours and awards came in a deluge. The Karnataka government brought to life his services in a ten-minute documentary titled *One Man's War* by filmmaker M.S. Sathyu. The Government of India conferred the Padma Bhushan on him.

His Skills

Modi's forte lay in his incredible swiftness. He was known for his dexterity as a surgeon and his diagnostic acumen. It was around the mid-seventies in the holy town of Tirupati that he performed 833 cataract operations in a day and entered the Guinness Book of World Records. The townsfolk had opened up all their choultires on the day at his service. He was the pioneer of mass eye surgery in India. He visited 46,120 villages and 1,21,18,630 patients, and performed a total of 6,10,564 operations till February 1993. 'When my time comes I would like to disappear silently,' he had concluded. He meant that when death came to him he would accept it wholeheartedly and die without troubling anyone.

Often, the very speed and the painlessness would make the patients doubt the success of the eye surgery. 'It was not unusual for the villagers to flee the camp throwing away the baggage in utter disbelief,' Dr Modi once told a journalist with a chuckle.[8]

Modi had observed, 'In the beginning the people were reluctant to undergo surgery, though it was quite simple, but those who regained sight became my ambassadors, mobilized funds and sent hordes of the blind and those with incipient blindness to me.'

His Philosophy of Life

For Modi, his mission was spiritual. 'I see myself as a *poojari* (priest). The patient is my God, every village is my place of pilgrimage, the operating table is my shrine and my instruments are the accessories of worship,' he said.

He used to organize three camps a month—two days for operations in each camp. 'I am always on the move,' he had told a journalist. A stickler for hygiene, he had a success rate of 99.5 per cent—the odd case of failure was because of the patient's ignorance. For instance, one villager gave his son's urine instead of his own for the pre-operative tests. Later complications arose as he was a diabetic.

Even after decades of service, the doctor did not tire. He would never postpone or cancel his eye camps. 'How can I rest when I know that every minute I work I can save a poor villager?' said the crusading missionary who was always busy on some project or the other for the rehabilitation of the disabled to make them self-reliant. Modi would say, 'My only desire is that I should be useful till my last breath.' No idle boast that, considering his unimpeachable track record of working among the sightless.

In his words, 'Like a circus company I have toured all over India since 1943 to provide free eye relief service. In the process I have examined over 10 million patients and conducted over 7,00,000 eye operations, which I am told is a world record. Somebody compared me to Henry Ford, saying I had brought conveyor belt technology to the field of eye care. My way of looking at things has not been affected by the ageing process at all. I am just an ordinary man. I will serve as long as God wants me to. For me, my patient is my God, the operating room is my temple and my instruments are my puja. My work has therefore been my pilgrimage.'[9]

DR DEVI SHETTY[10] (1953–)

Devi Shetty is the founder and chairman of Narayana Hrudayalaya Group of Hospitals. He was educated at St. Aloysius, Mangalore; Kasturba Medical College, Mangalore; Guy's Hospital, London; West Midlands Cardio-Thoracic Rotation Programme. Dr Shetty was awarded the Padma Bhushan in 2012 among many other awards.

He grew up in Mangalore and is the eighth of nine children. Doctors were gods in the Shetty household, swooping in to save his father when he fell into diabetic comas several times in the young boy's life. He had already resolved to be a doctor when his fifth-grade teacher told the class that a South African surgeon had just performed the world's first heart transplant. In that moment, Dr Shetty says, he decided to become a heart surgeon.

Early Life

After graduating from medical college in India, Dr Shetty trained in cardiac surgery at Guy's Hospital in London, one of Europe's top medical facilities. After working at that hospital for six years when the Birla family, leading industrialists in India, decided to start a heart hospital in Calcutta, Dr Shetty was brought in as the first director.[11] He then started with the Manipal Heart Foundation at Manipal Hospital.

Achievements

He is the first heart surgeon in India to enter into neonatal open-heart surgery, the first doctor in the world to perform open-heart surgery to close a hole in the heart, and the first user of an artificial heart in India.

Dr Shetty set about pursuing a heart hospital big enough to make a difference in a country where most of the people needing heart surgery couldn't afford it. His father-in-law, the owner of a large construction company, agreed to build and finance a heart hospital in his wife's hometown of Bangalore.

His most important contribution to medicine is not his surgical skills but his determination to make this huge industry of healthcare more efficient by applying Henry Ford's management principles. He believes that a combination of economies of scale and specialization can radically reduce the cost of heart surgery. His flagship Narayana Hrudayalaya Hospital in the 'Electronics City' district of Bangalore, is not far from GE, Infosys and Wipro.

The sheer number of patients allows surgeons to acquire world-class expertise in particular operations, and the generous back up facilities allow them to concentrate on their speciality rather than wasting their time on administration. By 2010 Dr Shetty had performed over 15,000 heart operations and other members of his team more than 10,000.[12] As a leader, Dr Shetty has been successful to motivate and instil the same drive which he has towards his vision in his team. At the 1000-bed Narayana Hrudayalaya Hospital, surgeons operate at a capacity virtually unheard of in the US, where the average hospital has 160 beds, according to the American Hospital Association. Narayana's forty-two cardiac surgeons performed 3,174 cardiac bypass surgeries in 2008, more than double the 1,367 surgeries the Cleveland Clinic, a US leader, did in the same year. His surgeons operated on 2,777 paediatric patients, more than double the 1,026 surgeries performed at Children's Hospital Boston. The hospital charges an average of $2,000 for open-heart surgery, compared with $20,000–1,00,000 in America, but its success rates are as good as in the best American hospitals, making it economically feasible for the underprivileged, who could never have afforded such a surgery otherwise.

Dr Shetty also founded the Nerayanma Nethralaya health city which was the centre for neurosciences, a children's hospital and a cancer research centre in Bangalore. He founded the Rabindranath Tagore International Institute of Cardiac Sciences in Kolkata. He later signed an MOU with the Karnataka government for building a hospital with 5000 beds with a budget of 1000 crores, close to the airport. His hospitals make use of economies of scale and perform heart surgeries for one-tenth the cost of what it takes in the United States. In Karnataka, Shetty has also crafted a unique, low-cost insurance programme, Yeshasvini, estimated to be the world's cheapest comprehensive health insurance scheme. Launched in tandem with the state government, it covers 4 million people who pay a premium of Rs 10 per month. 'There is no point in an innovation or a magic pill that is not affordable,' says Shetty, who is melding the charitable ideals of his role models Mother Teresa and Mahatma Gandhi with hard-headed business sense.

Next door to Narayana, Dr Shetty has built a 1400-bed cancer hospital and a 300-bed eye hospital, which share the same laboratories and blood bank as the heart institute. His family-owned business group, Narayana Hrudayalaya Private Ltd, reports a 7.7 per cent profit after taxes, slightly above the 6.9 per cent average for a US hospital, according to American Hospital Association data.

What Makes Dr Devi Shetty Super Effective?
1. His goal in life to 'not only become a great surgeon but use his skill and talent for the greater good.'
2. He formulated his own turning points in life which are the institutions he created: Narayana Hrudayalaya Hospital and the Yeshasvini health insurance scheme.
3. He recognizes his strengths and leverages them—he used his talent and business acumen to create a business model that changed the face of affordable healthcare in India.
4. He has always been a positive thinker.
5. He showed high perseverance as he never gave up even when he did not get financial backing from the government in his earlier attempts and later started Narayana Hrudayalaya Hospital with the help of his father.

DR PRATHAP REDDY[13] (1933–)

When Dr Reddy came back from the US, he had a disadvantage being a cardiologist—he could treat patients only to a certain extent. In case they didn't respond to medical treatment or, if they needed surgical treatment, there was no acceptable programme in India. So, he used to send those who could afford the expenses to the US, mostly to Denton Cooley in Houston.

'Dr Prathap Reddy came to India after serving as the Chief Resident of the Worcester City Hospital in the US to start his practice in Madras with a modest earning of Rs 100 per day.

The idea to establish Apollo Group of Hospitals came when Dr Reddy lost a patient who couldn't make it to Texas for an open-heart surgery. This inspired Dr Prathap Reddy to create world-class medical infrastructure in India and make it more accessible and affordable to common people. Dr Reddy's efforts bore fruit when he succeeded in setting up the first centre of the Apollo Hospitals Group in Chennai in 1983.'[14]

Driven by a deep urge to create world-class medical infrastructure in India and make it accessible and affordable to a large cross section of our people, Dr Prathap Reddy opted to give up his successful practice in the US to return to India in the early eighties.

That move led to the birth of the concept of providing in India the level of care with the same high quality but at a heavily reduced cost. Dr Prathap Reddy revolutionized the healthcare system in the country and pioneered the establishment of private hospitals.

The secret of Reddy's achievement is that: 'I have always believed that I should do the best possible to every person who comes to me. And to those who have trust in me, I should live up to their trust. For motivating our people, I have told them only one thing, "Don't do anything more than what you would have done to your own kith and kin. If you do that much, it is enough." This is where they say that Apollo care is great. That is because we are giving to everyone the same level of tender love and care that we would have given to our own most dear ones. This is inculcated in each one of us. So you will do your very best, automatically.'

And secondly, Dr Reddy says that there are three Ps behind the success: purity, patience and perseverance. You need patience if you want to do anything substantial. 'When I started this hospital, if there are a million bricks in this building, I had a million problems. They said, you cannot start a hospital in more than five hundred square yards. You can't fund a hospital. For importing your equipment, you should file twelve applications to twelve different offices. I had any number of such obstacles. So, I needed to have patience and perseverance. If these two are there and if your purpose is pure, success is yours.'

Dr Prathap Reddy started India's first hospital consultancy body, the Indian Hospitals Corporation, in 1982. He consequently commissioned two more tertiary health centres in India. The Government of India soon recognized his enterprising efforts leading to financial institutions amending their funding legislation to include hospitals and boards basing the scope of medical insurance.

From then onwards it was an upswing for the Apollo Group. It presently has over twenty-two centres in the major metros in India and has a combined turnover of $100 million.

The telemedicine technology has been successfully introduced by Dr Reddy and it will be a key enabler in transforming the healthcare delivery in India. His blueprint for the nation includes setting up of many rural hospitals. Dr Reddy is now looking at secondary health centres in semi-urban areas and smaller cities and has already identified twenty-three sites for the same. The maiden effort in this venture has been at Aragonda, his native village, and Dr Reddy envisages that this centre will serve as a model for all such projects of the Apollo Group in rural India. Today, in India there are not enough teachers in every discipline and the worst affected is health. There are not adequate numbers of teachers in medical colleges, nursing colleges and paramedical institutions. In order to remedy this lack, Dr Reddy created Medvarsity, a virtual medical university, eight years ago. This virtual university has the largest content, about twenty thousand hours of study material for undergrads, postgrads, practising physicians, specialists, nurses and technologists. 'Medvarsity' provides total access to experts in the field of medicine anywhere in the world, and 'MEDNET' provides hospital systems management packages. Both the initiatives are expected to transform the healthcare sector in India. Dr Reddy has good foresight and constantly works towards making healthcare more systematic.

Dr Reddy works in bringing quality healthcare to India by telling his team that if you are a wonderful factory, 99 per cent of what you produce is of excellent quality. The remaining 1 per cent is what you call the reject. 'So I tell them, please remember that the reject in a hospital is human life. So you will have to maintain 100 per cent efficiency and you should be probably able to help almost all of them.'

Recognizing his pioneering role in transforming the Indian healthcare industry, the Government of India awarded him the prestigious Padma Bhushan in February 1991. He was also presented with the Sir Neel Ratan Sarkar Award for medical excellence in June 1998. Nominated by Business India as one of the top fifty personalities who have made a difference to the country in the fifty years since Independence, the country has certainly recognized his contributions. The Royal College of Surgeons of Edinburgh has conferred upon him the award of fellowship Ad Hominem.

DR NARESH TREHAN (1946–)[15]

Dr Naresh Trehan, is a renowned cardiovascular and cardiothoracic surgeon. Born in 1946, Dr Trehan graduated from King George Medical College, Lucknow. He went to the United States in 1969. After graduating, he went on to practise at New York University Medical Center Manhattan from 1971 to 1988. He completed a thoracic surgery residency under Dr Frank Spencer at New York University. By the mid-1980s, he was earning over $1.5 million a year as a Manhattan heart surgeon. After a successful career in the US, he returned to India and started Escorts Heart Institute and Research Centre in 1988, a global landmark in cardiac care and a front runner in research, training and education. At present, he is serving as the chairman and managing director and chief cardiac surgeon of Medanta—the Medicity. He has served as personal surgeon to the President of India since 1991, and has received numerous awards, including the Padma Shri, Padma Bhushan and Lal Bahadur Shastri National Award.

'Specifically on the lines of a Mayo, Cleveland, Harvard and John Hopkins in its basics, Medanta intends to go beyond what any conventional medical institute has attempted,' the renowned heart surgeon says.

Within six months of its commencement the hospital was running to 100 per cent occupancy—something that conventional healthcare facilities normally achieve in two to three years' time. Around 300 doctors and 1100 paramedics have already joined the integrated healthcare facility comprising a hospital, a research centre and a medical and nursing school.

Patients from developed markets such as the US and European countries have also started trickling in, lured by the affordability factor. Treatment for diverse therapeutic areas such as cardiac, cancer, kidney transplant, diabetes and plastic surgery is being made available at one-tenth the cost of what is offered in the West. And given Trehan's reputation, critical specialties like cardiac care are already running to full capacity.

At a core level, Medanta is a conglomeration of multi-superspecialty institutes which are led by renowned medical practitioners who are front runners in their respective fields. Spread over 43 acres, the integrated healthcare facility includes a hospital, a research centre and a medical and nursing school. It has over 1,250 beds of which 600 are already operational. There are forty-five operation theatres catering to over twenty specialties. 'In a nutshell, we have built an institution which matches the highest standards of healthcare delivery across the world. It will offer not only the best technical facilities, but also clinical research, education and training,' he says. As an equity partner, Punj Lloyd developed the infrastructure for the sprawling healthcare facility.

Without any doubt, Trehan seems to have adopted a multi-pronged strategy in the creation of Medanta.

While in concept Medanta seems to be on course to match the standards of clinical care offered by the likes of Mayo, Harvard and Cleveland clinics, in reality, it will be an acid test for it to make treatments affordable for the general population in the long run.

His Inspiration

'My parents (both doctors) came from Pakistan in 1952 and we had no roof over our heads. I have vivid memories of shifting to a three-room apartment opposite Plaza Cinema in Connaught Place and having to share one room with my parents and sister because two of the other rooms were used by my parents as their clinics. I was around six then and used to happily pedal my toy car from K Block near Plaza to York hotel,' he reminisces.

But those were early years of initiation as well for an impressionable mind. Dr Trehan recalls patients coming to his parents' clinics with tears in their eyes and leaving the place with smiles. 'Many people in those days were refugees and had frugal means. My father used to treat them for free. That emotion of empathy sharing and feeling registered in my mind forever.' He decided against practising in an established hospital and found an industrialist to finance his vision of a private heart institute and research centre in New Delhi. The Escorts Heart Institute and Research Centre opened in 1988. Today it is among the largest of its kind in the world, with 325 beds, nine operating theatres and satellite operating rooms in five cities—although that means little in a nation of a billion people. At sixty-seven, Dr Trehan may be the most prominent heart surgeon in the country. He has won just about every award India gives for citizenship and service.

Why an Entrepreneur?

He wanted to create in India the same standard of healthcare, training and research that he saw in the US. 'I was doing well in New York as a coronary bypass surgeon earning over $1.5 million a year, but wanted to come back to provide the same standard of treatment that institutes like Mayo Clinic and Cleveland Clinic offered. I also wanted to provide affordable treatment for cardiac care,' says Dr Trehan, who has conducted more than 50,000 cardiac surgeries.

Contribution to Healthcare

He is a pioneer in the field of minimally invasive heart surgeries, including port access surgery for valve replacement/repair and atrial septal defect in India. He performed robotic heart surgery including total endoscopic CABG, transmyocardial laser revascularization surgery, and stem cell therapy for non-bypassable coronary arteries and heart failure for the first time in India.

He has been a part of the development of many new technologies and devices, including the coapsys, a device meant for mitral valve repair on beating hearts.

His views on healthcare for the underprivileged indicate an integrative mind where he has combined his skills to fulfil the needs of the nation in healthcare.

'Telemedicine is the only way to ensure healthcare at the doorstep of every last man in the queue in states like Bihar where poverty and remoteness make healthcare inaccessible to many.'[16]

He cited robotic surgery as another example. 'Robotic surgery is the future of all surgeries. It is very efficient and minimally invasive. It's currently costly, but the research is on to make it cost effective. Almost all surgeries from bypass to removal of fibroids, transplants and correction of sleep apnea can be done robotically.'

Who Is an Effective or Super Effective Doctor?

Dr M.C. Modi, who made it his life's singular mission to cure blindness, even making it into the Guinness Book of Records; who gave eyesight to many but has left only his story and values behind?

Naresh Trehan, who tries to provide high-class healthcare at perhaps expensive rates and has a beeline of patients who can afford his care?

Pratap Reddy, who has a chain of hospitals globally?

Devi Shetty, who has devoted his life to make available low-cost cardiac care and expanded to other fields?

In my view all of them are super effective doctors. Each one is super in his own way.

All of them came from reasonably humble beginnings.

All of them had a higher goal in mind from childhood. Some of them had missions which were more charitable in nature while for others the goal involved technology and not necessarily people. All of them set the best standards in terms of the quality of healthcare. Three of them focused on institutions which will continue even after they are gone. Dr Modi was so occupied with his service and application of skills that while he benefited millions and has left behind his values, he did not build strong institutions to carry on his legacy. Dr Trehan had an entrepreneurial approach, and Dr Shetty and Dr Reddy had both entrepreneurial skills combined with commitment to patients. Dr Shetty was thoroughly committed to the poor—a great deal more than Dr Reddy perhaps, but both of them had an interest in the poor and started with the intention of making hospital services more accessible.

All of them are good doctors. Dr Prathap C. Reddy, the visionary founder–chairman of Apollo Hospitals, is widely credited as being the architect of modern Indian healthcare. He is best described as a compassionate humanitarian, who has dedicated his life to bringing world-class healthcare within the economic and geographic reach of millions of patients. The institution he built and the values and vision he inculcated led to the private healthcare revolution that transformed the Indian healthcare landscape. The common characteristics among all of them are:

Technical skills: They are all excellent doctors in their fields. Domain knowledge builds credibility and gives rise to other aspirations which extend beyond the self and aim at serving larger humanity.

Leadership: They thought differently and always thought big.

Mission and vision driven: Each of them has a great vision. It extends to a larger number of people and humanity.

Entrepreneurial thinking: They thought like businessmen with only the exception of Dr Modi. Dr Mukesh, like many other doctors, was still young and perhaps was not exposed to the kind of background the others had to think big. He had his own clinics in Pune and also in Bandra and served many hospitals. He is an effective person and effective doctor and would have made it to be a VEP or SEP perhaps, had he lived longer.

Service orientation: They all exhibit a high degree of service orientation though some of them have specific target groups. Even someone like Trehan who focuses on serving those from elite groups, shows concern for the poor when they talk of telemedicine and the like. Dr Shetty demonstrates this in his own way and stands out among them all.

Achievement driven and extension motivated:[17] They all want to achieve something more—something higher and greater. They are never satisfied and keep moving on from one accomplishment to the next.

Perseverance and positive attitude: They possess the I-can-do-it attitude. It is these qualities that make a super effective person.

If I have to rank them in order in terms of their impact—all of them got recognition from the government; all of them serve a large number of people, Modi all by himself, Dr Shetty and Dr Reddy through their multiplying institutions, and Dr Trehan through his own institutions and through research and technological superiority.

Self-Assessment Tool for Doctors: How Effective Are You, Doctor?

Rate yourself using a five-point scale or get yourself rated by others on the following:

5 = Very high, 4 = High, 3 = Moderate, 2 = Low, 1 = Very low, 0 = Totally absent or Not true

EP/ED: How effective are you as a doctor according to the following criteria?

☐ 1. Depth of knowledge in your areas of work or specialization
☐ 2. Breadth of knowledge in your area of work or specialization
☐ 3. Ability to communicate effectively with the patient

☐ 4. Ability to listen and understand the symptoms and diagnose accurately the underlying causes

☐ 5. Ability to elicit all critical information required to diagnose the patient accurately

☐ 6. Keeping in touch with the recent developments in your field

☐ 7. Learning from various sources like fellow doctors, Internet, reading literature, magazines and journals, etc.

☐ 8. Ability to document the data and information accurately

☐ 9. Undertaking research studies on your own or use data to have new findings

☐ 10. Creativity or originality of thinking in your area of specialization

☐ 11. Working hard to ensure that you do justice to your job as a doctor and medical practitioner

☐ 12. Devotion to patients and going out of your way to help and treat them

☐ 13. Taking pride in guiding patients

☐ 14. Publishing and disseminating your work and points of view

☐ 15. Offering programmes and services that are well utilized by many people

☐ 16. Making an impact in any area that is acknowledged by many a cross the country or world

☐ 17. Extent to which your work and services are well acknowledged by the community around and you are a very popular doctor

☐ 18. Extent to which you are ethical, value driven and known for integrity and honesty in your practice

☐ 19. Promoting values like good character, honesty, integrity and search for truth as values for all

☐ 20. Extent to which you set an example for others to follow and live as a good doctor and role model

VEP/VED: What is the breadth and depth of your reach in terms of curative and other medical services you provide?

- ☐ 1. Treating a large number of people (thousands) in your lifetime in terms of curing or / and educating patients
- ☐ 2. Discovering new ideas and methods of treating patients or reaching out to potential users and benefiting a large number of people at present or in future
- ☐ 3. Writing and publishing to be read by a large number of people in the country and outside
- ☐ 4. Work by you is well talked about across the country in respective circles
- ☐ 5. Treating a large number of patients across the country or the state where you live
- ☐ 6. Reaching out to a large number in the society and carrying out a lot of service

SEP/SED: Have you established institutions or processes and systems that make your work and innovations and ideas available to many more people for future use and developing people?

- ☐ 1. Have established many institutions to multiply knowledge and skills and make them available to large number of patients and people
- ☐ 2. Have established at least one institution or agency that is doing well and is benefiting many people
- ☐ 3. A lot of research is carried out by people in the institutions that you have established
- ☐ 4. Ideas and messages reach a large number of people through the institutions you have established
- ☐ 5. Many people benefit from the institutions you have established

☐ 6. The institutions ensure that your skills and teachings reach a large number of people and help in the growth of knowledge

☐ 7. Other doctors and the medical profession also benefited a lot from your work

☐ 8. The institutions you have founded are helping a sizeable group of people

☐ 9. The institutions are globally acknowledged

☐ 10. The institutions carry an imprint of the contributions of the founders

3 Film Actors

I was invited a couple of years ago to give a series of lectures at the National Academy of Audit and Accounts at Shimla. Though I used to visit Chandigarh and Sanawar frequently, I sadly never took time off to visit Shimla. This time I was particularly interested to visit for a peculiar reason, and that was to go and have snacks at the Alfa Restaurant on the Mall Road in Shimla. The name of this restaurant was lodged in my mind since I attended a talk by Anupam Kher at the Ahmedabad Management Association a few years ago. For this talk, 'Face to Face with Achievers of Excellence', in August 2010, a team of students had prepared a collage of Kher's significant films starting with *Saaransh* to *A Wednesday* and *Wake Up Sid* released in 2009.

While delivering his talk Anupam Kher mentioned that his family would live in Shimla and when he was young his father would take them out once in every six months to Alfa Restaurant where they used to have mutton samosa, gulab jamun and espresso coffee. In those days school students would be automatically promoted to a higher class after the exams until the results were declared, and in the eventuality of their failing, they had to go back to the previous class and sit with the newly promoted students. I remember a similar practice in my village school in Akunuru, Andhra Pradesh in the fifties. Anupam Kher narrated an interesting incident after he completed his class ten

final examinations. The school reopened and he had to sit in
the eleventh class until the results were declared. His father
would work in the forest department and knew people in the
education department. A few days passed by when his father
suddenly came to the school one day in the middle of the classes
and took him away to Alfa Restaurant. They ordered mutton
samosas and gulab jamuns—the usual fare. Kher wondered why
they were having this feast so soon after the last one and asked
his father about the occasion. His father replied, 'Beta, you
failed your class ten exams and that is why I am celebrating.'
Kher was quite stunned and asked him again, 'Failed? If I have
failed, then why this celebration?' to which his father replied,
'I am celebrating this so that you will never be afraid of failure
in life.'

That was a touching story told by Anupam Kher and it left
an unforgettable imprint on me. I kept showing the video of
this talk in most of my classes, especially the narration of this
particular part of his speech while giving 360 Degree Feedback,
and I must have shown the piece at least thirty to forty times to
various groups to make a point on managing failures. The Alfa
Restaurant and Anupam Kher became a part of my psyche for
managing failure. Anupam Kher shared many more lessons from
his life, some of which are stated in his book, *The Best Thing
about You Is You,* published in 2012 by Hay House India. Some
other things I learnt from him as lessons from his own life are
to share your weaknesses with others so that you don't have to
be ashamed of them. He talked of how he had facial paralysis at
the time of shooting the film *Hum Aap Ke Hai Koun* and was
told by his doctor to go back to Shimla and take rest. He almost
decided to do that but then went on to the sets and announced
his problem to his friends. His friends gave him a lot of assurance
and the shooting went on without him having to go back to
Shimla. He also talked of how he did not know any acting when

he was young and how he discovered his interest after a few years and went on to pursue the same. One of the things we talk about in our leadership development programmes is the need for self-management. In fact Peter Drucker wrote an article on self-management in the *Harvard Business Review* which became a classic. In the article Peter Drucker makes the following points for those aspiring to be effective managers and leaders:

1. Know what you are good at. A person can perform only from strengths. One cannot build a performance on weaknesses, let alone something one cannot do at all. Put yourself where your strengths can produce results and work to improve them. Avoid intellectual arrogance—acquire skills as required. Remedy bad habits; have no lack of manners.

2. Successful careers develop when people are prepared for opportunities because they know their strengths, their method of work and their values. Discover where you belong. That knowledge can transform an ordinary person—hard-working and competent but otherwise mediocre—into an outstanding performer.

3. Do not try to change yourself (too much)—instead, work harder to improve the way you perform.

In many ways Anupam Kher was saying very similar things drawn out of his own experiences. Kher's book and his response to his father's death in 2012 have excellent lessons for all those aspiring to be effective.

Anupam Kher[1] was born in 1955 in Shimla, into a Kashmiri Pandit family. His father was a clerk and he had a modest upbringing. He received his education at D.A.V. School in Shimla. He is an alumnus and a former chairperson of the National School of Drama (NSD). Some of his early acting roles were in plays performed at the Himachal Pradesh University. He has acted in several hundred films and many plays. He has also appeared in acclaimed international films such as the 2002 Golden Globe-nominated *Bend It Like Beckham*, Ang Lee's 2007 Golden Lion-winning *Lust, Caution*, and David O. Russell's 2013 Oscar-winning *Silver Linings Playbook*. He has also held the post of chairman of the Central Board of Film Certification. In 2004, he was honoured with the Padma Shri by the Government of India for his contribution to Indian cinema. Kher has won the Filmfare Award for best performance in a comic role five times.

Kher made his acting debut in the 1982 Hindi movie *Aagman*. Then in 1984 came *Saaransh*, where twenty-eight-year-old Kher played a retired middle-class Maharashtrian man who had lost his son. He has hosted TV shows such as *Say Na Something to Anupam Uncle*, *Sawaal Dus Crore Ka*, *Lead India* and the recent *The Anupam Kher Show: Kucch Bhi Ho Sakta Hai*. He has had many comic roles but has also played the villain such as in his acclaimed role as the terrorist Dr Dang in *Karma* (1986). For his role in *Daddy* (1989) he received the Filmfare Critics Award for best performance. He has starred alongside Bollywood superstar Shah Rukh Khan many times in films such as *Darr* (1993), *Dilwale Dulhaniya Le Jayenge* (1995), *Chaahat* (1996), *Kuch Kuch Hota Hai* (1998), *Mohabbatein* (2000) and *Veer-Zaara* (2004).

He ventured into directing with *Om Jai Jagadish* (2002) and has been a producer. He produced and starred in the film *Maine Gandhi Ko Nahin Mara* (2005). He received the best actor award from the Karachi International Film Festival. His role of Police Commissioner Rathor in the critically and commercially acclaimed *A Wednesday* is also very much appreciated.

Kher is known internationally for *Bend It Like Beckham* (2002), *Bride and Prejudice* (2004), *Speedy Singhs* (2011), his appearance on the hit TV show *ER*, in *The Mistress of Spices* (2006) and *Lust, Caution* (2007). In 2012 he co-starred in the Academy Award-winning *Silver Linings Playbook*.

Kher has written and starred in a play about his own life called *Kucch Bhi Ho Sakta Hai*, which was directed by Feroz Abbas Khan.

In 2007, Anupam Kher, with his batchmate from NSD, Satish Kaushik, started a film production company, Karol Bagh Productions. Their first film, *Tere Sang*, was directed by Satish Kaushik. He was appointed in 2010 as the goodwill ambassador of the Pratham Education Foundation which strives to improve children's education in India.

The Anupam Kher Foundation is a public charitable trust which was founded in the year 2008 and is based out of Mumbai. This foundation aims to maximize the future opportunities for children from less privileged backgrounds by promoting and advocating good-quality education aimed at holistic growth.

In 2005, Anupam Kher established Actor Prepares,[2] an acting school for talented individuals who wish to pursue careers as actor-performers in the entertainment industry. This is the only school for actors in the world to be founded by an actor who is professionally active.

Kandaswamy Bharatan, executive director of Kavithalaya Productions started by the famous K. Balachander, teaches a course at IIMA, and in the last few years got to the classroom actors like Shriya Saran, Dhanush, Aamir Khan and others to share their experiences. Like Anupam Kher's story, every actor and actress has a story to share. Rajinikanth has a story to share and it got reflected in some ways in his Tamil version of the movie *Billu Barber*. Every life has lessons and some of the actors draw insightful takes from their own lives and share them for the benefit of others. These are more effective people than those that don't articulate lessons from their own experiences or even care to share. A year ago, Amitabh Bachchan visited the IIMA campus to share his experiences in advertising while promoting tourism for the Gujarat government. There are many lessons students drew from interactions with him. Kamal Haasan is another actor who shares his experiences for the benefit of others. In my view such an approach makes these actors more effective. Actors have large platforms and great reach to the public. These provide them with a good scope to take stands on issues of importance to the country and raise public awareness. For example, Deepika Padukone has done a great job of sharing how she was able to fight depression and has even started a service for others. The lives of some of the actors themselves are lessons to learn.

Lessons from Actors

Good actors are accomplished artists. The public relates to them through their movies and messages delivered through the movies besides the entertainment. Movies play a significant part in people's lives and influence society and culture. I am one of those people who have learnt a lot from movies. I only see Telugu and Hindi movies and rarely any English ones, and that keeps me more Indian. I don't miss any good movies and I re-watch them to draw out lessons. I particularly get moved by films that promote values. Those of us who were brought up in Andhra in the fifties and sixties have seen NTR, ANR and SVR movies and learnt a lot about family values, values (or lack of them) of the rich, qualities of a good leader, how good leaders should ensure that the poor are taken care of, etc. Films have a lot of impact on people through the messages they pass on in their stories as well as in the speeches of the actors. Actors are only one part of a film but they are the face, and the way they act is what makes an impact or imprint in your mind. They are a part of the 'Influence Professions'. Films have the potential to change the culture or create a new culture by virtue of the masses they reach. So actors are important and there are lessons to be learnt from their lives and conduct.

Who Is an Actor?

An effective actor is one who acts well and impresses you with their performance. In this book we are not merely looking at professional success but also the impact a person makes and the service they provide to society. So for the purposes of our assessment of actors as effective people, we need to look at them through the strength of their influence and what they give to the society.

An effective actor is talented and acts well. A more effective actor makes wise decisions about the films they agree to act in. Those who act in films with a message and deliver the message well to impact the values and culture of the country or society are more effective actors than those who merely act well. Those who influence millions through the creation of additional mechanisms and become role models for others are perhaps super effective. For example when Anupam Kher is using his acting talent to train others by starting a school that prepares actors, he is a super effective person as he is not only reaching out to people through his movies but also via activities that perhaps leave an even more lasting effect.

The following is an illustrative case study of some of the actors who have made a significant impact on the lives of many:

In recent years KANGANA RANAUT made a great deal of positive impact on society through the kind of films she picked up like *Queen* and *Tanu Weds Manu 2* on the empowerment and independence of women. For example the following are some of the things women can learn from the film *Queen*:[3]

1. 'You' are your biggest happiness.
2. Meet 'yourself'.

3. Take experiences as a part of life, and not *life* itself.
4. There is more to a tragedy. Maybe getting dumped or not having things turn out the way you had dreamt of them is for the best after all! At times, it is the worst things that can bring out the best in you.
5. Freedom is not to be able to do whatever you want, but to be who you truly are.
6. Never underestimate the role your friends play in your life.
7. You are not weak. Whether you see the ladies in your home or the ones running nations or those winning medals for the country, women are in no way 'weak'.

Ranaut has also demonstrated her high sense of responsibility by refusing to endorse a fairness cream brand. Such examples they set make actors role models for others.

AMITABH BACHCHAN is not only an acknowledged superstar all over the world but a lot can be learnt from his own life and the scope of his long career, the range of roles he has played, and the ups and downs he went through including an attempt to corporatize his name and achievements. Almost every movie he acted in had a message besides big entertainment value. Besides being a great actor he influenced the lives of many people through his game show *Kaun Banega Crorepati* which disseminated information and knowledge. Recently, he has also started promoting tourism by being the brand ambassador to some states, using his acting talent and name. The following are ten lessons suggested to be drawn from his life and work:[4]

1. Create a niche: Amitabh Bachchan entered the Indian film industry when it was dominated by actors like Rajesh Khanna, Dharmendra, Sunil Dutt and Dev Anand. While most were comfortable playing the romantic hero, he took

up the challenge of doing action films, thus creating a niche for himself.

2. Don't take no for an answer: It seems unbelievable that Mr Bachchan was once rejected for the role of a broadcaster in All India Radio because they did not like his voice. Ironically, today the actor's deep baritone and impeccable dialogue delivery have acquired an iconic status. He worked as a playback singer for twenty-nine movies and in 2005, even lent his voice as narrator to Luc Jacquet's Oscar-winning French documentary, *March of the Penguins*.

3. Accept failure, but never give up: In 1995, three years into semi-retirement from the film industry, he founded Amitabh Bachchan Corporation Limited, an event management and production firm. Although the company achieved considerable success in its first year, it subsequently suffered crippling losses, forcing Mr Bachchan to take up acting again in order to cope with massive business debts. In July 2000, he came back with a bang to host the first instalment of the reality series *Kaun Banega Crorepati*, which went on to become the most-watched TV show in the country.

4. Learn from everyone: He's worked with junior co-stars and directors half his age, but he's never reported to throw tantrums or push his weight around on set or otherwise.

5. Give everything your 100 per cent: His dedication to his craft is apparent in movies like *Black* and *Paa*. In *Paa*, to get into character, Bachchan had to spend four to five hours every day donning prosthetic make-up, post which he could not eat or drink normally—and it took two hours after each shoot to get rid of it. Despite his age and seniority, he did not complain once, which is the mark of a true professional. *Paa* remains one of his best performances to date.

6. Forgive and forget, and never lose sight of the bigger picture: To be sure, he has had his share of fall-outs, which

are inevitable—the Gandhi family, Shah Rukh Khan, Amar Singh, Anurag Kashyap, various media publications—but there's no denying that he does not believe in mud-slinging and has graciously moved on from most fall-outs, often extending a warm hand of friendship to former nemeses. He has never used the media as a tool, as so many celebrities often do, to lash out at his detractors.

7. You may be rich and famous, but you're never above anyone: His interactions with his fans and the press are generally warm and gracious, and he makes a visible effort to remain humble and grounded. And despite the constant attention, which can get to the most patient of people, he manages to keep his cool and handles the shutterbug invasion with a smile, posing for them, answering questions and leaving them satisfied.

8. Give back to society: From his decision to support the nationwide polio campaign to his association with various charity organizations, Amitabh Bachchan has always found the time to give back to society.

9. Respect thy parents: Big B finds special purpose in revisiting his father's poems—to him, it's a way of paying tribute to the man who raised him.

10. Have respect for other people's time and always be punctual: B-Town biggies have a notorious reputation for holding up shoots, strolling on to sets five hours late, throwing tantrums that cause setbacks to the schedule and delaying projects by months, sometimes, even years. Not Amitabh Bachchan. One of the very few stars known for their punctuality, he is apologetic even if he's kept you waiting a few short minutes.

AAMIR KHAN is known, besides his acting, for the social commitment he has shown by doing films like *Lagaan*, *PK*, *3 Idiots*, *Taare Zameen Par*, *Fanaa*, etc. and his TV show *Satyamev Jayate* which raises awareness on social issues. Like many others, the films he has acted in have a lot of messages. For example *3 Idiots* has significant messages that impress upon the youth to discover and pursue their inner passions and talents to become something in life. *Lagaan* is used in many management schools as a case study to teach determination, hard work, taking up challenges and teamwork.

His latest movie *PK* has given some interesting lessons like the following:[5]

1. Sometimes letting go makes you a bigger person.
2. Trust yourself and not someone who is a self-acclaimed manager of the almighty, trust your thinking and act accordingly.
3. Doubt what you see, read and hear.
4. Question what's in front of you and don't just stand blinded, accepting everything that's handed to you.
5. Apply your logic and brains and behave rationally not just because your religion says so, but because your mind says so.
6. Listen to yourself before you agree with something you aren't fully aware about.
7. Your mind holds the power, so give yourself a chance to be enlightened.
8. Rather than blindly following something that lies behind a fog, it's better to understand the hows and the whys of a thing you have been doing since your birth.
9. It's not a sin to be curious, so never be afraid to satisfy your thirst for curiosity.

There are lessons to be drawn from Aamir Khan's life itself:[6]

1. When you take on a project, give it everything you can. Be extremely committed to it. Focus is what differentiates the good from the great.

2. Diamonds are in the detail. Only when you focus on each and every bit of the project will you be able to create something that is a masterpiece and something that lasts forever.

3. Go with your gut feeling. Do not hesitate to try something different. If you want to create a niche, something that is different, you have to try doing things that no one else is doing. Yes, there is a lot of risk involved, but the higher the risks, the higher the rewards.

4. Good marketing without a good product might work sometimes, but good marketing along with a good product always works.

5. Be a responsible citizen. Aamir Khan is known to create responsible cinema. While making his movies he makes sure that they do not promote anything that might seem irresponsible or create imbalance in the society.

SHAH RUKH KHAN, having been a successful actor turned also into a producer and television personality disseminating his talent and impacting millions. He is often referred to as the 'Baadshah of Bollywood', 'King of Bollywood' or 'King Khan' and has acted in more than eighty films. Khan has a significant following world-wide in the Indian diaspora, and his work has earned him numerous prestigious awards including Filmfare and an honorary doctorate from the University of Edinburgh. Khan is co-chairman of the motion picture production company Red Chillies Entertainment and its subsidiaries, and is the co-owner of the Indian Premier League cricket team Kolkata Knight Riders. Khan's philanthropic endeavours have provided healthcare and disaster relief, and he was honoured with UNESCO's Pyramide con Marni award in 2011 for his support of children's education. He regularly features in listings of the most influential people in Indian culture, and in 2008 *Newsweek* named him one of their fifty most powerful people in the world. His fans consider him as an institution by himself and keep drawing lessons from his life and his tweets. He shared lessons from his own life and films while receiving an honorary doctorate from the University of Edinburgh.

Film personalities like the Khans, Bachchans and Kapoors who are considered as institutions themselves spread their talent, culture and values through production houses, acting and other forms of institutions including NGOs and educational centres.

There are many yesteryear actors from Bollywood and also from the south who are known for responsible cinema, going beyond what is expected of an actor. They include Dev Anand, Kishore Kumar, Pran, Rajesh Khanna, N.T. Rama Rao, Akkinenei Nagswara Rao, S.V. Ranga Rao, Sivaji Ganesan, M.G. Ramachandran, Gemini Ganesan, etc. Among those living include Dilip Kumar, Manoj Kumar, Vyjayanthimala, Shabana Azmi, Saira Banu and Kamal Haasan, just to name a few.

Actors are influential people. They influence our thought, values, ethos and culture and through them our choices and actions. Through their movies, dialogues, actions, what they do and don't do, what they approve and don't approve of, they affect the larger society. They are as influential as teachers—the difference being we have little choice in picking our teachers but we can choose what we want to see, hear and learn through movies. They also influence people outside of the cinematic space, especially in this hyper-connected world where the stars are so accessible to viewers.

Who Is an Effective Actor?

1. The first criterion is that an effective actor is one *who acts well as decided by the viewers*. That means an actor who provides an impactful performance in the film. Now the challenge is

how do you decide the impact of a performance? We may follow this criteria:

(i) The success of the film as per box office which is normally indicated by the revenues which also indicates the viewership and the duration of its run in the theatres;

(ii) The nature of reviews it has received and the credit given to the actor as a part of the reviews besides other variables like the story line, the dialogues, the songs, the settings, the editing, music and moral–social relevance at the time it has been made and released, and social impact;

2. *Magnitude and duration or span* of impact with which the acting tenure of the actor is linked. *The number of impact-making films* in which the actor has acted (male or female). This is a tricky criterion. A new actor may have acted in only a few films and then exited from the profession. For example, Bhagyashree acted only in one film, *Maine Pyar Kiya* and left a remarkable impression on all. But she got married soon after and did not act much. Do we include her as an effective actor? The normal response is that such an actor is effective only in that movie but can't be called as an effective actor for life, simply because she left acting. This reasoning holds unless she returns to acting again in the future. That means an effective actor is one who has made acting their profession and is available for a longer duration. The next question is how long? Generally cinema is perceived to be harsher on women, especially older women, than men, though this may not necessarily be the case. Whether you are a male actor or a female actor, there are many examples of being available for a long span of time and making an impact. Female actors like Asha Parekh, Wahida Rehman, Rekha, Saira Banu and Nirupa Roy in Bollywood and Anjali, Savitri, Janaki, Padmini and Bhanumathi in southern cinema had long and thriving acting careers. Singers of course have even longer

periods of impact. Male actors like Amitabh Bachchan, Rajendra Kumar, Dilip Kumar, Manoj Kumar, Ashok Kumar, Kishore Kumar, Raj Kapoor, Shammi Kapoor, Shashi Kapoor, Devanand, Pran, Rajendra Kumar, Rajesh Khanna, MGR, N.T. Rama Rao, A. Nageswara Rao and Satyanarayana continued to be available for acting roles all through their lives. For the purposes of this book, those who are career actors and available to make their impact for a reasonably long duration, leaving their imprints on the audience, and whose films are visited and revisited even today would be considered as effective actors. *Magnitude* of impact is a significant variable of effectiveness. Another dimension of the magnitude of impact is region/language specific. Actors from south India stand at a disadvantage as their audience is limited to a specific linguistic group. For example N.T. Rama Rao who used to be worshipped as Lord Krishna—every household had and still has his pictures in their homes and performs puja—is not likely to be known across the country or world as much as Amitabh Bachchan who acts in Hindi films. It is simply that the reach of Bollywood or Hindi films is much larger. We discount the linguistic limitations as we are not comparing statistics here but the relative impact in the groups for which the film or the actor's talent is meant. Nowadays the linguistic barrier is being broken slowly. For example, the recently released film of *Bahubali* with Prabhas in the lead role, backed by the popular film producer Karan Johar has hit record-breaking viewership across the country with a south Indian actor. Rajinikanth's films are also popular across the country.

3. It is said that female actors have a limited active screen life compared to their male counterparts; but the latter may have to learn to adjust to playing different roles as they get older and their popularity declines. An effective actor never retires.

Actors who manage their shelf life and keep bouncing back are more effective than those who fade into oblivion. Uday Kiran, after working in twenty-one successful films and even getting awards, ended his life when he was thirty-four. Of the twenty-one movies, *Chitram*, *Nuvvu Nenu* and *Manasantha Nuvve* were hits, earning him the title of 'Hat-trick Hero'. It was rumoured that he was going through depression due to lack of film offers and committed suicide.[7] Silk Smitha, on whose life *The Dirty Picture* was recently made, also committed suicide as she could not handle the ups and downs of her career.[8] Vijayalakshmi (1960–96), as she was originally named, worked predominantly in south Indian films. She entered the industry as an extra. She performed in various dance festivals and for various occasions like the Dussera in Mysore. Hema Malini started her own dance school to teach Bharat Natyam which is her skill base and she is trying to expand it by requesting for land in Mumbai. Ranga Shankara,[9] promoted by actor Arundhati Nag in the south, is a world-class theatre facility in Bangalore, and is one of the most affordable theatre spaces in India that is dedicated to the art of theatre.

Lessons for Effective People from Effective Actors: What Makes an Actor Effective (EP/EA), Very Effective (VEP/VEA) or Super Effective (SEP/SEA)?

1. Quality of acting: Popularity measured by fee charged and number of awards including recognition by various forums: Padma awards, National Awards, Filmfare Awards, etc.
2. Quality of impact, choice of films, and their influence on society: Socially aware films that have teaching and entertainment value and that don't propagate wrong values and culture.

3. Magnitude of impact: Duration of acting career and number of films.
4. Role model for the future: Upholding of Indian values and ethos by having model family, raising of children and role model for youth.
5. Charity and contribution to nation building: Working for a larger cause.
6. Institutionalization of talent: Contribution to culture, thought, art.

Translating these lessons, there could be an outline of ten action points for effectiveness of film actors:

1. You must master the art of acting and you must be good in your profession.
2. Have a long-term commitment to your profession.
3. Make choices that will bring out your talent and at the same time make a maximal impact on others. You should not only have skills but an attitude to influence. Aim at being the change maker. Make choices that gets you in the driver's seat as an agent of change.
4. Pass on a bit of your earnings to the less privileged.
5. Make your talent available to TV, newspapers and social media. Continuously learn from everywhere and from everyone.
6. Be positive. Never give up. If you manage the bad times, soon everything will pass and good times will come.
7. Discover your talent and spread it to others. Your students and followers will be your ambassadors. It is the legacy you leave behind.
8. Start institutions if you can as it is these institutions that will have a sustainable impact on society.
9. Never forget your values and ethics. We are what we are because of someone who helped us. Help people all the

time. Be associated with an NGO or start your own. Be an example and a role model for others.

Effective actors (EAs and EPs) act very well, are professional, stay long in the profession and continue to excel in their profession.

Very effective actors (VEAs or VEPs) extend their magnitude of effectiveness to many films by choosing the right ones and becoming popular and also getting involved in charity activities.

Super effective actors (SEAs or SEPs) are role models, they set standards for others, are highly committed to their profession, think about the society, extend themselves into society, start institutions, profess and leave values that are exemplary, build institutions that spread their message, are entrepreneurial and worthy of emulation.

Self-Assessment Tool: How Effective Are You as an Actor?
Use a five-point scale for evaluating:
5 = Very high, 4 = High, 3 = Moderate, 2 = Low and 1 = Very Low

EP/EA: How good are you as an actor in terms of the following criteria?

- ☐ 1. Skilled actor
- ☐ 2. Can perform any role with ease
- ☐ 3. Versatile actor. Can perform many roles
- ☐ 4. Carries out their job very well with sincerity
- ☐ 5. Delivers box-office hits
- ☐ 6. Can express feelings and takes the audience along, is identifiable
- ☐ 7. Understands and lives the characters assigned to them

☐   8. Has depth of knowledge of audience and their likes and dislikes

☐   9. Can cater to a variety of audiences in all cultures and impact them with their acting

☐ 10. Has creativity or originality of thinking and acting

☐ 11. Works hard and does justice to any role assigned to them

☐ 12. Offers movies that are well viewed and appreciated by many people

☐ 13. Acts in movies that are well acknowledged and written about

☐ 14. Value driven and known for integrity and honesty in work

☐ 15. Promotes values like maintaining good character, honesty, integrity and search for truth

☐ 16. Sets an example for others in following values

☐ 17. Lives as a role model

☐ 18. Carries out duties as a citizen: pays taxes, participates in events

☐ 19. Accessible to people and treats them with respect

☐ 20. Committed to the country; does not violate the rules of the land

VEA/VEP: Breadth and depth of reach through films and acting

☐   1. Acted in a large number of films

☐   2. Influenced a large number of people across the country in their language

☐   3. Impressed all people across the country in all languages

☐   4. This actor's work is well referred to across the world

☐   5. Popular in many other countries irrespective of linguistic barriers

SEA/SEP: Established institutions or processes and systems that make work and innovations and ideas available to many more people for future use and development of others

- ☐ 1. Have established many institutions to serve people
- ☐ 2. Have established at least one institution or agency that is doing well and is benefiting many people
- ☐ 3. A lot of good work is carried out by people in the institutions established
- ☐ 4. Ideas and messages reach out to a large number of people through the various media, books and articles
- ☐ 5. Many people benefit from the institutions established
- ☐ 6. Developed other people directly or contributed to the development of others

4 Civil Servants

Facilitating Development

The IIMA was set up to professionalize management in all sectors of society. It made significant strides in the industry and agriculture sectors and did some work in cooperatives and banking sectors. Education, health and government systems were next on the agenda. After stepping down as director of IIMA, Ravi J. Matthai was determined to work with education and introduce change and professional management in this sector. An Education Systems Unit was formed at IIMA in 1973 with Ravi Matthai, and myself as members, and Udai Pareek as coordinator. The three of us were invited in 1974 to attend a meeting at the Asian Institute of Educational Planning and Administration (now known as NUEPA University, ministry of HRD) at New Delhi, sponsored by UNESCO. The same workshop was also being attended by Mrs Chitra Naik, then director of education in Maharashtra, and Anil Bordia, joint secretary education, ministry of education, New Delhi. Between the sessions we went out for a meeting with J.P. Naik, Anil Bordia and Chitra Naik to discuss the interest of the education systems group in initiating change in the education department of any state. J.P. Naik was education adviser to the Prime Minister Indira Gandhi at that time. During the meeting Mrs Naik offered Maharashtra as a place of experiment for our work. We did not know what exactly we needed to do to initiate change but merely said that we would like to assist in professionalizing management through some innovations. It was during this lunch that Anil Bordia offered that Rajasthan could be a prime place for our work. As there was already a 'High Power Committee' in education with the minister of education as its chairman and they had already submitted a report of educational reforms in Rajasthan, there was a lot of scope for innovations in that state. He suggested that he could get the government of Rajasthan to extend all support and help them to implement it so that it would meet our objective. The state department's J.P. Naik (member Secretary, ICSSR) offered to support it as a research project. The meeting ended with the agreement that the work would be done in Rajasthan and the task would be to help the government of Rajasthan to implement the High Power Committee report. The project would be called as 'Educational Innovations in Rajasthan'. A steering committee was also formed with Ravi, Udai, myself, J. P. Naik, Chitra Naik, Anil Bordia, Inderjit Khanna (director of education), with the intention to meet periodically and review the progress.

A sum of Rs 50,000 was sanctioned by ICSSR to the project 'Educational Innovations in Rajasthan' to meet the travel and living expenses of the education systems unit from IIMA with Ravi Matthai as the project director.

We all met again in Delhi first and again in Jaipur and the work began in earnest. The High Power Committee identified many issues which have remained unresolved even after forty years: low school enrolment and high dropout rates, poor enrolment of girls, location and upgradation of schools, teacher transfers and transfer policies, quality of teachers and teaching, supervision and guidance to schools by educational administrators, etc. After studying the report we identified the school dropouts and quality of education as major areas. The three of us (Matthai, Pareek and I) chose the Ajmer and Jaipur districts of Rajasthan to understand the situation. We interviewed the top-level administrators and also visited many schools and villages. We concluded in 1975 that the educational administrators had little time to guide the teachers as they were mostly busy in administration, particularly teacher transfers and appointments, and rarely visited the schools to see the goings-on in the field. We also discovered that the schools are not seen as places of relevance by the locals and the villagers questioned the kind of education that was being imparted to the children. In fact, they complained that school education, the way it was being given, was responsible for unemployment—their wards who went to school stopped working in the farms and couldn't land any jobs either. We concluded that one of the ways to improve school enrolment as desired by the High Power Committee was to make what was being taught more relevant.

We worked out a three-pronged strategy to help implement the High Power Committee recommendations. First we were to release the administrative burden of the educational administrators by forming right policies and promoting the use of technology. Prof. T.P. Rama Rao and I worked on developing a computer model for teacher transfers and also for location of schools. The Dharampur Project experience came in handy for the location of schools. The minister of education, Rajasthan, even visited IIMA to see the Dharampur model and understand how teacher transfers through computers can ease the administrative burden. Of course the government may not have been convinced as perhaps using computerized solutions (MIS) for teacher transfers may have negated human control over the issue. We, in fact, explained that every genuine teacher transfer is accompanied by three to four unnecessary transfers due to limited and faulty MIS. This remained only as an experience and the reports of the two projects are still available in IIMA.

We set out to tour and study some blocks of the Ajmer district so as to get a clear picture of the educational needs of the communities. By the time we had toured and met people in some of the blocks of Ajmer district, the picture became clear. We did not even get to tour the other districts. We felt that education had become irrelevant for the villagers. It had to be made more useful and our work was charted out—how to make education more relevant to people in rural areas. It is this issue that led to a series of other questions. Ravi Matthai felt that to make it relevant again we had to identify local resources and create value addition in ways that the people could experience the same. It had to be done by and through the education department. We felt that this could not be done by mere recommendations to the government, as there already existed plenty of them, but through demonstration. We would have to demonstrate to them how to identify local resources, how to add value and how to make education linked to economic activity. Ajmer was chosen to demonstrate this. I still remember Ravi making a comment: 'We will demonstrate this in Ajmer district in six months and extend it to the remaining three districts in three years and leave it for the government to extend it to the rest of the state.' I was too young to have any views on this plan. It was an experience to work with Ravi and the other team members. I was overwhelmed to get an opportunity to work with some famous people like J.P. Naik. One of the places we visited at that time was Tilonia where the Social Work and Research Centre (SWRC) started by Aruna Roy and Bunker Roy was operating. Aruna left her civil service job and joined to work on non-formal education. Ravi Matthai also happened to be the chairman of SWRC. The main issue for discussion in those days used to be how to help the rural masses to get educated. We were naive enough not to realize that we were getting educated by the people instead!

After touring around the Ajmer district we chose the Jawaja block for the following reasons: It was backward and at the same time had some resources like agriculture (tomatoes used to be sold at Rs 2.5 a basket containing 5 to 10 kgs), sheep, tendu leaves, etc. which were amenable for economic activity. Local occupations like weaving, leatherwork and other such traditional methods were amenable for modernization. These and other details are documented in some of the case studies. (See, for example, the case study on 'Educational Innovations for Rural Development' by T.V. Rao and the book called *The Rural University* by Ravi Matthai.) When we presented our ideas to the ICSSR committee in the District Collector's office in Ajmer (R.S. Kumat was the District Collector), the committee, including Anil Bordia, were not convinced. They said that Ravi and his team should go ahead and do whatever they felt right but this would not help the High Power Committee much. Ravi argued that there was no easy solution to implement the committee report unless the basic issues were settled. I think it was at this time that the ICSSR committee started losing interest, except J.P. Naik who worked all his life on educational issues. I remember JP visiting IIMA a few years later and my taking him out to Vishala for dinner and having a long chat on these issues.

We set out to use Jawaja as an experimental block to demonstrate how education (primary and basic) could be made relevant to the masses. We tried many experiments including forming farmer cooperatives in agricultural produce, dairying, beedi making with tendu leaves, teaching new weaving skills to a group of defunct weavers, forming a cooperative society in Beawar Khas, and training a group of leather workers in leather processing using modern methods and making new types of products, etc. In all these experiments the education department, including the teachers and the deputy education inspector of schools from Beawar, used to accompany us. Many workshops were conducted to motivate schoolteachers to participate in the economic activity mobilization and curriculum development. For example, a number of them took part in conducting night classes in villages for mobilizing farmers producing tomatoes to form a society and sell their produce directly in city markets. Of all these, what stayed on was only the skill building of a group of weavers and leather workers. These are the products which even today are exhibited by AAJ (Artisans Alliance, Jawaja).

Ravi suffered a heart attack during one of the exhibitions of the Jawaja products in Mumbai. Subsequently, the need for developing the marketing skills of the NID-developed artisans to market their products, teaching them accounting, managing their accounts, helping them take loans from banks, working out repayment schedules, etc. became the main tasks. Both Udai and I dropped out from constant involvement in the project, and Tushar Moulik and Ranjit Gupta started participating actively in it and working with AAJ. Finally, only Ranjit stayed and from NID it was Ashok Chatterjee who continued to be involved with Jawaja passionately.

Jawaja produced many people who learnt a lot from it and are helping others. Mehmood Khan, Brian Pinto, Subramanian (MIDS), Arvind Khare and several others associated with Jawaja have contributed in their own ways to society from their learnings. NID continues to stay involved in the same.

The concept of self-reliance was at the heart of the Jawaja experiment: education that could help those whose lives are directed by others to take greater charge and make choices, and then realize at least some of the choices they make—and do this without greater dependence on others. The original article 'The Rural University' written by Ravi at that time explains the education system he had in mind very succinctly. This article was circulated by many vice chancellors in those days to their entire faculty. The fact that those Ravi chose to work with were at the very bottom of a highly discriminatory social structure is noteworthy. The Jawaja experiment had a lot of influence on so many others—the 'bottom of the pyramid' thinking is said to have begun with Jawaja. Vijay Mahajan was deeply influenced by the Jawaja experiment in starting and managing Pradan, an institution for professional management of NGOs. The project learning had a ripple effect beyond the IIMA family into so many institutions that have altered the course of development thinking in the country including Pradan, Utthan, NID, the Crafts Council of India and so many others through demonstration, as well as the 'Jawaja alumni'. As Ashok Chatterjee, former director of NID, puts it, 'The impact on NID was profound, influencing the way design education has been structured ever since. Ravi's involvement with NID is another whole story. It might not have existed today but for him, and his contribution is scarcely remembered beyond the Jawaja connection. In Jawaja, he gave NID a chance to test the relevance of design at the gut level of Indian poverty— the single-most important demonstration ever, to date. The demonstration came at a time of institutional crisis where the self-worth of an institution was at stake. And that of course was one of the intentions of The Rural University idea: to test the relevance of new disciplines emerging in the country and of young professionals from management and design to serve India's most basic needs of livelihoods and dignity.'

Role of Civil Servants:

I have started this chapter with this story because even after over six decades of Independence, India is struggling to find ways and means to make education relevant by up-skilling people, enhancing literacy rates, reducing school dropouts, ensuring women get their due, encouraging rural entrepreneurship, increasing agriculture production, becoming health and environment conscious, etc. We are still groping in the dark. Many of the people associated with the project died. J.P. Naik died in 1981. He served as member secretary of the Indian Education Commission from 1964 to 1966 and was educational adviser to the Government of India. Ravi Matthai died in 1984. Chitra Naik died in 2010. Both J.P. Naik and Chitra were Padma awardees. Chitra also served as a member of the Planning Commission. Anil Bordia died in 2012 and Udai Pareek in 2010. Inderjit Khanna lives in Jaipur. In my view, all of them—JP, Chitra, Khanna and Bordia offer excellent examples of effective civil servants. I have seen and worked with many civil servants. For me, Inderjit Khanna and Anil Bordia stand out. I will mention briefly their stories and then go on to discuss other effective civil servants.

INDERJIT KHANNA

Inderjit Khanna joined the Indian Administrative Service in 1966 in the Rajasthan cadre and after initial years as SDM, collector, deputy secretary and director of education, he spent fairly long periods of posting in the fields of rural development, education, planning and finance. This included two tenures of over six years each with the Government of India including secretary of UGC, and a spell of two years as a visiting professor at IIMA from 1981 to 1983. His last posting for three years was as chief Secretary, Rajasthan. After retiring in December 2002, he was appointed and worked as the state election commissioner, Rajasthan for five years. He is currently associated with the Gita Mittal Foundation which is running three centres for skill development of youth in Rajasthan. He is also on the committees and boards of seven institutions in the fields of health, education and rural development. Inder is a highly value driven person. After having worked for his entire life as an IAS officer, he leads a simple life in Jaipur as he followed all the values a civil servant should inculcate— honesty, integrity and commitment to public service. In his own career, when faced with the choice of going to work in the US or UK on study leave or to work at IIMA, Inder chose IIMA and worked as a visiting professor quite unlike many civil servants who would have preferred a stint at JF Kennedy School or some such place. The following is a quote from the paper he wrote in memory of Udai Pareek:[1]

'Corruption has emerged as one of the most pernicious threats to governance in India. There is a perception that it encompasses all spheres of governance. The bureaucracy, being under constant glare of the public has, therefore, necessarily to raise much above this perception by not only being honest but, as stated earlier, appearing to be honest.

'The basic objective of governance is to provide well-being, comfort and happiness to the people. This can be done when those who are entrusted with the responsibility to govern do so with a sense of responsibility, in an environment of transparency, exhibiting a culture of accountability and as people with integrity.'

ANIL BORDIA

Anil Bordia, though an IAS officer, is widely respected for his contributions to the Indian education sector and is considered a foremost Indian educationist and social activist. He played a proactive role in the formulation of a number of innovative education policies and programmes. His contribution in designing the New Education Policy—1986 and Programme of Action—1992, National University of Education, Policy and Administration (NUEPA), and launching innovative educational programmes such as, 'Mahila Samakhya', 'Shiksha Karmi', 'Lok Jumbish', 'Doosra Dashak', etc., is quite significant. '. . . He was passionate about taking education to the masses and making every Indian literate. In this endeavour, he roped in academicians, activists, journalists and educationists who would otherwise have maintained a distance from "government work",' wrote Rajesh Tandon in *Testing the Limits of the System*. He worked within the system to change it and subvert its regressive tendencies.

During his public service, he launched the Bihar education project from 1977 through 1980, where he assembled many voluntary organizations, academic institutions and public resource centres to work towards achieving total literacy in the state. He was also behind Mahila Samakhya, a women's education project which has participation from various women's movements. In 1987, he launched the Shiksha Karmi programme for eradicating illiteracy from the state of Rajasthan. Under the programme, society monitored schools with locally trained teachers were introduced, which was reported to be successful in the universalization of primary education in the state

After his retirement from government service in 1992, Anil Bordia embarked on an education programme for the young illiterates in Rajasthan which he conceptualized and named Lok Jumbish. He guided the program me till 1999 and it was stated to be a highly successful initiative. In 2001, Bordia launched another movement, Doosra Dashak, which was aimed at the education and development of the youth. He also headed a committee, Right to Education (RTE), which submitted a detailed report with suggestions to synchronize the norms and strategies of the RTE with that of the Sarva Shiksha Abhiyan, a government programme mandated to achieve Universalization of Elementary Education (UEE), so that operational synergies are achieved. He was also vocal about women's role in society and girls' participation in primary education.

Krishna Kumar, a noted educationist, had the following to say about Bordia:[2]

'One can hardly think of an educational initiative launched by the Union government during the last quarter of the twentieth century which did not carry Anil Bordia's mark. As a civil servant, he distinguished himself by identifying with the cause of educational reform, and then by redefining what governance in education might mean. He was an endearing man, exuding passion for his work and always keen to find ways to get things moving. He wore his status lightly, so lightly that a stranger might well feel confused on being told that Anil Bordia was a civil servant. There was nothing awkward or assembled about his modesty. One knew instantly that he cared.'

Anil Bordia tirelessly encouraged a mind-boggling range of ideas and initiatives. Many of them, indirectly and often invisibly, allowed deeper creative forces that the system was used to ignoring, even crushing, to be released and accommodated.

Civil Servants and Their Role and Obligations

Civil servants in India include several services: the IAS, IPS, IFS, IRS, IAAS, etc. The various civil services at the union and state levels can be classified in three broad groups—central civil services, all India services and the state civil services. The central services function under the Union government and are generally engaged in administering subjects which are assigned to the union under the Constitution, whereas the all India services are common to the union and the states, and the state services function only under the state governments. The central civil services administer subjects like post and telegraphs, railways, customs and central excise, income tax, telecommunications, etc. The Administrative Reforms Commission report lists fifty-eight such services including some specialist services like the Indian Revenue Service, Indian Accounts and Audit Service, Indian Information Service, Indian Foreign Service, etc. As per the administrative reforms report there are 55,184 civil servants in India classified under group A of all India and central services. The Indian Administrative Service, Indian Police Service and Indian Forest Service are considered as all India services. IAS and IPS officers play a major role in the country. The specialist services also play a significant role. For the purposes of this discussion I have largely drawn cases from the IAS and IPS—lessons drawn here are equally applicable to other services. I have also included specialist services like the IRS while discussing some exceptionally effective people.

'Civil servants have special obligations because they are responsible for managing resources entrusted to them by the community, because they provide and deliver services to the community and because they take important decisions that affect all aspects of a community's life. The community has a right to expect that the civil service functions fairly, impartially and efficiently. It is essential that the community must be able to trust and have confidence in the integrity of the civil service decision-making process. Within the civil service itself, it needs to be ensured that the decisions and actions of civil servants reflect the policies of the government of the day and the standards that the community expects from them as government servants. The expectation that the civil service will maintain the same standards of professionalism, responsiveness and impartiality in serving successive political governments is a key element of the way our democratic polity functions.

'In a democracy, an efficient civil service must have a set of values that distinguishes it from other professions. Integrity, dedication to public service, impartiality, political neutrality, anonymity, etc. are said to be the hallmarks of an efficient civil service.'[3]

The Administrative Reforms Commission (ARC) suggests the following principles in the Code of Ethics for civil servants in India:[4]

- Integrity: Civil servants should be guided solely by public interest in their official decision-making and not by any financial or other consideration either in respect of themselves, their families or their friends.
- Impartiality: Civil servants in carrying out their official work, including functions like procurement, recruitment, delivery of services, etc., should take decisions based on merit alone.
- Commitment to public service: Civil servants should deliver services in a fair, effective, impartial and courteous manner.
- Open accountability: Civil servants are accountable for their decisions and actions and should be willing to subject themselves to appropriate scrutiny for this purpose.
- Devotion to duty: Civil servants maintain absolute and unstinting devotion towards their duties and responsibilities at all times.
- Exemplary behaviour: Civil servants shall treat all members of the public with respect and courtesy and, at all times, should behave in a manner that upholds the rich traditions of the civil services.

The amended rules state that every member of the all India services, which includes the IAS and IPS, shall be courteous and responsive to the public, particularly the weaker sections, and ensure accountability and transparency in discharge of his duties.

Let us now look at some outstanding civil servants and study their effectiveness.

N. VITTAL

A Maharashtrian, N. Vittal was born in Thiruvananthapuram and was educated in Tiruchirapalli and Chennai. He graduated with BSc (Hons) in Chemistry from Loyola College, Madras in 1958. He belonged to the IAS batch of 1960, and is one of the eminent public servants of India, who has held important positions in the Government of India, the most prominent of which was that of the Central Vigilance Commissioner.

N. Vittal has held a number of assignments at the state and Central government. As Secretary to the Government of India, he initiated policies for boosting software, setting up software technology parks and strategic alliances with the corporate sector. He was successful in introducing the electronics hardware technology park scheme, whereby, mini Hong Kongs and mini Singapores could be created in India to boost manufacture of electronic hardware. He made the department of electronics a front runner in adjusting to the new industry-friendly policy, encouraging Foreign Direct Investment (FDI) from IBM, Motorola, etc. As chairman, Telecom Commission, he initiated the process of liberalization in the telecom sector and played a major role in getting the National Telecom Policy 1994 approved and announced.

Some of the other major achievements during his career are: Revival of the Kandla Free Trade Zone, opening of the Dahej Port in Gujarat, and the emergence of the Gujarat Narmada Valley Fertiliser Company (GNFC) not only as an efficient business enterprise but also as a model for what a public sector unit can do for backward area development, especially in education, health, culture and environment, and management. GNFC was a zero pollution plant. He set up the single window service for the industry promotion bureau in Gujarat, which was adopted later by other states. As Secretary (civil supplies), he set up the Gujarat State Civil Supplies Corporation and as Additional Chief Secretary (Home), initiated the proposal for setting up the Gujarat Police Housing Corporation. As chairman, Public Enterprises Selection Board, he initiated measures for greater transparency and speed in the functioning of the PESB. He headed the committee which resulted in the cancellation of 696 obsolete guidelines hampering the autonomy of the PSEs.

Widely travelled, Vittal's interests also lie in application of management principles in organization, in the public and private sectors. He has written more than 400 articles on various subjects relating to management, public relations, human resources development, management of technology, public sector management, etc. in many journals and magazines.

His Values: He has always fought for transparency in the system. Vittal valued reading and writing. He kept in touch with all developments of the field wherever he was posted. He was known as a creative civil servant, upright, transparent and accessible.

According to Mr Vittal, the strength of an IAS officer is his ignorance. It allowed him to learn to function better. His long experience in the government taught him that each individual had something to give that could bring joy. A close associate of Mr Vittal and former civil servant of the Gujarat cadre, G. Sundaram, said Mr Vittal believed in transparency and putting politicians in their place.

VINOD RAI[5]

Vinod Rai (born in 1948), famous as CAG (Comptroller and Auditor General) of India, is the epitome of the anti-corruption movement and has been credited with having turned the office of the CAG into a powerful force for accountability and transparency in contemporary India. Rai holds a master's degree in economics from Delhi University and in public administration from Harvard University. He is a 1972-batch IAS officer and he started his career as the sub-collector of Thrissur district. He was called the second Sakthan Thampuran for his role in the development of Thrissur city. Prior to his appointment as CAG, he served as Secretary, financial services and additional Secretary in the banking division including banks and insurance companies under the ministry of finance. According to Dr Anil Khandelwal (in a personal communication with the author) Mr Rai is a 'learning bureaucrat who is humble, a good listener and always open'. Dr Khandelwal attributes the success of the Bank of Baroda to the proactive support provided by Vinod Rai as secretary of banking (*Dare to Lead*, Anil Khandelwal, New Delhi: Response Books, 2013). A few months after Mr Rai took over as CAG, I happened to listen to his keynote speech on the Civil Services Day in Vigyan Bhavan when he spelt out his mission of creating a new image for audit as a 'proactive tool'.

Rai was instrumental in setting up the India Infrastructure Finance Company and was director on several boards including the State Bank of India, ICICI Bank, IDBI Bank, Life Insurance Corporation of India and Infrastructure Development and Finance Company of India. He is the chairman of the United Nations Panel of External Auditors and member of the governing board of the International Organization of Supreme Audit Institutions (INTOSAI). The United Nations Secretary-General Ban Ki Moon has appreciated the panel and the yeoman service rendered by the external auditors in improving governance in the United Nations system.

Forbes described Rai as being among that rare breed of civil servants who knows how to get work done in the government. A former colleague says Rai has an uncanny ability to cut through red tape. He was appointed as Comptroller and Auditor General of India with the backing of finance minister P. Chidambaram. But he has served up uncomfortable audit reports that have pinned many government departments beyond the baseline.

As a part of his duty, Rai has many a times raised questions on the faulty policymaking of several state governments and the Union government run by the Congress-led United Progressive Alliance and BJP-led governments in Chhattisgarh and Gujarat. He wrote a book after his retirement—*Not Just an Accountant: The Diary of the Nation's Conscience Keeper*, which speaks about how the political system was exploited to violate laws.

D.R. MEHTA[6]

D.R. Mehta is an IAS officer of the 1961 batch. He held numerous important positions initially in the government of Rajasthan and later in the Central government. Mehta served as chairman of SEBI from 1995 to 2002. During Mehta's tenure, a slew of economic reforms were introduced making the Indian capital market one of the most modern and efficient ones in the world, attracting both local and foreign investors in large numbers. From 1992 to 1995 Mehta served as the deputy governor of the Reserve Bank of India (RBI). Still earlier, from 1991 to 1992 he was the director general of foreign trade, Government of India, and ministry of commerce. Prior to this, from 1989 to 1991, Mehta was Additional Secretary to the Government of India in the ministry of finance, dealing with banking.

From 1974 to 1989, except for a period of five years in between when he was serving the ministry of finance in the Government of India, Mehta served the state government of Rajasthan in various senior positions as the Secretary to the government in the departments of industries, mines and special programmes for the poor, etc. During this period he was the Secretary to the chief minister of Rajasthan.

D.R. Mehta has been active in the social field throughout his life. He set up Bhagwan Mahaveer Viklang Sahayata Samiti (BMVSS) in Jaipur in 1975 and is now its full-time honorary volunteer. Under his leadership, BMVSS emerged as the largest organization for the handicapped in the world, providing artificial limbs/calipers and other aids and appliances for free. More than one million people have been its beneficiaries so far. Harvard and Michigan universities use it as a case study.

Mehta's focus on combining social service with science led to an MOU between Stanford University and BMVSS, resulting in the development of a new knee joint called the Jaipur Knee. It was hailed by *Time Magazine* as one of the 50 Best Inventions of the World for the year 2009.

Mehta is also a well-known animal rights activist. He has started and has been associated with some animal rescue homes, and has also published literature on animal welfare.

D.R. Mehta has been honoured at national and international levels including a Padma Bhushan by the President of India. Mehta received the Tech Museum Award for Innovation and Its Use for Humanity in Silicon Valley in November 2007. He is also a recipient of the Indian for Collective Action Award, Diwali Behan Award (conferred by the Dalai Lama), CNBC Award for Social Enterprise, Satpal Mittal Award, etc. Mr Mehta is also a director on the Europe/Asia Board of the Alfred Sloan School of Management, MIT, USA. D.R. Mehta has also been bestowed the Rajiv Gandhi National Sadbhavana Award this year. The award, which carries a citation and a cash prize of Rs 5 lakhs, has been given for his outstanding contribution towards the promotion of communal harmony, peace and goodwill. In 2013 he was conferred with the Rajasthan Ratan by the Rajasthan government.

E. SREEDHARAN

Elattuvalapil Sreedharan is a retired Indian Engineering Service (IES) officer popularly known as the 'Metro Man'. He served as the managing director of the Delhi Metro from 1995–2012 and was chosen for the prestigious Lokmanya Tilak Award 2013.

Sreedharan's star quality began to show early in his career. He trained as a civil engineer in Kakinda, Andhra Pradesh. At Indian Railways he made his mark by restoring a storm-ravaged bridge in forty-six days which might have otherwise taken six months. He went on to help design India's first metro in Kolkata in 1970 and then served as head of the Cochin Shipyard in Kerala.

He officially retired in 1990 but was lured back to work to build the Konkan Railway, which runs through mountainous terrain to connect strategic ports in Mumbai and Mangalore.

The quest for excellence came naturally to Elattuvalapil Sreedharan. In school, he would vie with T.N. Seshan, the former chief election commissioner, to come first in class. The seventy-three-year-old managing director of Delhi Metro Rail Corporation set a scorching pace for his co-workers to follow. That competitive streak in him has motivated the 1650-strong workforce to avoid delay or cost-overrun and to transform the Delhi Metro into a technological marvel. His no-nonsense, bureaucracy-busting efficiency helped him to accomplish what had seemed impossible in India: finish building the initial $2.3 billion subway system in 2005 under budget and almost three years ahead of schedule. If anyone can pull off this daunting $4.25 billion project it is a man whose humble serenity is not incidental; he wakes up well before dawn every day to meditate and read the Bhagavad Gita, does yoga each morning and walks for at least forty-five minutes in the evening. A plaque in his office quotes from the Indian scripture *Yog Vashisht*: 'Work I do; not that "I" do it.'

In one of his visits to his alma mater, BEM Mission higher secondary school, Palakkad, in 2009, Sreedharan suggested that the school curriculum should include imbibing moral values, developing integrity and learning the importance of our culture. He also mentioned that he owed a lot to his teachers in the school who helped him develop values and confidence which made the government entrust him with the Konkan Railway project and the Rs 20,000-crore Delhi Metro Rail project. Despite achieving such great feats in his career, E. Sreedharan is a humble man who never forgot his roots and used his skill and knowledge to overcome obstacles and to make contributions for the betterment of his nation and its people.

KIRAN BEDI[7]
Kiran Bedi is India's first woman IPS officer (1972–2007). She joined the Indian Police Service in 1972. Her experience and expertise include more than thirty-five years of tough, innovative and welfare policing. Kiran Bedi is a role model who has inspired and shaped many of India's current women achievers.

She got her doctorate in 1993 from the Indian Institute of Technology, New Delhi for her thesis, Drug abuse and Domestic Violence. Kiran Bedi was posted to Tihar in 1993–95; and converted the high-security prison into a Reformatory, a transformation of a magnitude unparalleled in the history of prison administration anywhere in the world. Her courageous and holistic approach towards prison governance became a major factor in her earning the prestigious Ramon Magsaysay Award for Government Service in the year 1994. The process of transformation of Tihar is documented in Kiran's book, It's Always Possible.

Traffic police postings came to Kiran in early years of her service. She was unsparing in enforcing discipline on the roads.

Due to the presence of a large number of cranes to remove wrongly parked vehicles—including that of a former Prime Minister—she was nicknamed 'Crane Bedi'. She rewarded honesty and cooperation to motivate others. The citizens of Delhi still remember her for this posting.

She initiated sharing of information on narcotics through a magazine called *Narcontrol* of which she was the editor. The magazine carried information, which hitherto was considered confidential. To date, this is the only official magazine on narcotics in the country. Along with her official duties, she continued working on drug abuse prevention with Navijyoti, a non-profit organization, she had set up during her earlier tenure.

With her posting in the Police Training College in June 1998, she transformed it from a neglected police training school to a fully equipped, techno savvy, innovative and vibrant institution. During Kiran's posting as Special Secretary to the lieutenant governor she set up a system called the Public Redressal Unit. It enabled anyone to reach the LG office through phone, mail, fax and even personally.

After quitting the police services—she retired in 2007—she launched Saferindia.com which is intended to be a bridge between the police and the complainant, where one can only send in a grievance when it has not been heard by the former.

'My idols are values. My future is developing. The effort goes on. Let us see where this effort becomes destiny,' says Kiran Bedi.

K.P.C.H. GANDHI: TRUTH LABS[8]
Dr Gandhi has degrees in subjects ranging from physics to Gandhian thought to criminal justice from universities in India and abroad. He joined the Central Forensic Science Lab,

Government of India in 1970 and was elevated to the rank of IGP, Police Scientific Services, the first such distinction in India, and director of the Andhra Pradesh Forensic Sciences Laboratory (APFSL) by 1992. He achieved 'Zero Pendency' in the APFSL in 100 days by clearing all cases, some of which had been pending for several years. Dr Gandhi has been responsible for the successful investigation of a number of sensational and sensitive crime cases in the past like the 'Noida Nithari' murder case, 'Tehelka Tapes' case, Godhra aftermath riots case, etc. He got recognition and rewards from various government and non-government bodies including the Union Home Minister's Award for 'Excellence in Forensic Sciences' and several other international and national awards. After retiring in 2007, Dr Gandhi chose to make use of his expertise and started two non-profit organizations—Crime Stoppers Foundation India and Truth Foundation, to enable people to fight crime. He continues to work for this cause and hopes to see a crime-free society some day.

Truth Labs, a subsidiary of Truth Foundation, is a laboratory exclusively set up in the quest of truth and pursuit of justice, to help, assist and guide the victims of crime and injustice. Truth Labs provides legally valid expert services by accredited experts to individuals and institutions directly without the need to come through the police or courts.

Recently the *Economic Times* wrote about Dr Gandhi:[9] 'Sitting across the table and sipping his filter coffee at a restaurant in Bengaluru, Gandhi is every bit the 50s Hollywood detective, with a pencil-line moustache and sharp piercing eyes. It is in his nature to pay attention to detail and he speaks in a measured metre. Normally, he is known as a cool customer. At the same time, there is a justice activist side to the man, which causes some agitation and animated remarks. He vents anger at the scale of corruption, repeatedly pointing out how difficult it is for the honest to survive and repeatedly starts his comments in that typical manner of middle-class India with an indignant "In this country . . ." Gandhi has examined the viscera of many a scam and knows the nature of the manipulations and now that he has retired from government service, he says, he feels the need to speak out.'

NAGABHAIRAVA JAYAPRAKASH NARAYAN[10]

Narayan is a former Indian public administrator, well known for his role in electoral reforms and the Right to Information (RTI) Act. He has also written columns in Indian newspapers, such as Times of India, The Economic Times, Financial Express, The Hindu and Eenadu, and hosted television shows covering elections and politics such as Pratidhwani. JP joined the IAS in 1980, emerging the all India topper and worked on agriculture, irrigation, technology and youth rehabilitation projects in various capacities and in various districts of Andhra Pradesh.

Dr Narayan's experience in the government convinced him that the faulty governance process is the biggest hurdle in India's path of progress and Indians achieving greater success. What India needs today is a fundamental change in the rules of the game and not a periodic change of players. In order to translate his vision into practical reality, he resigned from the IAS in 1996 so that he could work on the grass-roots movement for good governance. Dr Narayan is the founder member of the Foundation for Democratic Reforms (FDR) and currently serves as its general secretary. FDR is one of India's leading think tanks and research resource centres for formulating and promoting fundamental reforms in political, electoral and governance spheres and in critical areas of state policy. He started the Lok Satta Movement in 1996 to educate the citizens of India about voting, rights and government. The Lok Satta movement has also been a driving force in achieving quite a few governance reforms in recent years, among others: improvements in voter registration, disclosure of candidate details, political funding reform law of 2003, Right to Information Act, 2005, National Rural Health Mission (2005).

There are many civil servants in India who have done marvellous work but are not included here as it is meant to be illustrative and not exhaustive. D.J. Pandian, a 1981 batch IAS officer in the Gujarat cadre, was responsible for starting the Pandit Dennadayal Petroleum University in Gandhinagar. As described by Dr P. Selvaraj, one of his long-term associates from his village in Tamil Nadu, 'He is sincere, honest, a man of clean habits, god fearing, cheerful, energetic, bold, emotionally sensitive, positive, hard-working, enterprising and humble. A simple attempt to map his personality applying David McClelland's theory would result in the following score; Need for Achievement: 90, Need for Power: 25, Need for Affiliation: 80 and Need for Extension: 90.

'DJP's thirst for social service did not stop with discharging his duties as an IAS officer. He inspired his eldest brother Shri. D. Jagaveerapandian, to establish a charitable society, Navajeevan Educational and Welfare Society, in the year 1989 and Navajeevan Educational and Awareness Trust in the year 2000; both in Thiruthangal, Virudhunagar district. The society has established and is running a child development centre in Madurai (1998); a high school in Madurai (1998); and, a teacher training institute (2007), a college for education (2009), and an arts and sciences college (2012); all in Kannirajapuram village. All are service-oriented, poor-friendly, not-for-profit organizations in the real sense.'

Abhayanand[11] is an IPS officer and educationist who conceptualized Super 30 with Anand Kumar to teach poor students to crack IIT JEE. Following his graduation from Science

College, Patna, Abhayanand was selected as the IPS officer for the Bihar cadre after clearing the UPSC Civil Services Examination in 1977. He was the ADG (headquarters) in 2006 and as such he concentrated on the speedy trial of Arms Act cases in Bihar. Later, during his tenure as the ADG of Bihar Military Police, Patna, he motivated the constables to donate generously from their salaries to metamorphose a dilapidated government hospital into a modern nursing home with state-of-the-art facilities for treatment of the police force and their family members. From 2003 to 2008, Abhayanand used to coach the students along with Anand Kumar. However, he split from Anand Kumar in 2007 and then wanted to take his social experiment to a wider forum so that more underprivileged but talented children could benefit out of it. He started a programme called Rahmani 30 where underprivileged Muslim students were selected and then coached for the JEE. In the inaugural year of Rahmani 30, all of the ten students who took part in this programme in 2009 cleared the JEE. In 2010, four students out of twelve cracked the entrance test. Three out of fifteen Rahmani 30 students cleared the exam in 2011.

B.N. Yugandhar and K.R. Venugopal are two interesting IAS officers who are examples of total devotion to development. Both of them served in Prime Minister P.V. Narasimha Rao's government and continued their development activities even after their retirement. Both of them help NGOs to carry out various projects in rural development. The development orientation of Yugandhar is reflected in the way he raised his son Satya Nadella who is now the CEO of Microsoft. Moreover, Yugandhar preferred his only son to be connected to his village. 'Yugandhar used to take Satya to the fields whenever they would visit Bukkapuram,' Hari Prasad, a villager, now settled in Bangalore, told a newspaper.[12]

What Do We Conclude from All These Cases of Effective Civil Servants?

1. Effective civil servants, whichever service they are in, seem to take their job very seriously and deliver results in whatever posting they get. They have internalized their role and work with devotion. They are not rebels but carry out their duties well. Some of them may have reformist attitudes but they serve with commitment as all reformist attitudes are meant to serve larger causes. Only in stray cases when they feel that they can't do systemic reforms from within, they leave the service midway and start doing things differently. They demonstrate high role efficacy.[13]

2. They are highly value driven. They understand the civil service code and follow it well. They are followers of the system and not system breakers.

3. They set examples for others in the way they carry out various activities, tasks and functions associated with their job. They go beyond the rules and maintain the spirit of the rules. They are more purpose driven than merely rule driven. They make the mission of the organization their personal mission.

4. They follow the code of conduct of the civil services, but operate within the allowable framework. They do not limit their work to office hours and they use all the available time in a day as their work hours.

5. They get agitated if the purpose for which the civil service exists is not fulfilled. When they see too much injustice and when things are not being done, they quit the civil service to pursue their mission. They acquire the mission from the way they discharge their duties. They become role models in the way they do things inside and outside.

6. They are creative and innovative and have a high concern for the society.
7. The super effective ones set up their own institutions. They are institution builders: Gandhi set up Truth Labs, D.R. Mehta the Bhagwan Mahaveer Viklang Sahayata Samiti (BMVSS), Anil Bordia the Lok Jumbish and many others. Jayaprakash Narayan set up Lok Satta. Kiran Bedi started her own NGO.
8. They work for larger development goals.
9. They are humble except for those that have left the service who may sometimes become activists..
10. They are restless and hard-working.
11. They are widely travelled and are ready to talk and propagate their points of view.
12. Many of them document their experiences and write books. They fit well into the leadership qualities outlined by Noel Tichy. Leaders have points of view and they keep influencing others with those points of view.

Assessing the Effectiveness of Civil Servants
Use a five-point scale to rate yourself:
5 = Very high, 4 = High, 3 = Moderate, 2 = Low and 1 = Very low

ECS/EP: How good are you as a civil servant in terms of the following criteria?

☐   1. Depth of knowledge as an officer in civil services or in your areas of work (for IAS as a generalist and for IPS, IRS and others as a generalist within the specialized service)

☐   2. Breadth of knowledge in your area of work (as a generalist or specialist)

☐   3. Desire to learn whenever posted to a new area or function

☐   4. Speed of learning in every posting

☐   5. Speed in decision-making

☐   6. Quality of decision-making

☐   7. Verbal communication skills with public (media, talks, etc.)

☐   8. Writing skills in carrying out duties

☐   9. Ability to study situations and make up a diagnosis of needs on your own

☐ 10. Creativity or originality of thinking or innovative ideas

☐ 11. Working hard to do justice to the job

☐ 12. Devotion to people or communities to help them and guide them

☐ 13. Taking pride in guiding public and communities or customers

☐ 14. Publishing and disseminating your work and points of view or what is desired

☐ 15. Offering schemes, programmes and projects that are of relevance to people

☐ 16. Making impact in any area that is acknowledged by many across the country

☐ 17. Carrying out work that is well acknowledged and written about

☐ 18. Extent to which you are value driven and known for integrity and honesty in work

☐ 19. Promoing values like maintaining good character, honesty, integrity and search for truth as values for all

☐ 20. Sets an example for others in following values of civil service and lives as a good civil servant and a role model

VECS/VEP: Breadth and depth of reach of service—in terms of implementation of schemes or projects, carrying out job requirements, or innovations or experiments and other services provided

- ☐ 1. Aims at servicing a large number of people (thousands) in their work
- ☐ 2. Mission driven in carrying out work to benefit communities
- ☐ 3. Actions and services benefit a large number of people present or in future
- ☐ 4. Writes and disseminates work and values and is read by a large number of people in the country
- ☐ 5. Publications that are well referenced across the world and by international agencies
- ☐ 6. Experiments, innovates and undertakes development projects for larger use

SECS/SEP: Established institutions or processes and systems that make work and innovations and ideas available to many more people for future use and developing others

- ☐ 1. Established or supported many institutions
- ☐ 2. The institutions established or agencies supported by this person are doing well and benefiting many people
- ☐ 3. A lot of work is carried out by people in the institutions established
- ☐ 4. Ideas and messages reach a large number of people through the institutions they have established
- ☐ 5. Many people benefit from the institutions established, projects promoted or systems and processes initiated

☐ 6. Institutions ensure that talent, teachings and lessons reach a large number of other people and help in growth of knowledge

☐ 7. Contributed to the growth and development of others in the profession

☐ 8. Mentored many and left lasting impact

5 Educational Entrepreneurs

There are many young people in the country who begin to think differently after they embark on their professional journey. They may be management graduates, design experts, IIT graduates, doctors or lawyers—they can be from any profession. They work for some time, feel restless about what they are doing, or see a gap and adopt 'making things happen' as their mission. The fields they usually choose pertain to education, health, or employment promotion, etc. These professionals can be called educational entrepreneurs. In this chapter, we study effective people who have started schools, educational testing services, educational methods or a series of educational programmes and so on. This chapter deals with people like Kiran Bir Sethi, an NID graduate who started a school with a difference; K.K. Nair, who made the Ahmedabad Management Association an institution of continuing education for several types of people in the community; Sridhar who started an educational testing service to uplift the education standards of schoolchildren; Sharat Chandra, an IIT and IIM graduate, who started making tools for teaching science and mathematics to ordinary schoolchildren for their better understanding of these subjects; Manjula Shroff, who started Calorx University for teacher training besides higher secondary schools; Amitabh Shah, who uses young people to teach other youth through an agency called 'YUVA Unstoppable'; and Dr Ashok Agarwal who started the Indian Institute of Health Management and Research. These are excellent examples of educational entrepreneurs who are serving masses of schoolchildren as well as adults at various stages of learning.

KIRAN BIR SETHI

Born and brought up in Bangalore, Kiran's parents had a significant influence on her life. Her mother, Asha Bir, was one of her earliest role models and her father, Raghbir Singh Bir, ignited her then nascent interest in design. Two of her greatest sources of inspiration, Kiran's parents motivated her to take the same career path.

During a visit to Italy, Kiran came across a place called Reggio Emilia. The city had its own approach towards education, with the entire community taking responsibility for the education of their children while believing in their ability to think independently. They also believed in giving a child the freedom to shape their own identity, and explore themselves and their surroundings to their heart's content. Creative, innovative and unique, this approach contrasted sharply with what Kiran had seen at her son's school.

When Kiran's five-and-half-year-old son, Raag, started going to school, she discovered, to her dismay and surprise, that teachers were de-motivating and discouraging their students. Children were repeatedly told that they 'could not' do several things, and reprimanded if they attempted to explore or learn something on their own. In addition, they were made to think competitively and vie for marks and academic achievements. Stifled under an iron fist, children were disheartened and cognitively handicapped, to the point where eight- to nine-year-olds were still struggling to confront any unfamiliar task given to them. When she realized this, Kiran concluded that the existing system was flawed, and destroying the innate potential of children. Parental expectations and pressure, coupled with a competitive mindset and the threat of punishment, were ruining the inherently playful attitude of children, and making them afraid and shy of taking risks.

Kiran decided to find another school for her son; one that she hoped would teach in a freer way, but she could not find any that satisfied her requirements. Most parents, upon finding that there wasn't a school that matched up to their ideals in their city, would simply opt to stick to the school their child was already enrolled in. Kiran, on the other hand, took matters in her own hands. She created a brand new learning centre that followed a completely new education system—one that was exploration-oriented, emphasized on free, independent learning, supported creativity and nurtured innovation: The Riverside School.

With Kiran believing in a literally open learning environment, the students of Riverside spend more than a third of their time outside the school walls, going for nature walks and exploring, or even simply sitting on a log and having a lesson in a classroom of trees. Most Indian schools follow 'periods', a concept where each lesson, regardless of subject or topic, is limited to a pre-decided time. However, Riverside did away with the idea entirely. Instead of settling for a time limit, the length of classes in Riverside is decided a day earlier by the teachers depending on the subject that is being taught, or whether a new topic or unit is being introduced for the first time. Therefore, every lesson is taught for an optimal time, one that is best-suited for the students, the teachers and the lesson itself.

Aside from the regular, day-to-day classes, Riverside's teaching approach is not restricted to lessons. To give a whole, complete education, one focuses as much on being a good human being as a good achiever. Riverside emphasizes as much on attitude and community service—with the Citizenship and

Persistence programmes—as on skills and academics. To give the students a chance to showcase and test the skills they accrue over the school year, the students are often given projects, tasks and challenges that range from designing a home-made water filter to organizing a sports day or even to the writing of this very article. Everyone has different strengths and skill sets. By encouraging and pushing a child to participate in different events and activities, one can give them various opportunities to recognize and nurture their individual skills and abilities, and train them in their particular field of excellence.

Apart from pushing them, these projects also give them the satisfaction of having their work approved and employed. The seventh-grade students of Riverside were given a client project by the manager of the Vastrapur Lake Park to design trash bins to ensure that the park becomes clean. The third graders were asked to design an itinerary for Ahmedabad that emphasized on the city's heritage, its most acclaimed and famous sites as well as ideal rest stops and restaurants. Likewise, tenth graders studying Business Studies designed a new ice cream flavour, deciding on a price and developing a marketing strategy to create a detailed and comprehensive proposal that was accepted by Pradeep Chona, the marketing director of Havmor. These projects provide platforms for the students to utilize their skills and to develop theoretical knowledge, emphasizing on practicality and execution.

With Riverside, Kiran noticed that children are closely connected to their environment, and love to stay out playing as long as they can. However, with industrialization and urbanization, the environment is no longer safe for children to play in. Once again trying to alter an unsatisfactory situation, she founded an initiative called 'aProCh: a Protagonist in every Child', in 2007. aProCh's aim is to work *for* the children, *with* the children, addressing their needs and wants by including them in every step of the process. Slowly, the initiative's success grew to the point where it became manifest in child-friendly zebra crossings and an event called 'Street Smart', wherein an entire road is blocked for vehicles and turned into a playground for children, replete with activities and games. 'aProCh's work helped Ahmedabad acquire the tag of India's first "child-friendly city", even as it grew to host many more events from "Movie'ing Experience" to "Parents of the Park". Of course, the names are pretty much self-explanatory.'

Kiran believes that if anyone wants to make a difference, they need to be shameless. Instead of needlessly worrying about society and 'what everyone else will think', you should do what you think is necessary. On being asked to convey a message, she responded, 'Take care of today and it will take care of tomorrow.' Kiran has always believed that change cannot be wrought overnight. One has to be persistent, determined and perseverant, even when everything explodes in your face. Stay with your idea, with your passion, and you will succeed.

MANJULA SHROFF

Manjula Pooja Shroff is founder chairperson of the Ahmedabad-based Calorx Group which comprises of fourteen Calorx preschools, two DPS schools in Ahmedabad, eight K-12 Calorx public schools spread across Gujarat, Rajasthan and Maharashtra, and also the Calorx Teachers University, with an aggregate enrolment of 8,000 students instructed by 450 teachers.

An alumna of Utkal and Delhi universities and IIMA, Shroff moved to Ahmedabad after her marriage. In 1996 she promoted the first Delhi Public School Society franchise school in Gujarat—DPS, Ahmedabad, and for almost a decade thereafter, dedicated herself to nurturing the fledgling school before promoting the IBO-affiliated Calorx Global School, Ahmedabad in 2006. Calorx is a name synonymous with education par excellence. It believes in empowering children while helping them to succeed in all spheres of life.

An entrepreneur, she is regarded by many as the change agent for schooling in the state of Gujarat. As chairperson of Calorx, she has been instrumental in founding and managing several premier schools. She is the recipient of several awards, among them, the prestigious Secular India Award from the President of India, Shri Shankar Dayal Sharma and Woman of the Year by American Bibliography Society, North Carolina.

Altus Learning, which Mrs Shroff heads, is a professionally managed education company based in Gujarat that delivers education services in the P-12 segment to the Calorx Group, which has been running K-12 schools and preschools for over sixteen years.

With K-12 growing at a phenomenal rate in India, Altus Learning is filling the professional gap by providing management services to pre-schools and K-12 schools in areas of HR and training, systems and IT, infrastructure development, academic research and business development. Altus Learning is currently focusing in areas of Gujarat but is also expanding its footprint across India and seeking opportunities in the Asia Pacific region.

Kaizen's Equity Private Limited's investment in Altus is a reiteration of the company's sound processes and system-based approach that is transforming the education sector and bringing about more transparency and professionalism.

In an interview with us she said the following:

Source of Inspiration behind Her Work: 'One of the things that inspires people is their own life experiences. Things that happened in their life and things that made an impact while one was growing up are the factors that affect you the deepest and stay with you for the longest time. I come from a very conservative royal family in Orissa where I was educated in a good school. A convent school. My mother lived in "parda". The reason a girl was educated was to make her more marketable in the marriage market. So, very few people went to college and got higher education. Girls were allowed education till the tenth class and then were married off at a very young age. When this happened with my sister, I realized that this is not the kind of life I want to lead. I did not know that education was my liberation but I knew that education higher than the tenth class was important for me to become something in life. My first battle was to do my undergraduation and then later my graduation. Thus when you cannot take things for granted you realize how worthwhile they are. I had to make a few compromises like going to an all girls' college as it would have been blasphemous if a girl from my family went to a co-ed. This was also one of the inspirations for the career I chose. So I got my calling very early in life owing to how my life had treated me. I never wanted to become a teacher or make a career in it. The only aim I had was that I wanted to build this ammunition inside me called EDUCATION.

'After my graduation I went to Delhi University to study computers (PGDEC). There the teachers and professors were not trained in computers so I used to train them as well as study. So I was not a teacher per se but I was a reasonably good trainer. And in Delhi also I was not doing education at all. I was doing industry; I was handling contracts, finance, real estate, etc.

'However, when I came to Ahmedabad I knew I had to do something in education. There were so many high places of education here like NID, PRL, IIM, C.N. Vidyalaya, CEPT, etc. So in any field in education, Ahmedabad was leading. However, when I started Delhi Public School around two decades ago, contemporary education was not quite up to the mark. That gap became very stark for me and once I got into it I realized how much I enjoy education. Moreover, I consider myself more of an entrepreneur than an educationist as I'm not an academic worm but I'm much more a managerial, strategic kind of a person.

So I do have this business mindedness which I'm blending into the field of education.'

On Her Strong Points: 'I'm a good leader. I carry my team with me. I never insult or demean my subordinates nor do I let anyone else be rude to them. In order to inspire people and empower them RESPECT and TRUST are the two main factors. I genuinely respect and trust my team members and so the effect shows. I never distrust until I have a reason to. I care about their self-respect. I have been told that I am a visionary. I am sticky. I must get the job done whatever the situation. I am a task master. I think I have an ability to be detached. This lets me think rationally and effectively. This allows me objectivity. So, I'm not a partial person. I'm just focused on merit and work. I don't get emotionally involved. I'm a multi-tasker. I try to live in all the components of the Wheel of Life. Be it career, social, emotional, spiritual all of it. I try living a very wholesome life.'

Qualities People Should Cultivate to Make a Difference to Others: 'Only one word: GIVING. And this givingness does not come in the way of your career, social life, etc. And there is a certain understanding of giving where the other person doesn't feel inferior while taking that help from you. Once you have understood this giving you can imbibe it in a charity or workplace anywhere. Social organizations like Visamo Kids and Prerna work on this belief.

'After the earthquake in 2001 when I had come back home to my two-year-old son who had been with the maid when the earthquake had hit, I felt so much gratitude towards life that I threw myself into social work. There are four stages of disaster management: Rescue, Restoration, Rehabilitation and Reconstruction. And without knowing it I had been involved in all the stages. And in the Rehabilitation stage I had built *visamo* (shelter in Gujarati) for the homeless survivors. And later people requested me to continue with the idea and use it for a cause. I then connected it with education for underprivileged children and Visamo Kids was established.'

Messages She Would Like to Give for Others to Become an Effective Person: YOUTH: 'They need to start focusing on a career early in life. That choice may not always be right. It should be made nonetheless. I feel it's healthy that parents and children discuss career options and make decisions keeping in mind the interest and expectations of both sides. Children need to narrow down choices. But more importantly you need to build discipline. One has to have integrity. Shortcuts may help you reach your goal early but in the long term it has a lot of fallouts. Youth should have VALUES. Values are what make you. Family, friends and finance, if these three are ruled by your values then I feel you can be very effective in life.'

Women: 'I feel women are very sacrificial. They feel that their entire life is about sacrifice. As a daughter, as a wife, as a mother she sacrifices. I feel love and sacrifice are two different things. Why should one quell one's own love and abilities to love their dear ones? One should live for oneself because if you do that you are happier and in turn will make other people around you happy. If you are unhappy and tired of all the sacrifices you have made, you'll feel drained. Then how will you make others happy. So women can be effective if they take care of their inner self. I also believe they should be financially independent.'

Professionals: 'I have seen that people get very fixed in their approach and are not flexible enough. They get caught in egos. This can be very detrimental. One should keep the long-term aim in mind. "We have to give up the WAR to win the BATTLE." That's how one carries a team and becomes effective. As an entrepreneur I say this. There are opinions and facts. Facts are alright but one also has to carry one's intuition with them. They should also have the ability to stand alone.'

K.K. NAIR

K.K. Nair is an unusual person. While Dr Vikram Sarabhai founded the Ahmedabad Management Association (AMA), K.K. Nair has made it a living organization that relentlessly serves all categories of people with continuing education. Starting with managing it from a single room accommodation in a crowded area, he with the help of continuously changing office bearers brought it to the level of conducting postgraduate courses in various disciplines, and short-term to long-term courses for all categories—housewives, students, teachers, civil servants, scientists, vice chancellors and retired and retiring citizens of Ahmedabad and Gujarat. A person who started with simple beginnings and ever remains simple and unassuming, he is an illustration of a silent revolution in learning and education in Ahmedabad. The learning facilities of AMA are unparalleled and the pricing is affordable to anyone and is often free. Wisdom from all sections of society is made available at AMA for an interested person at all times.

Born in a humble family in Kerala, K.K. Nair faced many hardships since his childhood like lack of proper education and his father losing his job when K.K. Nair was only ten. However, his thirst for knowledge and a dream to get out of Kerala and achieve something propelled him onwards.

He took SSC and HSC through correspondence and then acquired a bachelor's degree. He had an option to go for IAF, but by then he had received a call from IIMA to join as administrative staff, so he took up the job. He shared that he was inspired by the story of Keshav Menon—the editor and founder of *Matrubhoomi*.

At IIMA, he was heavily influenced by the professors with whom he worked as a secretary and particularly Prof. P.S. George, in the Centre for Management in Agriculture, who inculcated in him the habits that he owes his success to. For example, he wanted everything to be done quickly without any delay. Nair also learnt from him that to achieve something there has to be a 'willingness' to do the work, and the general attitude one has towards it matters. He also gives credit to the conducive environment that was provided at IIMA. When asked about his journey at AMA and how he managed to take it to the heights he said that he achieved it through honesty, innovativeness, having no expectations and willingness to go the extra mile. For instance, he is planning to open a facility for research and development in order to help interested students. This shows his integrative mindset and innovativeness to give more and be at par with competitors despite being a not-for-profit organization.

When asked about goals in life and his opinion about them, he had a very clear reply that goals are not necessary in life. But, it is important to have passion. If you have passion, you will automatically have something to do. That something will lead to something else and so forth. All that is required is the willingness to do things without expecting anything in return. Work is how one proves oneself. If and when you get an opportunity, grab it, do it perfectly and prove yourself. Have small goals, work towards them with integrity and passion. Large goals do not always work.

When asked how he managed to bring in so many well-known speakers like C.K. Prahlad, Kumar Birla, etc. he said that when people see the sincerity with which someone is doing his work without any expectations they respect that and are willing to help.

He also mentioned that time management is a very important aspect when it comes to being effective in one's work. Even after so many years his working hours are long, comprising ten to twelve hours, wherein he constantly tries to make the training programmes and lectures more innovative and diverse in nature.

His advice to the younger generation with regard to being more effective at work and in life is to be sincere to their job. He also believes that the upbringing of people is of great import.

The point and the philosophy of his life is, 'If you are honest, if you have integrity, people will recognize your efforts and grant your requests. Whatever T.V. Rao says about my skills to get things done, I attribute it to this value.'

One needs to be constantly self-analytical to discover one's strengths and weaknesses. But, it is also important to be humble. At the same time, one should inform others about their weaknesses and help them get rid of them or improve themselves. He mentioned a few instances like when he had told the washroom cleaner at AMA that if the washroom was clean, he would get the credit. Nair had to keep checking the washroom again and again but he made his point. Similarly, he had explained to the AC technician that it is inefficient to keep coming back and that he should check all the ACs and get them repaired all at once.

SRIDHAR RAJAGOPALAN[1]

Sridhar Rajagopalan has a BTech from IIT Madras and PGDM from IIMA. He is an educational entrepreneur who has helped change the way student learning outcomes are seen in India. He worked in IBM India for two-and-a-half years before co-founding and running the Ekalavya School in Ahmedabad.

Established in 2001, a company called Educational Initiatives (EI) believes in making a difference in education through personalized learning and ensuring that students learn with understanding. 'Our detailed research has proven that children today respond to rote-based questions relatively well, however, they fail to answer unfamiliar or application-based questions due to unclear core concepts. Our team consists of professionals who have vast experience in the field of school education. The team members have taught in leading schools, been members of the state textbook committees and designed and taught courses at the school as well as at teacher-training level. We believe in learning through understanding, so that the education lasts the students for a lifetime as a tool to help them in all their endeavours. Through our other interactive tools like Mindspark (digital self-learning programme), ASSET, detailed assessment, CCE certificate course, teacher evaluation programme, teacher sheets and more, Educational Initiatives assists thousands of teachers in improving their students' achievements.'

In the last fourteen years, EI has assessed over 2 million students, with more than 65,000 students experiencing personalized learning through Mindspark in cities like Lansing and Michigan, USA.

'The school was started before education became a profitable business and making money was not the motive at that time,' he recalls. Several initiatives to impart quality education were introduced at Ekalavya. Twenty-five per cent of the seats were reserved for poor children. Classes were divided not into sections, but by subjects such as maths, science and social studies. It was found to make learning exciting as the ambience in these classes was different. Teachers owned these classes and they took extra care to provide the materials useful for children to learn the specific subjects.

Finding teachers was one of the biggest problems and so a teachers' training institute was founded to address this. Rajagopalan headed this division. 'We started with the lower classes and kept adding a level each year. When I left six-and-a-half-years later, the school had classes till eighth standard and today, it is a full-fledged school,' he explains.

In 2001, after the Bhuj earthquake in Gujarat, the team also got involved in rural education and realized that running a school did not solve the problem of education. The biggest problems that the nation faced were those of the learning methodologies used by schools—encouraging rote learning—apart from finding good teachers.

The question that plagued Rajagopalan was this—how could he use his experience to contribute to alleviating these problems?

Today, EI boasts of schools such as Ryan International School in Mayur Vihar, Delhi; Amity International School in Saket, Delhi; Arya Vidya Mandir in Bandra (West), Mumbai; La Martiniere for Boys, Kolkata; and Presidency School, Bangalore, among the schools that subscribe to its products.

Customizing Questions: Mindspark was developed three years ago and is a computer-based question paper. In this, the student's level is assessed first before questions to test the student at that level are generated by the system. 'For instance, if a child is in class five, but his understanding of a particular topic matches that of a student of class three, then the questions are administered accordingly,' says Rajagopalan. This is especially popular in government schools.

Detailed Assessment, the latest addition to EI's product range, allows a teacher to test on specific topics within a subject to assess a student's understanding level of that specific class. 'This one is especially popular in Singapore,' states Rajagopalan.

The team at EI has been developed around the need to research learning patterns and develop products around that understanding. 'We have a team of 200 people, double of what we were two to three years ago. Most of these are bright youngsters as we realized that teaching experience is of no value here,' he points out. Nearly 120 members of the team work on test question development and are trained through interactions with children to understand how they think and learn.

Wide Reach: Currently, ASSET is the most popular of EI's products, with 1500 schools as members not only in India, but abroad as well. Mindspark is used in fifty-five schools currently. The focus for the coming years is going to be in supporting schools to use these products and bringing out improvements in the existing products. 'Mindspark can be very disruptive, needing two hours of school time and space for computers. Both for this and ASSET, we are looking at a tablet version,' explains Rajagopalan. ASSET is a paper-based test currently.

He also believes that there is a huge potential across the globe and existing clientele have shown that the changes needed to adapt to the US markets are very trivial. Currently, Mindspark for maths and languages are available, and EI is looking at incorporating other subjects. There is one planned for teachers as well. 'Just developing these products will keep us busy for seven to eight years,' says Rajagopalan.

The primary goal for EI is to change the education scene. Rajagopalan firmly believes that if it achieves this, then it will become a large company, but that is not the main thrust. The company also wants to work with boards to improve assessment methodologies. With parents and educators concerned about the stress on marks and rote learning, EI gives schools a viable alternative to rethink their teaching methodology. By constantly reviewing and improving its products, EI hopes to keep its first mover advantage and bring about a meaningful social impact through its initiatives in education.

K. SHARAT CHANDRA

K. Sharat Chandra's father was in government service, working with a public sector company, NTPC. Sharat Chandra had strong values injected by his parents. After getting his bachelor's degree in chemical engineering from IIT Bombay, he worked for two years at KPMG as a business analyst. He then joined IIMA for PGDM. He did his summer internship in Citibank Treasury and then went on an exchange programme from IIMA to Germany where he had very little work. What impressed him most was the amount of innovation that was evident in various sectors and businesses in Germany, which he realized was because of the education system followed there that encourages students to think out of the box. And this was a complete contrast to the Indian system, where the application of what is learnt is completely ignored, with a greater focus on learning for exams. He realized that right from childhood, if children are encouraged to innovate and develop their own products, this would create the confidence to experiment as adults. He also felt that he was lucky to have gone through IIT and IIM education because his roots in education were good thanks to his parents who worked with a NTPC that gave him access to study in a good school (Delhi Public School). What about the millions of bright minds who study in municipal schools and village schools and do not have access to a good education, especially in mathematics and science?

Convinced that the need of the hour was to move away from traditional teaching methods, K. Sharat Chandra started working on developing low-cost experiments that can be used for project work in schools.

He felt that if Germany could build itself as a wonderful country, why were Indians lagging behind? He went on thinking of this as a challenge to build competencies in India through education. On returning to IIMA, Sharat was influenced by the economics professor, Sebastian Morris, and the entrepreneurship professor, Sunil Honda. He took up the challenge of doing something different. He says, 'I know the corporate world. Having worked for two years at KPMG and having pursued summers at Citibank and an exchange programme in Germany,

I know what I did not want to do. I did not want to do the kind of things we do in the corporate world.' While at IIMA, the work done by Ekalavya Foundation and Sridhar, the other alumnus of IIMA who had formed educational initiatives and managed them so well, inspired him. With this entire experience, he did not want to go for placement in a corporate job. He was toying with some ideas and finally settled on the area of improving educational standards.

Sharat and his team's work began by demonstrating to students on subjects like motion, inertia, magnetic fields, etc. 'Children were seeing the practical explanation but even that wasn't hands-on,' says Sharat.

Then one day, 'Things just changed. After one such demonstration, the principal of Bharatiya Vidya Bhavan asked me how I could make this into a hands-on activity. It was possible but I wasn't ready with a kit each for the children from Class VI to X at that point of time. I took some time but met the deadline,' smiles Sharat. Now students across the state learn science and maths with these kits developed at Butterfly Fields, a company started by Sharat for promoting low-cost learning tools in science and mathematics.

Butterfly Fields isn't just about science projects since it is designed by an IIT+IIM. There are fun games as well and, 'my favourite is the trump card game where I beat most of the challengers,' he says with pride. 'That's also because I have designed it,' he says cheekily.

Butterfly Fields is currently present in Andhra Pradesh, Karnataka and Tamil Nadu. It works with 3000 government schools in Andhra Pradesh and an additional 1000 schools spread across the private sector in the three states. Sharat Chandra states that government school requirements are more intense, so he intends to create a foundation before expanding aggressively. In the government segment, budget becomes a big constraint and the focus is to deliver products in a box so that there is less of a programme/service component.

The company also works with corporate entities that focus on education as part of their corporate social responsibility (CSR) activities. In the CSR segment, it works with several private companies such as GMR group, Chennai-based Ramky, Microsoft and Sarah Dell Foundation, which are active in supporting education for the underprivileged. Butterfly Fields works with around seventy schools in this category. In the private segment, Butterfly Fields focuses on mid-range schools with school fees in the range of Rs 12,000 a year. In all three states, the company focuses on the top two cities. In the next fifteen months, the company plans to reach out to ten states.

Butterfly Fields is also active in providing hands-on training programmes after school hours and is targeting an expansion in this segment. Many private schools too opt to encourage this since then the regular fee is not affected and the decision to send the child for these classes lies with the parents. It's also working with partners for this, and the Hyderabad-based Eenadu Group is already a partner and does workshops in twenty districts in Andhra Pradesh. By the summer of 2012, the company had seventy summer camps under this model, with thirty through the Eenadu tie-up. The plan is to expand the reach across the geography. Since 2012 summer camps are being conducted regularly. Butterfly Fields clearly has an eye on profits, but also has a social purpose, which it fulfils through its work with government schools and companies active in CSR. Most importantly, it aims to bring the children up to speed and fulfil the Indian dream of enabling the youth of tomorrow to innovate.

DR ASHOK AGARWAL
Born in 1955, Dr Agarwal established IIHMR (Indian Institute of Health Management Research) in 1984 and concentrated

only on social work for a decade thereafter. Along with IIHMR, he devoted his time and energy to BCT (Bhoruka Charitable Trust), a trust started by his father in 1963. BCT is guiding an intensive rural development programme in 500 villages of Rajasthan. It has implemented HIV/AIDS programmes in Karnataka, Andhra Pradesh and Rajasthan.

IIHMR has completed three successful decades of research in the healthcare sector and has transformed itself into a university with four schools. Throughout these years, the IIHMR University has conducted more than 500 research projects and studies at the national and international levels. These have high relevance to health policies and programmes. The IIHMR University has extensively worked on assignments/consultancies for studies and projects funded by various bilateral agencies, the Government of India and state governments. The areas of research/studies included during these decades were health systems, human resources and training, family welfare, maternal and child health, medical education, health management information systems, evaluations, education and communication, information technology survey, project implementation plan, health economics and financing, drugs, strategy planning, HIV/AIDS, nutrition, communication behaviour, national health policy, health insurance, quality assurance, operations research, reproductive health and gender health.

Dr Agarwal does not believe in individual rewards, hence, he has never received any personally. He has always received awards on behalf of his companies and IIHMR/BCT. 'I have been recognized by the people, villagers, beneficiaries and my own staff,' he says. He is a trustee on eight boards, such as Bhoruka Mountaineering Trust, Kolkata; Bhoruka Public Welfare Trust, Kolkata; Qimpro Foundation, Mumbai; Disha Foundation, Jaipur; Environmental Sanitation Institute, Ahmedabad and others.

Qimpro Foundation works towards recognizing Indians serving as role models for world-class quality leadership in business, education and health care. Disha Foundation helps in carrying out the task of education, rehabilitation and vocational training to mentally and physically challenged children. Bhoruka Mountaineering Trust is the first non-profit trust to promote trekking and mountaineering in India.

In 1982, Dr Agarwal instituted the first non-profit, voluntary donor-based blood bank and special investigation centre called the Bhoruka Research Centre for Hematology and Blood Transfusion in Kolkata.

Dr Agarwal did his MBBS from Calcutta National College in 1980 and received his MPH from John Hopkins University, USA in 1984. He did his residency in Internal Medicine and Emergency Care at Chittaranjan Hospital, Kolkata.

Dr Agarwal is also the director of ABC India Ltd, Kolkata, which has been a pioneer in the field of logistics since its inception more than thirty-eight years ago. Moreover, he is the director of Transcorp International Ltd, TCI Industries Limited and Sharma East India Hospital and Medical Research Ltd. He is the chairman of the Medical Research Committee of Jindal Naturopathy Institute, Bangalore, India. This institute is the oldest and the biggest for providing treatment as well as undertaking scientific research in the area of naturopathy and yoga science.

He is the vice chairman of the Centre for Micro Finance, Jaipur; Comprehensive Health Project, Rangabelia; Tagore Society for Rural Development, West Bengal; and Bhagwan Mahaveer Viklang Sahayata Samiti, Jaipur. The latter is the largest organization globally to provide free artificial limbs, Jaipur Foot, polio calipers, crutches and prosthesis to 60,000 amputees and disabled people each year, both in India and abroad.

Apart from these, he is the member of many other organizations such as the Rajiv Gandhi Water Development and Conservation Mission, Jaipur; Health Advisory Board, John Hopkins University; Bloomberg School of Public Health, Baltimore, USA; Governing Board Aapni Yojana, Jaipur; Governing Board, BRCM College of Engineering and Technology, Bahal, Haryana; Sobhasaria Engineering College, Sikar, Rajasthan.

Dr Agarwal believes that leadership is a continuum. It is never a part-time job or for office hours. Leaders in Asian countries need to be less paternalistic and more professional. They should be clear of their expectations from people and should not meddle in the regular affairs of their team members.

Dr Agarwal is a straightforward person. He is fair in his assessment of people and situations. Keeping calm and taking care of emergencies—medical, accidental or otherwise are some of his strengths. He also believes in getting periodic feedback from others who work with him using 360 Degree Feedback tools. He says that he has become more aware of his strengths and weaknesses through the 360 Degree Feedback tool. In 2015 he is going through another round of such feedback.

AMITABH SHAH[2]

Amitabh Shah was born in Ahmedabad, Gujarat to affluent parents. He was a state-level tennis champion at the age of fifteen and his dream was to be a professional tennis player. His parents found out a way for him to go to the United States in a student exchange programme, to a small town called Talladega, in Alabama. The incentives for the young Amitabh were that the host was a tennis coach, and he had received a full scholarship. Amitabh excelled in education, securing top rank in school and then he joined the University of Alabama to do his bachelor's in computer science. He topped the university exams. Even in Alabama, he was a member of the Rotaract club, which is a part of Rotary International. The club promotes the culture in young people to address the social needs of their communities. He topped the class and joined Hewitt Associates as a lead system configuration analyst in 2001. Like any other young person he enjoyed his carefree life in Atlanta, Georgia working with Hewitt Associates. His father was unhappy with his lifestyle and asked him to do a master's in Business Administration to get some meaning and direction in his life. Taking his father's advice he applied to the University of Texas where he got a full scholarship. He decided to visit Ahmedabad for a month before joining the course.

On his way to India in the year 2004, he was watching a Hindi movie, *Swades*, in the aeroplane. The story of the protagonist who comes from NASA and changes the lives of the people in his rural village touched his heart. That was probably one of the pushes that he needed. Amitabh Shah was raised by his nanny Kamlaben who was close to him. Buoyed by *Swades*, he got off the plane and straight went to meet Kamlaben. He found her sitting on the road of one of the city squares in a miserable physical state. Amitabh felt bad. He took her to his home where he came to know that Kamlaben's son used to beat her and make the eighty-two-year-old lady do all the household chores. She used to get food only one time a day and weighed just 25 kilograms then! Amitabh nursed her and within two weeks she showed signs of improvement. Thus began a pivotal journey in his life. He took her to Suvarna Mandir, an old age home, near the Iskcon temple in Ahmedabad. Here he found many such people whom their families had abandoned. He met Savita Bai whose son had left her with the promise of taking her back home after two days. There were numerous others who were ditched by their families.

Amitabh mobilized his friends, young as himself, who were mostly preoccupied with playing sports or hitting the gym. They started visiting the old age home every evening and soon he had forty-five people visiting the old age home, which was housing forty people. He had just asked his friends to come with him, but indirectly he gave a platform or a cause to his friends, the youth who were ready to be of help to society, but did not have a direction. Indeed, a visionary person is one who permeates his vision among all. He understood that youth from all the social strata can easily contribute two hours a week for societal causes. He realized that with the largest number of young people in the age group of 18–30 years in the world, India can do magic by utilizing its youth base for a variety of causes.

Amitabh had a full scholarship from the University of Texas for his MBA and his non-refundable flight ticket was also ready. He had suddenly found a new calling in his life, to dedicate his life in his own way for societal causes, and he enjoyed his work. He started YUVA Unstoppable in 2005 with the aim to mobilize the youth to dedicate their time for creating a better world. Slowly people started to join his cause. His father was not happy with his decision to miss out on his MBA and do societal work, but he convinced his father that he would do his MBA, but only from Yale University, as its focus was on leadership and management and the institute was number one in non-profit management. Two years after starting YUVA, Amitabh went on to do his MBA at Yale, but he had already gathered enough momentum for his cause. He was coordinating the activities of YUVA through Skype from his college. He also had good support from his friend, a firm believer in the cause—Marmik Joshi, a co-founder and the current president of operations in India. After his MBA stint he declined a half a million dollar job from JP Morgan, to work in Wall Street—all because he was motivated to do something for the people of his country. He came back and had a small stint of six months with Mr Narendra Modi who was then the chief minister of Gujarat where he learnt a lot, and then he diverted his full attention to YUVA.

Amitabh feels that his own positive mindset was partly responsible for the success of the programme. In his words, 'I see a half-filled glass of water as partially filled with water and partially filled with air.' He says that we are always taught from childhood to have a positive frame of mind and he has actually trained himself to see the good in every situation. Like a bodybuilder training his body every day for physical rigours and stress, he trains his mind every day by writing down ten things that he is grateful for that day in his diary. This he has been doing for the past seven years. In his words, 'I brainwash myself with positivity.' He sees opportunity in every situation. 'If someone owes money to me and is not paying, I see other options.'

He has received the Prince's prize for innovative philanthropy from Prince Albert II of Monaco for his commitment in mobilizing the youth to stand up and work towards the development of society. His dream is to replicate this model of two hours of social service across the world, through mobilization of youth to create a sustainable model for development. This model can have huge benefits wherever it is applied and this international honour will certainly help him move forward with his dream.

YUVA Unstoppable is working in forty cities in India, has more than 1,25,000 volunteers for its cause, and has helped 2,50,000 children in their education by teaching students at various municipal schools. Through its work he intends to promote kindness among the youth, to develop a better society. He perceives 'kindness is like exercising; if you practise it becomes a habit'. The IIMA case study on the volunteers of

YUVA Unstoppable reflects that individuals dedicating two hours a week for a year have 30 per cent less probability of being corrupt, their confidence goes up by 50 per cent and compassion level goes up by 84 per cent. In a society riddled with corruption scandals this is very bright news.

According to Amitabh, 'Compassion is the sign of a great leader,' and leaders can be from any field.

Lessons from Effective Educational Entrepreneurs

All the people described here are effective people. Kiran, Shroff, Sridhar, Sharat, KK and Ashok are all different types of educational entrepreneurs. They have sound educational backgrounds from institutes like NID, IIT, IIM, John Hopkins, Delhi University and the like. They have made a lot of difference to society. They thought differently and chose a path less trodden—one that has raised awareness and elevated people through education. The following lessons and insights may be drawn from the qualities of effective educational entrepreneurs:

1. They think differently. They would like to constantly question their experiences and look around for what is needed. They like to do unusual things. They have a larger purpose in mind.
2. They work hard and are visionaries. All of them have larger societal goals in mind. While making money is an important consideration as they acknowledged, it may not be their primary goal. Manjula Shroff, Sharat or Sridhar are all interested in building enough financial gains but feel that the work they do is more important than what they earn. Their goals are super-ordinate.
3. They observe the world around them and try to imbibe lessons—Sharat learnt from his professors and visits to

Ekalavya School, Sridhar from his own experiences, Kiran from the experiences of her own kids, and Manjula Shroff from her childhood struggle.

4. They are highly self-aware and are constantly introspecting and thinking about themselves and others.

5. They are innovative problem solvers. They aim at solving the problems and issues of the society. When faced with larger societal problems like the quality of education, etc., they aim high to provide solutions for a larger number of people in the community.

6. They are mission driven. From a small beginning Ashok built IIHMR University and also campuses in four other cities besides Jaipur. The way Manjula branched out from school to university and Kiran started undertaking various projects, indicates that effective people are restless and keep moving from one issue to another converting problems into opportunities. Their mission is set by the nature of experiences they have had. For example, Amitabh Shah demonstrates how *Swades* and Kamlaben influenced him. So does Manjula's childhood experiences and Sharat's later experiences. Sridhar's experience in Ekalavya Foundation and later in his own work led him from one issue to another and expanded his activities as issues came up and lessons were learnt. But instinctively, all of them seem to have some compassion for the neglected sections of the education sector in society.

7. They are optimistic change managers. They believe that change can be brought about in the society. All of them express optimism and positive thinking in their interviews. They persist and do not give up in the event of difficulties including family pressures.

8. All of them are institution builders and build institutions that have lasting effect. They also spend a good part of their

time delegating and empowering their juniors to carry out their work.

Effective Educational Entrepreneurs
Use a five-point scale for evaluating
**5 = Very good/High, 4 = Good/High, 3 = Moderate,
2 = Low and 1 = Very low**

1. How good are you as an Educational Entrepreneur in terms of the following criteria? (EEE/EP)

☐ 1. Depth of knowledge in your areas of work (making children literate, developing low-cost teaching methods, creativity in education, new methods of teaching, skill development, self employment, etc.)

☐ 2. Breadth of knowledge in your area of work (extent of awareness of how others are doing, experiences, lessons, etc.)

☐ 3. Extent of passion due to conviction and commitment to work in a sustained way in the areas of education

☐ 4. Extent to which you are willing and prepared to face ups and downs in the education field and in your experiments and new initiatives

☐ 5. Communication skills to convince and enrol people to use the services you offer: schools, colleges, government, teachers, parents, administration, etc.

☐ 6. Knowledge of the area—geographic, where you plan to work—in terms of various stakeholders or users of your products and services, their learning attitudes, culture and habits and possible resistance

☐ 7. Ability to read, tour, visit other places and learn from experiences of others on your own

☐   8. Creativity or originality of thinking in your area of work

☐   9. Working hard to ensure that you do justice to your potential users or beneficiaries through your work

☐ 10. Taking pride in helping others

☐ 11. Respect for student or adult learners and other stakeholders (teachers, students, headmasters, administration etc.)

☐ 12. Skills in presenting your work, philosophy and intent, etc., or publishing or disseminating your work and points of view to various agencies: schools, colleges, government, funding agencies, etc.

☐ 13. Ability to come up with and offer new products, services and other interventions that are appropriate for the education sector you are serving

☐ 14. Extent to which you promote values like maintaining good character, honesty, integrity and search for truth as values for all

☐ 15. Extent to which you set an example for others in following values of educational entrepreneurs and live as a good teacher and role model

☐ 16. Extent to which you possess administrative and management skills to run your enterprise as a profit-making or self-sustaining organization

☐ 17. Extent of commitment to education and its role in the economic development of a nation or society

☐ 18. Ability to convert problems and issues you face into opportunities for intervention, change and development

2. What is the breadth and depth of your reach in terms of the services you provide (VEEE/VEP)

☐ 1. Reaching a large number of learners or beneficiaries in terms of products and service offered and the ideas and points of view

☐ 2. Studying, understanding means to benefit a large number of learners at present or in future and aiming at the same

☐ 3. Writing and publishing about your products and services to be used by a large number of people in the country and outside

☐ 4. Getting large-scale acknowledgements for the innovations, creativity of your products and services

☐ 5. Promoting others to start products and services that are complementary to yours

☐ 6. Expanding your reach to other geographical areas (states, districts, colleges, schools, etc.)

☐ 7. Expanding your reach to other learners or groups (from schools to colleges, from primary to middle schools or higher secondary schools, etc.)

3. Established institutions, organizations, agencies or processes and systems that make your work and innovations and ideas available to many more people for future use (SEEE/SEP)

☐ 1. Networking with many institutions, professional bodies, and administrative agencies like the boards of secondary education, UGC, AICTE, state governments, ministry of HRD, etc. to disseminate and participate in your work

☐ 2. Establishing at least one organization, institution or agency that is doing well and is making products and services in a sustainable way to benefit many people

☐ 3. Vastness and variety of the products and services and service delivery-related activities and their reach

☐ 4. Extent to which the philosophy, vision, mission, ideas and messages reach to a large number of people through the organizations and networks that are established

☐ 5. Many people are trained to carry on the work through the enterprises or agencies and institutions established

6 Professors

Often he would ask me, 'You are young, decide what would you like to be remembered for.' I kept thinking of new impressive answers, till one day I gave up and resorted to tit-for-tat. I asked him back, 'First you tell me, what you will like to be remembered for? President, scientist, writer, Missile Man, India 2020, Target 3 billion . . . What?' I thought I had made the question easier by giving options, but he sprang on me a surprise. 'Teacher,' he said.

—Srijan Pal Singh on Dr A.P.J. Abdul Kalam

India has produced some excellent teachers. These are teachers in schools, colleges and universities titled as professors. Notable among them are: Professors C. Rangarajan, V.S. Vyas, Samuel Paul, Anil Gupta, Bakul Dholakia, Pritam Singh, Udai Pareek, Durganaid Sinha, Prayag Mehta, C.K. Prahalad, Vijay Govindarajan, Pradip Khandwalla, S.C. Kucchal, Indira Parikh, Pulin Garg, Nitish De, B.L. Maheswari, Suresh Srivastava, D.M. Pestonejee, E.G. Parameswaran, K. Balakrishnan, Amar Kalro, S.K. Chakravarthy, M.B. Athreya, Fr E.H. McGrath, Sharad Sarin, Dharni Sinha, Sasi Misra, D. Tripathi, V.L. Mote, M.N. Vora, S.K. Bhattacharya among others in what comprises a long, long list. Some of them are sadly no longer with us.

Many have retired and many whose names are not mentioned here are still young and doing well, on their way to making remarkable contributions. Having worked at IIMA and lived in Ahmedabad for the last forty years, my experiences and contacts are skewed towards IIMA and management education. The people included and mentioned here are only illustrative of the kinds of things professors do or should do which make them effective and outstanding. These kinds of professors can be found in each of the fields mentioned here and not merely management. They can be found in basic sciences, engineering and technology, humanities, social sciences, art, music, dancing, law, commerce, fashion, etc.

DR SAMUEL PAUL (1930–2015)

Almost two and half decades ago Bangalore witnessed an interesting phenomenon—a kind of silent revolution which crept up upon its citizens and changed the face of public services like transport, health and education among others. In early 1992 a survey was conducted in Bangalore to measure the degree of citizen satisfaction with transport, telephone, electricity, water, education, health and other such public services. The survey covered 480 middle-income and 330 low-income (slum dwellers') households. The city was stratified into two categories according to the time of their existence. Six localities were selected, and within each locality households that had interacted with any public service provider in the preceding six months were chosen. Eight agencies were selected: the Electricity Board, Regional Transport Office (RTO), the Water and Sewerage Board, Bangalore City Corporation (BCC), Telecom, public sector banks and hospitals, and Bangalore Development Authority (BDA). The survey revealed that the public satisfaction with the performance of some of the service providers was as low as 1 per cent and dissatisfaction was as high as 65 per cent (BDA).

Agencies such as the Bangalore City Corporation, Electricity Board, Water and Sewerage Board, and Telecom had only single-digit satisfaction figures. Corruption was widespread in almost all public agencies. A third of the urban poor surveyed had paid a bribe to public officials in the previous six months. Customer satisfaction in middle-income households was low in regard to public service aspects such as staff behaviour, problem resolution rate, and number of visits made to the agency to get their work done. The situation was worse for the urban poor, who had to make multiple visits to agencies, were ill-treated by public officials, and had a lower problem resolution rate (38 per cent) than the middle-income households (57 per cent). The report estimated that citizens of Bangalore spent a lot of money to take care of the unreliability of public services and the money spent by them on activities like buying generators to take care of the power breakdowns and water shortage, etc. amounted to many times the entire tax collection of the Bangalore city. The study results were interesting and when they were shared with the agencies there were reactions but there were efforts to improve. The study was initiated by Professor Samuel Paul, a former professor of IIMA.

The study was repeated in 1999 and there were partial improvement in services such as telephones and hospitals. 'However, overall citizen satisfaction remained low, with most of the performers scoring less than 50 per cent for satisfaction levels. People seemed even less satisfied with the way staff interacted with the clients. Bangalore Telecom, for instance, had the highest overall satisfaction rating of 67 per cent, but this dropped sharply to 30 per cent among a sub-sample of people who interfaced with agency personnel to solve a specific problem. The scale of corruption also increased during this period. Although no dramatic improvement in quality of service was witnessed between 1994 and 1999, attempts were made to respond to public dissatisfaction. In telephones, electricity and water supply, bill collection was streamlined and new systems were introduced for the registration of routine breakdowns of service. The BCC initiated a joint programme with local citizen groups and NGOs to improve civic services. With the assistance of the PAC [Public Affairs Centre], BCC introduced a new grievance redressal system. As a result, a new training and orientation programme for the concerned officials was carried out.'[1]

The report card findings, by Prof. Paul and team, following heavy media coverage, substantially contributed to raising public awareness on issues such as quality of service delivery, corruption levels, and so forth. This has led to the formation of active civic groups that are keen to effect reform for improved governance. From thirty such groups present in the city before the 1993 exercise, the number has grown to 200 in 2003. The report card exercise has been replicated in other Indian cities such as Chennai, Pune, Ahmedabad, Baroda, Kolkata and Mumbai. Nine countries like the Philippines, Vietnam and Ukraine have adopted this model for the purpose of ensuring accountability in public agencies.

Surveying citizens' satisfaction with public services has become a significant part of life. All this work by Prof. Paul and his team gave birth to an institution in Bangalore called the Public Affairs Centre. 'The Public Affairs Centre (PAC) is a not-for-profit, non-partisan organization dedicated to improving the quality of governance in India by promoting the active engagement of citizens. PAC's research activities are organized under two main themes: public policy and participatory governance. PAC undertakes and supports research, disseminates research findings, facilitates collective citizen action through awareness raising and capacity building activities, and provides advisory services to state and non-state agencies. The Centre is globally known for its pioneering *Citizen Report Cards*—benchmarking studies used to improve public services—as well as for its work on electoral transparency, public works quality monitoring tools and approaches, and audits of the Right to Information Act and the National Rural Employment Guarantee Act in India. PAC's uniqueness lies in synthesizing research and action in its activities and approaches. Its research aims to provide a stimulus for action and its action, in turn, is powered by knowledge derived from research. PAC's work is organized primarily around the premise that an informed and active citizenry is the key to improved governance. While conventional policy research concentrates on policy issues and administrative processes, PAC's work has focused on governance as experienced from an average citizen's perspective.'[2]

Dr Samuel Paul is a scholar, and economist, and was a visiting professor at Harvard Business School, and an adviser to the World Bank and the UN Commission on Transnational Corporations. He was a professor at IIMA in the early sixties and then for a second time from 1972 to 1978. He has also taught at the Kennedy School of Government and the Woodrow Wilson School of Public Affairs, Princeton University.

On his return from Washington to India in the early nineties, he pioneered the creation of citizen report cards, a tool for social accountability. He later went on to be the founding chairperson of a new think tank, the Public Affairs Centre, that has taken his work forward. Other organizations that he helped launch are the Public Affairs Foundation, the Coalition against Corruption and the Children's Movement for Civic Awareness. He has also been on the Boards of the State Bank of India and several international research centres. In recent years, his focus has been on public governance and related issues. He is the first Asian to be awarded the Jit Gill Memorial Award by the World Bank, in 2006. Paul was also the recipient of the Fred Riggs

Award of the American Society of Public Administration, and the Nohria Award of the All India Management Association. The Government of India honoured him with the Padma Shri in 2004.

ANIL GUPTA (1958–)

Dr Anil K. Gupta, a doctorate from Kurukshetra University, 1986, is currently a professor at IIMA. His unique work analysing indigenous knowledge of farmers and pastoralists, and building bridges to science-based and indigenous knowledge has led to the honour of him being elected at a young age to India's National Academy of Agricultural Sciences. He has earned the recognition of the Pew Conservation Scholar Award of $1,50,000, 1993–96, from the University of Michigan. Biodiversity conservation through documentation, value addition and dissemination of local peoples' innovative resource conservation practices is the thrust of his work.

His desire to develop a platform to recognize, respect and reward grass-roots innovators was the stimulus behind the creation of the Honey Bee Network. Honey Bee Network is a crucible of like-minded individuals, innovators, farmers, scholars, academicians, policy makers, entrepreneurs and non-governmental organizations (NGOs). To help provide support structures for grass-roots innovators and link formal and informal knowledge systems, Srishti, a global initiative and an NGO, to network local innovators was established in 1993 by Prof. Anil Gupta. It provides organizational support to the Honey Bee Network in over seventy countries. Prof. Gupta also helped establish the National Innovation Foundation, India (NIF) in February 2000. With an initial corpus of Rs 20 crores its aim was to help India become an innovative and creative society and a global leader in sustainable technologies by scouting and sustaining grass-roots innovations.

Prof. Gupta has been walking around 6000 km across India for a week or more every summer and winter for the last twelve years as a part of Shodh Yatra (journey on foot to celebrate creativity at the grass-roots level) to learn from grass-roots innovators. In fact, Shodh Yatra, which is a second-year course, is one of the most popular courses taught in IIMA.

He continues to take on other responsibilities at IIMA besides teaching, starting new and innovative courses and managing Honey Bee, Srishti and NIF. Anil Gupta was Kasturbhai Lalbhai Chair Professor in Entrepreneurship, IIMA (2003–08); Chairperson, Ravi J. Matthai Centre for Educational Innovation, Indian Institute of Management, 1993–94.

Prof. Gupta is invited by many countries across the world to teach and share his knowledge (European Business School, Frankfurt; University of Natural Resources and Applied Life Sciences, Vienna, Austria; Tianjin University of Finance and Economics, Tianjin, China; etc.). He has received many awards including the Padma Shri in 2004 for distinguished achievements in the field of management education; he was adjudged one of the fifty most influential people in the field of intellectual property rights around the world in 2003; and as one of the Star Personalities of Asia among the fifty leaders at the forefront of change by *Business Week*, New York in 2001.[3] He was nominated for the World Technology Award, (Environment) 2001 UK, and is currently a member of the jury for these awards; he was nominated for the Stockholm Challenge Award, 2000, and he received the Asian Innovation Award Gold from *Far Eastern Economic Review* (26 October 2000) for coordinating Srishti and Honey Bee Network and served as a judge for the same and the Asian Young Inventors award in 2001.[4]

Regarding the strengths that helped him to achieve, Anil says, 'Hard work (sleepless nights). I may not have a very good mind but hard work had always been there. There is no short cut to hard work. Many don't acknowledge the hard work; they feel the person is very bright. However in reality, intelligence is not it (the key). One should have the ability to switch the mind on and off. Many fail to do that and are not able to give their best.' He says, 'If you are working on something and if you give your full energy to it, some breakthrough is likely to happen.'

He feels there is no one goal in life and it is important to have multiple goals to evaluate oneself or one would burn out very quickly. The energy that one gets to move forward is through these goals. They may be short term, medium term or long term. It is vital to achieve the short-term ones in order to get to the long-term ones. Thus, different kinds of milestones are required to keep oneself motivated.

Managing time for work is not the same as managing time for life. Effectiveness is not just how one is perceived in the eyes of the world. One should find a good balance in one's personal life too and not be a workaholic. He quoted the example of Gandhi saying, 'Gandhi failed as a husband, as a father but he's still bigger than any one of us. People overlook these failures. But the truth is that he did fail. He was not kind to his wife. Later on he may have developed some compassion but he was still inconsiderate towards her.' Integrative minds are able to see connections between events in most cases. If one doesn't see those connections, she/he may get lost and will not learn much. He said that, 'Intelligence is nothing but connecting the unconnectable.' Thus, the ability to see connections is important. There is a difference. To integrate connections is just to make them coherent. However, connecting may not always be coherent.

SHANTHA SINHA[5] (1950–)

Prof. Shantha Sinha worked as a professor in the department of political science in Hyderabad Central University and is the founder of Mamidipudi Venkatarangaiya Foundation—named in memory of her grandfather—popularly known as the M.V. Foundation. She headed the National Commission for Protection of Child Rights for two consecutive terms (three years each from 2007 to 2013) and returned to resume her work as a professor in the university. After continuing her work for two years, she retired in early 2015 from the university. She continues to do research work at the M.V. Foundation. The M.V. Foundation itself has moved on even in her absence as its director.

She has made an immense contribution in the area of child development. She has strived hard for eliminating child labour. She has played a pivotal role in universalizing elementary education. These days, she is working in close association with government teachers, non-governmental organizations, women's groups, local bodies and youth associations.

Early in her career when Sinha was teaching at the University of Hyderabad, she was not wholly satisfied with classroom teaching. As a result, she began to look for ways to pursue her interest in working-class people and their rights. This led her to propose a project to the Government of India in connection with a programme called Shramik Vidyapeet, or 'workers' education'. Her proposal focused on workers' education for villagers. Sinha chose the villages of Uppal Mandal, near Hyderabad where she began organizing women agricultural workers for minimum wages. When the employers of these women were paying far less than the minimum wages set by the government, Sinha urged the women to go on strike. Instead, they devised a labour action designed to mobilize a moral force behind their demands. For twenty days, they continued to work but refused to accept any wages. This impressed Sinha. 'That was the first lesson I learnt from the women. They needed that daily wage—five rupees in those days, but they said no, we will not [take it]. When that happened, I knew I had a lot more to learn.'

Ordinarily, employers in a situation like this would bribe the labour officials to decide the dispute in their favour. But the officials were so humbled by these women that they resolved the issue in favour of the women workers.

Confronting egregious cases of child-labour abuse in Uppal Mandal, Sinha decided to act. She and her Shramik Vidyapeet colleagues rescued a couple of children from bondage. For the next few months they sheltered them in the university greenhouse, waiting for the tension to ease in the village from which they had been rescued. No provisions had been made for the children in advance. There was not even a light in the greenhouse. But Sinha managed to arrange regular meals for the children and visited them daily. Soon, the children were learning gardening skills and the older ones, carpentry and plumbing—from contractors carrying out construction projects on campus. From these improvised beginnings at Hyderabad University, a successful literacy programme for rescued child workers grew. One out of the original group of rescued children eventually became a clerk (secretary) at the university.

In 1989, Sinha completed her work with Shramik Vidyapeet and soon rejoined her department to teach political science. To avoid confusion and conflict, the M.V. Foundation set up its programme in villages where Shramik Vidyapeet was not present. It chose as its pilot area the Ranga Reddy district, an hour's drive from the university.[6]

She gained the internationally renowned 2003 Ramon Magsaysay Award for community leadership. She has also been awarded the Padma Shri (1999), and the Albert Shanker International Award (1999) from Education International. A rights activist, her contribution to a phenomenal reduction in child labour in nearly 500 villages of Ranga Reddy district in Andhra Pradesh is perhaps unparalleled.

As a result of the M.V. Foundation's work the following had been achieved in a short period of time by 2005: About 4,00,000 children withdrawn from work and mainstreamed into formal schools in Andhra Pradesh; 15,000 bonded labourers have been released; 25,000 adolescent girls have accessed schools; 80,000 volunteers and members of Child Rights and members of Child Rights Protection Forums on a voluntary basis; 2500 government teachers involved actively in abolition of child labour.

In an interview with the author of this book on 30 July 2015, Dr Sinha maintained that the universities and other institutions where professors work are the platforms that support any good work they do. There is no dichotomy between the kind of work you do in working with the society and your responsibilities as a professor. She maintained that in her own case the university had always been supportive. She did her share of teaching, research and writing papers and continued her work. She says work in the community helped her to teach better if anything. Principles of democracy and participation, etc. can be better taught when experienced practically. She said that constant learning and conceptualization take place when you work with the communities. For example, you gain new insights and question assumptions, you learn that our assumption that child labour leads to poverty is a discovery while it is for long assumed to be the other way. It is stimulating to teach and constantly learn. You learn from different sources, and community work helps you to learn from practice. She said that she never compromised on her duties as a professor and always taught the required courses and guided many students for their dissertation and thesis work. She felt that professors owe it to their universities and other institutions where they work to do an excellent job and come up with new concepts, theories and philosophies. There are a lot of professors whom she respects who have designed and implemented such interventions.

She says that she was able to build the M.V. Foundation and leave it to be managed on its own mainly due to the fact that she worked in a university system. But for the university such institution building was not possible. She mentioned that professors like Sharmila Rege, who started the Centre for Women's Study at the University of Pune, are examples worthy of emulation.

Shantha's case demonstrates beyond doubt that professors can be super effective if they recognize the larger responsibility they have to the society and lift themselves up to serve society. Institutions are platforms to multiply and apply your talent. You grow by helping others to grow. Commitment combined with a desire to learn constantly from multiple fields raises professors to do greater things.

KIRAN SETH (1949–)[7]

Kiran Seth is a professor emeritus in the department of Mechanical Engineering at the Indian Institute of Technology, Delhi, where he has worked since 1976. He is most known as the founder of the Society for the Promotion of Indian Classical Music and Culture among Youth (SPIC MACAY) which he founded in 1977. SPIC MACAY is a non-profit organization which promotes Indian classical music, Indian classical dance, and other aspects of Indian culture, among youth the world over through its about 500 chapters and conventions, baithaks, lectures and musical fests.

In 2009, he was awarded the Padma Shri by the Government of India for his contribution to the arts. Seth was one of the toppers of mechanical engineering (BTech) from IIT, Kharagpur in the year 1970, after which he did his MS in 1971 and PhD in 1974 from Columbia University in New York. He started his career working as a Member of the Technical Staff (MTS) at Bell Laboratories, New Jersey in 1974, and returned to India in 1976 to teach and do research work at IIT, Delhi, where he has been working ever since.

SPIC MACAY is the biggest, non-profit, voluntary, cultural youth movement in independent India. Its contribution to Indian classical music and dance is unparalleled. Generations of Indians are today aware of Indian classical music and in a position to appreciate it thanks to the efforts of Seth. Today the movement conducts thousands of concerts, lecture-demos, talks, yoga workshops, classic film shows, theatre shows and craft workshops all over in schools and colleges so that young people are inspired and awakened.

Kiran Seth engineered a cultural movement on campuses. He deconstructed the myth that classical art forms could not strike a chord with uninitiated young listeners. He taught them how to keep in touch with the past even while securing the future. And 'notes' assumed a new meaning in the life of school and college students across the country. Academics apart, many of them learnt to appreciate the classical and folk arts.

Though SPIC MACAY began with classical music, over the years, its agenda has widened to include folk music, yoga and meditation, crafts, talks by writers, painters, philosophers, social activists and environmentalists, walks to monuments with historians, theatre, classic films and even holistic food. Seth's take on it? 'After all, art is about bringing rhythm to life!'[8]

TRILOCHAN SASTRY[9] (1960–) and JAGDEEP CHHOKAR (1941–)

Professors Trilochan Sastry and Jagdeep Chhokar are two noteworthy professors who have been fighting to bring accountability and transparency into governance through making the political systems better—ethical and transparent.

Trilochan is currently a professor at IIM Bangalore. Prior to this he taught at the ISB, Hyderabad, for a short period and also at the IIMA where he also was a part of the 1981–83 batch. Trilochan graduated from IIT Delhi at the age of twenty-one years. Both at IIT and IIM Trilochan was bothered by the amount of subsidy the government was giving to educate students. At IIT in 1976 itself his director once announced that per year about Rs 50,000 was spent on each student by the government. He always had a feeling that he should pay it back to the society. At IIMA he chose to work in rural areas. He spent a couple of months in Kherwara, Rajasthan surveying the government departments and found that they did not work well at all. Through his work in Kherwara he started developing new perspectives on life and work. He joined MIT in the US and completed his PhD. He returned to India in 1992 and joined IIMA as a professor in Operations Management and continued work on development issues. At IIMA Trilochan taught a few courses, published papers and also pursued his other interests. It was around this time he continued to be bothered by politicians and ministers getting implicated in criminal cases and felt strongly that they were looting the country. He decided to file a PIL. With the help of some colleagues and other professors he formed the Association for Democratic Reforms (ADR) to fight corruption and bring democratic reforms.

Professor Jagdeep S. Chhokar worked as a professor at IIMA for over twenty-two years and retired from there in 2006. He has a PhD in management and organizational behaviour from Louisiana State University (USA), an MBA from Delhi University, Graduate Engineer from the Institution of Mechanical Engineers (London) and the Institution of Production Engineers (London), and an LLB from Gujarat University. At IIMA Prof. Chhokar also acted as a Director In-charge and Dean. Prior to joining IIMA, he worked with the Indian Railways in a number of engineering and managerial positions for twelve years; and as an international marketing manager in a public sector company for four years. Professor Chhokar makes an interesting case of an effective professor as he did his law at the fag end of his career at IIMA. He was offered the possibility to continue at IIMA but preferred to do his work with ADR and pursue other interests after retirement at IIMA. While at IIMA Professor Chhokar was a sincere, hard-working and no-nonsense teacher who was very devoted to his work. He taught as well as carried out his research work very dutifully as evidenced by his research and publications. His contributions at ADR are indicators of his commitment to nation building.

ADR[10] was established in 1999 by Trilochan and Jagdeep along with a few other professors from IIMA. In 1999, a PIL was filed by them with the Delhi High Court asking for the disclosure of the criminal, financial and educational background of the candidates contesting elections. Based on this, the Supreme Court in 2002, and subsequently in 2003, made it mandatory for all candidates contesting elections to disclose their criminal, financial and educational background prior to the polls by filing an affidavit with the Election Commission.

The first election watch was conducted by ADR in 2002 for the Gujarat Assembly Elections, whereby detailed analysis of the backgrounds of candidates contesting elections was provided to the electorate in order to help the electorate make an informed choice during polls. Since then ADR has conducted election watches for almost all state and parliament elections in collaboration with the National Election Watch. It conducts multiple projects aimed at increasing transparency and accountability in the political and electoral system of the country. ADR continues its mission of fighting for people's rights and bring some honesty and transparency in politics and Indian politicians.

Today ADR has its office in Delhi and has thirty employees. Trilochan continues to work at the IIMB taking sabbaticals off and on whenever he can and continues his work. His work is now focused on fund-raising for ADR and another body, the Centre for Cooperative Development (CCD), which he started to benefit farmers in rural areas. The CCD attempts to organize the farmers into product groups, form cooperatives and sell their products through the cooperative to get value for their produce. They may also set up food processing factories for further value addition. Today the centre is working in around 200 villages in Andhra Pradesh and the effort is spreading to other states. Trilochan spends his energies, besides teaching at IIMB, to mobilize talent to manage the NGO and its activities as it grows.

Trilochan feels that it is the IIMs that have helped him to formulate and accomplish his goals and mission. He feels that the experience he gains and the activities he undertakes give him more credibility as a professor than anything else. The students Google about their professors and get to know the work they do and therefore have a different level of motivation in their classes as they know their professors are not merely preaching but also doing something for the society. Trilochan keeps using the fieldwork he is doing and the data generated there to write papers and encourage others to do their master's and doctoral dissertations. Hence the work is integrated. Trilochan also attributes a lot to the IIMs, both at Ahmedabad and Bangalore, for the nature of opportunity they offer to network with other prominent people in the industry and government that helps in carrying out any development work. For example IIMA alumni like Nachiket More (ICICI Bank) and Shika Sharma (Axis Bank) support him in his activities.

For Trilochan, 'IIMA gives a platform to follow your heart and do interesting things. A lot of things can be done if one wants to be an effective professor. Professors should find out what they are passionate about and go after the same.'

ADR was given the Social Impact Award by the Times of India Group in January 2013, the Indian of the Year Award for Public Service by CNN-IBN in December 2013, and the Indian of the Year Award for Public Service by NDTV in April 2014. ADR and Jagdeep Chhokar were prominently featured on the fifth and final episode of Aamir Khan's show *Satyamev Jayate* on Criminalization of Politics on 30 March 2014. He is also the founding chairperson of Aajeevika Bureau, a not-for-profit organization based in Udaipur that works on migrant labour issues.

The following survey is an illustration of the nature of service ADR is doing for the country:

ADR Daksh National Voters Survey is the largest ever survey in India with over 2,50,000 respondents in 525 constituencies of the Lok Sabha. It is perhaps the largest survey ever done in the world in one country. The purpose of the survey is threefold: To find out voter priorities in terms of governance issues like water, electricity, roads, food, education and health; to rate the performance of MPs and to highlight voter priorities so that elections in future are fought on voter issues, and more importantly, the governance agenda of future governments reflects voter priorities. ADR expects that this is a long-term effort and this survey will have to be repeated several times before the larger goal is achieved.[11]

P.N. KHANDWALLA

Pradip N. Khandwalla was educated at Bombay University (BCom), Wharton School, University of Pennsylvania (MBA), and Carnegie-Mellon University (PhD). He is also a member of the Institute of Chartered Accountants of India and an honorary member of the National HRD Network.

Professor Khandwalla taught at McGill University, Canada, for several years before returning to India in 1975. Thereafter he was a professor at the IIMA until his retirement in 2002. He held the L&T Chair in Organizational Behaviour at IIMA from 1985 to 1991. He was the director of IIMA from 1991 to 1996.

Professor Khandwalla has authored sixteen professional books and over 100 papers and articles in Indian and foreign journals. His book, *The Design of Organizations*, was an international textbook used in nearly 100 management schools around the world. Another book, *Fourth Eye: Excellence through Creativity*, stimulated the creativity movement in India. His books on the public sector include *Excellent Management in the Public Sector; Social Development: A New Role for the Organizational Sciences; Organizational Designs for Excellence; Innovative Corporate Turnarounds; Management Styles; Revitalizing the State: A Menu of Options; Turnaround Excellence: Insights from 120 Cases; Corporate Creativity: The Winning Edge* (also available in Mandarin language); *Lifelong Creativity: An Unending Quest; Management of Corporate Greatness: Blending Goodness with Greed; Creative Society: Prospects for India.*

Professor Khandwalla has served on the editorial/advisory boards of several of the world's leading journals of management and organizational research, including *Administrative Science Quarterly* (US), *Journal of Management* (US), *Organizational Science* (US), *Organization Studies* (UK) and *Asian Journal of Management* (Singapore). He was editor of *Vikalpa*, India, and served as guest editor of special issues of *International Studies of Management and Organization*, US. Professor Khandwalla's books and contributions have been acclaimed by many forums and he has received many awards for his writings and contributions.

Professor Khandwalla is an ideal professor in terms of his thoroughness, research, writings and classroom teaching. He is a symbol of what professor of excellence or professor par excellence represents.

KAVIL RAMACHANDRAN[12]

Professor Kavil Ramachandran did his MCom at the University of Calicut in 1978 and completed his PhD in Business Management at Cranfield University, UK (formerly Cranfield Institute of Technology) in 1986. He has been a professor at the Indian School of Business since 2001 and was a professor at IIMA between 1986 and 2000. He worked for a year at St. Joseph's College, Calicut, as a lecturer and also with the APITCO as a consultant for four years.

He designed, developed and taught courses in entrepreneurship and strategy at different points in time. He also teaches family business managers' courses and programmes on managing growth transformation, perpetuating family business and strategies for growth of enterprises.

Prof. Ramachandran has written six books, all related to entrepreneurship and family business. Ram has also published a number of papers in books and journals and has been very productive in pursuing the cause of entrepreneurship and family business. Ram has been regularly organizing annual conferences on family business for Asian participants at the ISB since 2008.

On institution building, he says, 'I believe one of my key strengths is in this area, and I have been closely involved in the process of institution building in various capacities. Conceptual understanding of entrepreneurship and strategic management has been blended with the practice of institution building effectively to create a valuable resource base.'

At ISB he carried out many institution building activities besides teaching entrepreneurship to students, entrepreneurs, potential entrepreneurs and family businesses. As Executive Director, Thomas Schmidheiny Centre for Family Enterprise (since 2015) and Thomas Schmidheiny Chair Professor of Family Business and Wealth Management (2008–2014), he was responsible for creating an identity and making ISB known as one of the best resources for family business in Asia. As Founding Chairman, Wadhwani Centre for Entrepreneurship Development, ISB (2001–04) he led a small team, which initiated a number of activities including designing a MBA teaching programme, business plan competition, entrepreneurial mentoring, linking with venture capitalists, entrepreneurs and major technology institutions, research on entrepreneurial leadership and opportunity identification, and an executive training programme. He established the ISB Knowledge Hub (ISB K-Hub)—a semi-virtual business accelerator that offers mentoring support to hi-tech start-ups. It has obtained funding support from the state and Central governments. It works on network resource principle with least fixed cost investments. The model has been widely acclaimed as somewhat unique and it currently has eight firms being incubated. There are new applicants in the pipeline.

He is founding coordinator and general secretary of the Society of Entrepreneurship Educators (SEE) since 2003. He identified the need to develop a pool of entrepreneurship educators (to start with India) to facilitate growth of entrepreneurship education. SEE has more than 250 members, and has organized a series of workshops for the faculty of management and technological institutions.

M.S. PILLAI[13]

Professor M.S. Pillai is an unusual professor-cum-institution-builder. He is included here for the unusual thinking and effort to build character and values as part of management education. M.S. Pillai (MA, LLB and MBA) served as the founder-director of the Symbiosis Centre for Management and Human Resource Development (SCMHRD), Pune, from 1993 to 2004. When SCMHRD was founded in 1993, it had thirty-two students. When M.S. Pillai left in 2004, the institute had almost 21,000 applicants and was one of the top management schools in India.

After his abrupt departure from SCMHRD in 2004, many of his former students came together and provided him financial and moral support to start Sadhana Centre for Management and Leadership Development (SCMLD) in Pune. He is currently Principal Director at SCMLD, Pune.

SCMLD is a quiet, no frills, high-quality, low-cost, absolutely transparent institute for the honest and hard-working who can challenge themselves to emerge extraordinary despite constraints and past circumstances. The approach to grooming at SCMLD is of a finishing school for overall higher-level skills and healthy habits development to make its students employable/entrepreneurial by focusing on bridging the gap in terms of attitudes, personality, functional knowledge, professional skills, perception, applied insights, integrity, interpersonal sensitivity, character, holistic health—physical, mental, emotional, spiritual and social—discipline, good habits, hard work, self-motivation, continuous learning, community and customer sensitivity, environmental awareness, being responsible and taking initiative and so on. It attempts to re-construct its students for leadership behaviour through paradigm change and competency building. In short, it strives to make the ordinary and the less ordinary extraordinary in a world where the above qualities are fast becoming extinct. It is a Herculean task.[14]

Professor Pillai's philosophy is, 'Nurture the roots and the fruits shall fall.'

What Makes an Effective Professor and a Super Effective or Outstanding Professor?

An effective professor should have the following characteristics:

1. Good knowledge of subject matter
2. Good communication skills

3. Patience with empathy and understanding of students
4. Aptitude to disseminate and influence the thinking of others
5. High ethical standards
6. Research skills and competencies
7. Ability to provide guidance and mentoring with patience and understanding
8. Initiative and drive
9. Creativity
10. Kindness

Effective professors also seem to do the following:

1. Teach well or effectively wherever and whenever they teach, and influence the thinking of a variety of students. For a management professor the variety may include youngsters registered for degrees, diplomas and certificates, managers of all levels starting from young managers to CEOs and chairmen of boards and even ministers and politicians.
2. Discover what they don't know through research. Disseminate what they discovered through their writings, books, articles, presentations in conferences, classrooms and discussions, meetings, etc.
3. Manage their own time and have respect for other people and their time and talent.
4. Influence the thinking of as many people as possible through application of their own research, learnings and what they know by offering extension or consultation services or consultancy practice.
5. Set a personal example for others to emulate by maintaining the high ethical standards required of teachers.
6. Build institutions, mechanisms or practices that will be lasting and available to the society even after them.

Dr A.P.J. Abdul Kalam meets all of the above criteria and is a great teacher by all standards.

If you teach well and influence a number of students you are an effective teacher. If you teach well, you write and influence a larger number, you are still an effective teacher and perhaps a very effective teacher. If you establish institutions that amplify your efforts and reach greater numbers and as a teacher your lessons extend beyond the classroom, then you are a super effective teacher or an outstanding teacher. Anil Gupta and Samuel Paul, who lived largely in India, fall into the category of effective professors as do worldwide recognized management gurus C.K. Prahalad and Vijay Govindarajan. Both Professors Prahalad and Govindarajan were faculty at IIMA and I had the privilege of being their colleague and working with them. Prahalad and I were planning a research study on organizational culture before he left to settle in the USA and Vijay Govindarajan and I worked on the reorganization of Bank of Baroda in the early eighties along with Professor N.R. Sheth. They are not discussed extensively despite their considerable achievements for they did not live a large part of their life in India. Among the Indian professors many meet the above criteria. Their most distinguishing criteria among the above are points 5, 6 and 7.

I have had the good fortune of working with many of them and closely observing others. I draw from my own experiences as well as their published works and their association with many activities. Of the professors studied in this chapter, Anil Gupta and Samuel Paul are super effective professors as they have developed a legacy behind them and the institutions are likely to continue even after them. People like C.K. Prahalad and Vijay Govindarajan bring a good name to the country and leave behind a legacy of their academic contributions. All the others are very effective professors. They are good in their field and in the classroom.

Lessons of Effectiveness

1. Effectiveness to begin with for a professor stems from his subject matter knowledge or expertise in the field. Without the depth and breadth of knowledge one can't be an effective teacher and communicator.

2. The desire to influence others is an important quality for a professor. Teaching is a human services profession and the desire to influence others is the core of teaching. All these professors had a tremendous desire to influence others. Some of them went beyond the classroom to become even more effective.

3. Long-term commitment to the profession is another quality required. Some have left the profession in the middle and joined executive roles like the late K.K. Anand, or Tarun Sheth who joined Hindustan Lever, S.K. Bhattacharya who set up his own consulting firm, Kamal Chowdhary who joined the Ford Foundation first and later the Government of India. Those who continue till they retire have a lot of scope to make an impact through their teachings, writings and the extensive work they do. Professors like Ravi Matthai are impactful—he came from the industry and stayed on in the teaching profession till he died. So is Jagdeep Chhokar who worked in railways and other corporations for a long time before he joined academics. Almost all the professors we included here continued to teach and make their mark.

4. The institutions they work with are normally supportive of the innovative work they do. In fact most universities and institutions support even action-based work like the IIMA supported Anil Gupta, Trilochan Sastry, Jagdeep Chhokar, and the author for starting the National HRD Network and the Academy of HRD, Hyderabad University, Shantha Sinha's work on education and so on. It is also the professor

who has to take the initiative and mobilize support from the institution where he works. As Trilochan says, the institution is an opportunity. If you have interest and passion you can do many things and the institution is the first and best resource you have.

5. Continuous education, awareness creation and spreading of knowledge are the main contributions of effective professors. They do this by many means including writing books, teaching in programmes, attending and organizing conferences and seminars, starting new bodies and so on. Research and writing is a good way to disseminate knowledge and effective professors do this.

6. More effective professors seem to be restless and create their own avenues for their research, consolidation and dissemination. Khandwalla, Ramachandran, Trilochan Sastry, Samuel Paul and Anil Gupta are excellent examples of this. They try to reach out to a larger canvass of people through their writings and talks.

7. Super effective professors focus on building institutions that carry on their work and meet the needs of the nation. Paul built the Centre for Public Affairs and a foundation; Shantha Sinha built M.V. Foundations; Anil Gupta built the Honey Bee Network and Srishti; the author National HRD Network and the Academy of HRD; Trilochan Sastry ADR and CCD; Dharni Sinha, Udai Pareek and team ISABS; Pulin Garg built ISISD; Indira Parikh built Sumedhas and Flame; Dharni Sinha built AMDISA (Association of Management Development Institutions in South Asia) and Cosmode; B.L. Maheswari built the Centre for Organization Development; Joe Philip built the Association of Indian Management Schools and after that the Xavier Institute of Management and Entrepreneurship in Bangalore. Thus institutions help to maintain, generate and disseminate knowledge.

8. Super effective professors seem to be value driven, passionate and exhibit commitment to whatever they undertake. They integrate the knowledge they gain from these experiences into their classroom teaching.

9. Super effective professors also seem to move from one area to another as the need develops and as they learn. They are constantly learning, experimenting and sharing.

10. Super effective people also build the next generation of professors and institution builders to take their work forward. Trilochan Sastry recruits competent people to head the NGO he has set up so that he can expand and the work goes on. Shantha Sinha, Samuel Paul and Anil Gupta have trained a number of people to take charge of the organizations they built in their absence.

Self-Assessment Tool for Professors: How Effective Are You as a Professor?

Rate yourself using a five-point scale or get yourself rated by others on the following:

5 = Very effective, 4 = Effective, 3 = Somewhat effective, 2 = A little effective, 1 = Not at all effective

EP: How good are you as a professor in terms of the following criteria?

☐   1. Depth of knowledge in your areas of specialization
☐   2. Breadth of knowledge in your area of specialization
☐   3. Classroom communication skills in the subjects you teach
☐   4. Writing skills in the area of your specialization
☐   5. Undertaking research studies on your own
☐   6. Creativity or originality of thinking in your area of specialization
☐   7. Working hard to ensure that justice is done to your job as a teacher and researcher

☐ 8. Devotion to students and going out of your way to help them and coach them

☐ 9. Ability to listen, understand, empathize and assess student needs

☐ 10. Taking pride in guiding them

☐ 11. Able to empower the students and learners and respect them

☐ 12. Keeping in touch with the recent developments in their field

☐ 13. Learning from various sources like fellow professors, the Internet, reading literature, magazines and journals, etc.

☐ 14. Publishing and disseminating your work and points of view

☐ 15. Offering programmes that are well attended by many people

☐ 16. Making an impact in any area that is acknowledged by many across the country or the world

☐ 17. Well acknowledged, and the work done by the professor is extensively written about—a lot is written about your work

☐ 18. Value driven and known for integrity and honesty in work

☐ 19. Promoting values like maintaining good character, honesty, integrity and search for truth as values for all

☐ 20. Setting an example for others in following values, and lives as a good teacher and role model

VEP: What is the breadth and depth of your reach in terms of the teaching and other services you provide?

☐ 1. Teaching a large number of people (thousands) in your lifetime so far in terms of disseminating knowledge, ideas and points of view

☐   2. Researching in areas of use that will benefit a large
       number of people at present or in the future
☐   3. Writing and publishing to be read by a large number of
       people in the country and outside
☐   4. Publications that are well referenced across the world or
       used in the country where they are relevant
☐   5. Reaching out to many other people besides the direct
       students through other activities and fora

SEP: Established and developed institutions or processes and
systems that make your work and innovations and ideas available
to many more people for future use

☐   1. Associated with many institutions and contributing to
       their growth
☐   2. Established at least one institution or agency that is
       doing well and is benefiting many people
☐   3. A lot of research is carried out by people in the
       institutions you established
☐   4. Ideas and messages reach a large number of people
       through the institutions that have been established
☐   5. Many people benefit from these institutions
☐   6. The institutions ensure that your skills and teachings
       reach a large number of people and help in growth of
       knowledge
☐   7. The institutions founded are helping a sizeable group of
       people

7 Social Workers

I recently visited a hospital called T.T. Ranganathan Clinical Research Foundation (TTRCF) and met its chief trustee and founder director Shanthi Ranganathan. Shanthi has spent all her life devoted to this 100-bed hospital that treats substance-dependent people like alcoholics, drug addicts, etc. An addict is taken in once they volunteer for a medical treatment for a week and is then counselled and rehabilitated for a month and then discharged. When I visited this hospital in the morning and went around I found a lot of activity. The hospital looks like a school with several classrooms, a gym, and a treatment centre, etc. It is neat and clean with groups of people sitting in different rooms and listening to their coaches. The employees are all pleasant to talk to, every one of them smiling and eager to answer your questions or provide any help. It is estimated to rehabilitate over a thousand people a year. I thought it was well organized and neat.

The T.T.K. Hospital was born of Shanthi Ranganathan's personal experience and determination. At the prime of her youth, her husband, Ranganathan, fell victim to alcoholism. In 1979, T.T. Ranganathan, the thirty-three-year-old grandson of industrialist and former Union finance minister T.T. Krishnamachari, died in the USA where his family had taken him to treat him for alcoholism.[1] Nobody, neither his parents—

Padma and T.T. Narasimhan of the T.T.K. group—nor his young wife, Shanthi, was able to help him fight his dependence. This led Shanthi to start a rehabilitation hospital—a mission born out of compassion and personal grief. Her vision of giving a new life to thousands of individuals affected by addiction and rebuilding their broken families became a reality due to the generosity and support of the T.T.K. group of companies.

Social Work as a Mission

It is said that social work grew out of humanitarian and democratic ideals. Its values focus on respect for the equality, worth and dignity of all people. Social work practice has focused on meeting human needs and developing human potential. The profession strives to alleviate poverty and to liberate vulnerable and oppressed people in order to promote social inclusion. 'The social work profession addresses the barriers, inequities and injustices that exist in society. Its mission is to help people to develop their full potential, enrich their lives, and prevent dysfunction. Professional social work is focused on problem solving and change. As such, social workers are change agents in society and in the lives of the individuals, families and communities they serve.'[2]

There are many categories of social workers. There are many schools of social work that prepare students to be professionally trained. There are over fifty of them in India and the most famous of them include: Tata Institute of Social Sciences; Madras School of Social Work; MS University School of Social Work; Delhi School of Social Work; Nirmala Niketan; Loyola School of Social Work, etc.

Normally these schools prepare candidates for employment as indicated by their placement bureaus. Rarely do they prepare them to start their own NGOs. There are a number of individuals who end up doing the work of professionally trained social workers without any qualifications for the same. It is mostly these cases that start out of a genuine concern for making a difference. Some of them start out of a personal tragedy or experience of some traumatic nature. Such individuals spend their lifetime with high commitment to their cause and make a difference.

The mission of the social work profession is rooted in a set of core values. These core values, embraced by social workers throughout the profession's history, are the foundation of social work's unique purpose and perspective: 'service', 'social justice', 'dignity and worth of the person', 'importance of human relationships', 'integrity' and 'competence'.

GAGAN SETHI

Gagan Sethi holds a master's in social work from Maharaja Sayaji Rao University, Baroda and has also interned in behavioural sciences under the tutelage of Father Heredero, of St. Xaviers College, Ahmedabad. In his twenties, he met Father Heredero, and it was this charismatic personality who planted the seeds of institution building in him. He says, 'Father firmly implanted in me three fundamental principles, which he himself practised with rigour. First: Getting into your team people better than you or having a skill that you yourself do not possess. Second: pursuit of excellence in detail. Third: Dialoguing to the nth degree.' Gagan still practises these three principles and attributes his work to them.

Armed with these principles and with the association of Professor Contractor who was working at the Behavioural Science Centre of St. Xavier's College, Ahmedabad, he started Jan Vikas: an NGO based out of Ahmedabad, which aims to ensure justice to marginalized people and give them the opportunity and support to live a life with dignity and equity. Jan Vikas was bolstered by efforts to motivate and train youth to start new initiatives for social transformation. Gagan Sethi maintains that 'to be effective, organizations should limit themselves to three structural levels'.

What started out as a journey for women empowerment, political education and natural resource management, branched out to other areas like human rights, legal education, social justice and environmental education. Gagan Sethi's working methodologies have been successful and have led to the creation of seventeen bodies of national and international significance like Kutch Mahila Vikas Sangathan(KMVS), Centre for Social Justice (CSJ) and HID Forum. They focus on nurturing organizations at the grass-roots level with development professionals. He has an uncanny style of thinking and organizational development, which have been influenced by his love for the work of Paulo Freire: a philosophy combining humanism and Marxism. The Centre for Social Justice (CSJ) was started in the year 1994, as a project of Jan Vikas. CSJ was started to pursue justice and uphold human rights in the country. CSJ adopts a unique approach by ensuring social justice through legal awareness, alternate dispute resolution, and challenging laws for not being sensitive to the needs of the underprivileged. CSJ mainly focuses on Dalits, women, tribals and under-trial prisoners. 'I believe that trust begets trust. There are exceptions to this principle and we should learn to take the consequences.'

Gagan Sethi has worked at the grass-roots level and his clear understanding with a strong ethos has fostered the creation of institutions which are creating ripples in society. We hope that many more young people follow in the footsteps of Gagan Sethi.

THOMAS RAJA

A large section of India's population is poverty ridden. Though the state of the poor weighs on many minds, few take any active initiative to better their state. T. Raja is one among a selected chunk of people who have taken it upon themselves to help underprivileged people. He shelters around 350 destitutes in his trust named New Ark Mission of India in the Doddagubbi village in Karnataka. He founded this trust with the help of some Christian missionaries in 1997. He picks up people who are starving, stinking, with fatal diseases like AIDS, cancer, mental diseases, etc. and are not wanted and touched by anyone, lying unattended on the roads. The number of such people picked up from the city of Bangalore has reached the count of 450 now and on an average, the overall count of such persons in the last eighteen years is found to be around 4000. As the numbers began to increase, a Home of Hope was built in a larger area donated by some missionaries. The aim of the Home of Hope organization is to rescue the lives of the homeless.

When asked about his early phases of life, Raja related that he fell under bad influence. At an early age, he began to steal and got into smoking and drinking. He sold his mother's *mangalsutra* to drink and watch movies with his friends. He was disowned and he ran away from his troubled home life only to serve a hellish stint in prison. Ill, broken and hopeless, he was eventually helped out by his parents who found him.

After spending some time as an auto driver, Raja realized something which changed his entire life. After leaving his house, Raja had spent a lot of time on the unforgiving streets. He could feel sympathy for the poor and people close to death, lying beside the roads. While some of those unattended fellows were thrown out of their houses, others were disowned by their families, like Raja was, once upon a time. He said, 'I saw hundreds of people lying on the road in miserable conditions. They didn't have food, clothes or any money with them. I wondered what I could do with them. No one was there to help them. People used to run away from them because of the bad odour coming from them.'

He was often criticized by his neighbours for bringing these poor people home. He explained the situation, 'I thought of Mother Teresa at that time. I started feeding them. One day I saw a man lying naked. He had nothing to eat. From that day onwards, I started taking these people to my own house. Initially I took 2–3 people; my parents started scolding me. They thought I was mad and also they felt I was creating a scene in the society. I used to go to people, explain to them about my service and asked them for donations.'

It was then that a person named S.R. Manohar gave him 10,000 rupees and asked him to take a house on rent. Then gradually the Marwari and Jain communities extended hands of support to him by financially helping him and assisting the poor ones to access medical care. Raja stays in the same campus of the Home of Hope with his family and inmates and today he is called the daddy of Home of Hope, for which he is very happy.

JADAV PAYENG

In 2012 at a public function in Jawaharlal Nehru University, the vice chancellor Sudhir Kumar Sopory named Jadav Payeng the 'Forest Man of India'. On 8 April 2015 he was honoured with the Padma Shri from the Government of India. Born in Assam, Mr Jadav relates how he came about to start his mission of saving India's forest. 'I attribute the social institution as my inspiration, i.e. my community's culture. We as the Mishing tribe take from nature and give back to the nature. We live in line with the nature. Our lifestyle is sustainable. In 1979 when the floods of Brahmaputra brought hundreds of snakes to the island, it was then just a sandbar. When the rains subsided and summer approached, these snakes started dying one after the other on the hot river sand bed. This painful death of snakes on the sand afflicted my young mind. I started relating myself with the pain the dying life forms might be going through. I started questioning the situation: Are these snakes meant for dying like this? Why are these snakes dying? What is missing? Can we intervene? What best can be done? If something can be done, why not start it? How to start it? Whom to approach? The learning I received was if the life has to survive, this earth has to survive first—with its ecosystem intact. Trial and error, suggestions from elders, persistent efforts and every other challenge there after seem to be a mere process than obstacles.'

He asked the people from the forest department to plant trees, but they insisted that he do it himself. He started planting saplings in an island on the banks of the Brahmaputra with 100 bamboo shoots. A few years later, the sandbar got transformed into a big bamboo thicket. When the bamboo survived, under the shade of these shoots he planted other local plant varieties of saplings. He planted them, watered them and ensured their survival. He spread the seeds on new lands before the rainy season on a regular basis for approximately thirty-six years which resulted in a full-fledged forest.

By 1980, Mr Jadav, having left his home and education, had already started growing plants and transporting the red ants of his village as he believed that these ants could change the properties of the soil. After some time he started working with the forestry division of the Golaghat district when it launched a drive of tree plantation in around 200 hectares. After the project was over, he stayed back to plant more trees and to take care of them. The area was transformed into a forest and the area came to be known as Molai forest after his pet name Molai. This forest now shelters rhinoceros, Bengal tigers, apes, deer, birds, rabbits, etc. A herd of approximately 100 elephants have given birth to around ten calves in this forest in the past few years.

When asked about a message he wants to give to the residents of planet earth, he says, 'Inspiration is very subjective, differs from person to person. There are many who know what is happening around. Doing makes the difference. Doing is the real measure of inspiration. My inspiration is life, mother earth. I did it for mother earth, not for me, not for you, not for money but for the nature as the subject to be served. All the while we were consuming the nature, we were not letting it heal, I wanted to give back more to my mother so that all life forms can still have a better floor.'

AYYAPPA MASAGI

Water scarcity has been a menace in the lives of many city dwellers, and for farmers it has been a torture to their daily livelihood. India is naturally endowed with many rivers but the irresponsible manner of water consumption and wastage has deteriorated the condition. Compounding to these practices has been the vagaries of the monsoon. Ayyappa Masagi, a technologist, farmer and social activist, is harvesting every drop of water to replenish the subsurface water level in villages as well as cities.

An agrarian family is where he came from, and from childhood he had seen his parents practise water conservation at home as well as in agriculture. 'As a farmer's son, I had the dream of applying science and technology for rural development.' While working in L&T, in the year 1994, he purchased six acres of land in Veerapur village in Gadag district and started his innovative practices of agriculture. 'I wanted to prove to everyone that rain forest crops like coffee, rubber, etc. can be grown in the Deccan Plateau, popularly known as Bayalu Seeme, and also prove that more crops can be grown with whatever rain happens in that particular area despite flood or famine.' Ayyappa Masagi started off well, with good crops blessed due to regular rains. Next year, there was severe drought and his crops failed. The following year it was the other extreme and there was a severe flood. 'The floods engulfed my entire farm and I had to take shelter on a tree for an entire night.' Ayyappa Masagi was not the one to give up. He had embarked on a journey with the mission to make India water sufficient and he was determined to achieve it. He was too strong-willed a person to give up. He saw opportunity in the floods! He thought why not collect all this flood water and conserve it for the subsequent years.

Ayyappa Masagi reached out to experts in this field like Rajendra Singh and innovated borewell recharging techniques. Till then he had only known about rainwater harvesting techniques. Borewell recharging techniques became an answer to harvesting rain water by sending rainwater directly to the groundwater table. Traditional rainwater harvesting systems do not have an answer to surplus rainwater and follow the percolation method, whereas rainwater percolates into the layers of the earth and takes significant time before reaching the groundwater table.

He began to write about his new method and propagate this new way of harvesting water. Ayyappa Masagi continued his work irrespective of the problems it created for his family, and it is at Ardeshanahalli village near Doddaballapur that he got his biggest success. The water table in a 2 km radius had been contaminated by the effluent from one of the pharmaceutical companies which let the contaminated water flow into the dry borewells thinking they were dead. Ayyappa, through his borewell recharging technique, converted the contaminated water into potable water within a short span and this attracted the attention of Rajendra Singh—the Waterman of India. With the collaboration and guidance of the Ashoka organization, Ayyappa Masagi started the Water Literacy Foundation in 2005. Before this he was working alone to solve all the problems;

but now he has a team and this enables him to reach people and industrial organizations that are benefiting from his result-oriented projects.

His mission is to make India water efficient by 2020. For this mission he requires more and more farmers to adopt his practices. His aim is to conduct more and more workshops to train water warriors like him.

NARAYANAN KRISHNAN

'All it takes is just one moment to change you forever.' This recitation is truly manifested in the story of Mr Narayanan Krishnan.

Narayanan Krishnan, a bright, young award-winning chef of a five-star hotel group was shortlisted for an elite job in Switzerland. Being the proud bearer of a renowned degree, he was all set to embrace the new opportunity, longing for a bright future. Unaware of his subsequent destiny, he set forth on his journey in high spirits. Before heading towards Europe, on the street of his hometown Madurai, he saw a very old man eating his own human waste. The sight of this despairing act scandalized him. The level one can stoop to just to satisfy one's hunger was frightening. This agonizing incident made him stop and realize the impact of poverty on his fellow human beings at his own hometown, Madurai. Absolutely bewildered, he immediately purchased some idlis from a nearby restaurant and gave them to the man. Within a few seconds, the man gulped down the idlis. After eating the idlis, the man glanced at him with admiring gratitude. The smile on the face of the old man revolutionized his thoughts. It was a moment of self-realization and of examining the rationale behind one's existence. The satisfaction that he could bestow on the poor old man became the turning point which transformed his entire life and made him decide to take up 'Helping the helpless' as his sole mission.

With this initiative in mind, he returned home to set a
path for his new destination. His parents didn't support his idea
at the beginning. His relatives told his parents to take him to
a psychiatrist or a priest. As stated by Narayanan, 'They had
to undergo a lot of pain because they had spent a lot on my
education.'

In 2002, investing from his personal savings, Narayanan
Krishnan fed around thirty people. This continued for some
days until Krishnan founded his non-profit Akshaya Trust in
2003. Talking about neverending human compassion, the
facts and figures reflect that, from 6,300 meals served in 2002,
the number hiked to 36,000 meals in January 2010. With the
unconditional support of his team members, till now he has
already served more than 1.2 million meals including breakfast,
lunch and dinner to India's numerous homeless ones who are
mostly elderly people abandoned by their families and who
often fall prey to unending miseries and abuses.

Another fact about him is required to be highlighted. In
2005–06, he observed that the unattended dead bodies of many
poor people lay on the roads. No one bothered to cremate
them. Hence he himself started cremating those dead bodies
and so far he has cremated more than 450 bodies. After some
time, another issue cropped up in front of him, i.e. after a year
or two, around 2008, he witnessed many mentally ill women
being harassed and sexually abused, and this increased the ratio of
babies lying abandoned on roads, crying. To solve this problem,
he purchased about 3.2 acres of land in the outskirts of the city
by selling all his assets, and with support from a few corporate
companies he built a rehabilitation centre on that land.

He says, 'One always discovers one's strength at times of
great trouble. Life and its journey make you take help and you
cultivate your strengths.' He also believes that any unaccustomed
initiative is always shadowed by thousands of obstacles. It requires

courage to convince one's dear ones about new ideas and to gain their support. Apart from this, the bigger issues arise while dealing with the uncertain society. Any good which comes free is always questioned and accompanied by mistrust and suspicion. But still Krishnan believes that only by establishing a belief in himself and his dreams, he can beat all the accusations without worrying about the faceless, nameless enemies that still lurk.

Narayan an Krishnan is an inspiration to many, and will continue to make this world a better place through his generosity and desire to change the world, one step at a time! When asked about his feelings about all the work he has accomplished, he replied that till now, he has not done anything great. Hunger and poverty are two unsolved miseries. Though these unending miseries cannot be absolutely eradicated, still he hopes that via his work he will inspire if not all, at least some, helping them to come out of their state of despair.

LAXMI GAUTAM

Vrindavan, a town holy to the Hindus, is located on the banks of the Yamuna in Uttar Pradesh. There are many abandoned women, especially widows, who come to Vrindavan to find peace in the land of Krishna. That is the reason behind Vrindavan being named as the 'the city of widows'. Dr Laxmi, an academician who teaches ancient culture and history in the Institute of Oriental Philosophy, has dedicated her life to serve these unfortunate women. She says that she has been observing these widows since her childhood, as Vrindavan is her birthplace, and she feels connected with them.

Dr Laxmi Gautam resides in the alleys beside river Yamuna. Her day begins by walking the alleys in search of dead bodies of the widows of the place. On finding a dead body, she arranges for a cremation and performs the rituals. There have even been circumstances where she has lifted the dead bodies herself. Till date she is given the credit to have carried out more than 500 cremations.

Her service doesn't end there. Apart from carrying out such unusual social initiatives, she also acts as a blessing in disguise to the countless abandoned widows of Vrindavan. There have been instances when she has paid from her earnings for the treatment of these destitute widows on being refused free medical help by the government hospitals. After being discharged from these hospitals, she makes arrangements to send them back to their homes. If the widows are hesitant to return, she provides shelter to them in one of the local ashrams like the Apna Ghar Ashram of Rajasthan. She also knocks on the doors of the police, state government and even Central government to provide justice to several rape victims.

There are widows who are too old to take care of themselves and they don't have any place to go. Dr Gautam brings them to her own house and takes care of them as if they are her parents. She feeds them and emotionally supports them through her foundation named Kanak Dhara NGO which she has named after her late mother-in-law. She does not accept donations and her NGO is supported by the help of her near and dear ones.

BALAJI SAMPATH

Balaji Sampath's parents were in the government service; as a result he did his schooling in various schools across India. As a student, wherever he went he faced difficulty in understanding the concepts of science due to ineffective teaching practices. Teachers themselves were not clear about concepts and their styles of teaching did not facilitate comprehension of the subject but rote memorization. This probably was because of the education system prevalent in India. His parents encouraged him to analyse this and come up with a solution for it.

Balaji Sampath had mastered the comprehension of subjects, which is evident from the fact that he secured an all India fourth rank in the IIT-JEE exam. He got admitted to IIT, Madras, and it is from there that he first started his journey of teaching poor kids. While at college, he taught these children in a village called Thiramani, near the IIT, Madras campus. After completing his doctoral programme from the University of Maryland, USA, Balaji returned to India to work full-time as a volunteer to reform the education system in his own way. Balaji was very clear in his goals; he knew the biggest problem in the education system was how education was delivered to students.

Balaji started teaching poor children, in a temple on the roadside, and the next day a local offered him space on his rooftop. All this work led Balaji Sampath to start Aid India in 1996, a not-for-profit organization devoted to improve the quality of education in schools.[3]

One of the major challenges Balaji faced in India are the many bureaucratic hurdles in processes. Still he has received collaboration from some areas through which his programme is functioning in 400 schools in Tamil Nadu and has been approved by the government in Tamil Nadu. He is also working in states like Kerala, Andhra Pradesh and Bihar.

Balaji's reach and teach strategy involves low-cost curriculum and teaching materials by assessing the children's current level of learning. These learning aids, using videos, low-cost kits and recorded sessions, are easily comprehendible and very useful for students coming from low-income groups. The Eureka science low-cost experiment kit: a collection of 300 experiments covering all sessions and developed by Balaji, has been very popular among students and teachers. It comes with a manual to disseminate and demonstrate the teaching techniques. Being a firm believer of teamwork, he has involved volunteers from Tamil Nadu Science forum to train them and disseminate the teachings to rural students. He is also working towards training of teachers in government schools so as to improve their teaching techniques so that students find it easy to understand.

He has started a coaching class, ahaguru.com, where a nominal sum is charged for ten lessons and these are provided free for government schools. One computer in a village school is all it takes for education for all. 'When I first meet children, they say that they can't learn, one year later somebody wants to be a teacher or a doctor. This transition is what gives me happiness and drives me.'

Balaji Sampath has been selling dreams to numerous children and also helps them to realize those dreams. His innovative ways of teaching have definitely helped people enjoy learning and take education seriously. He indeed is giving people the opportunity to grow and kick-start a cycle of progress in the country.

UTTAM TERON

Uttam Teron was born in the Karbi dominated village of Pamohi, 20 kilometres away from Guwahati. His father was a train driver and his mother a homemaker who never went to school. This did not stop him from pursuing education and he successfully completed his graduation from a city college. It is here that the first seeds of societal work were planted in his life through working in Guwahati Zilla Moina Parijat, a local group which coached children in leadership, music, physical education, etc.

The children in Uttam's village and those from nearby ones hardly went to school and Uttam wanted to do something about that. He had saved 800 rupees by giving tuitions. He just wanted to help educate the children and bring more and more children into the stream of education. Thus in 2003, he used the money had he saved to construct classrooms with tin and bamboo, and with the rest of the money he bought desks and benches from the village carpenter. This simple act of grit and determination resulted in the humble beginning of Parijat Academy in a cowshed with four students in it. Initially one of the difficulties he faced was to convince the parents to send their children to school.

Uttam was not bogged down by challenges and maintains, 'If one wants to do something good for the people; one should not expect results quickly.' The school that started with four students now has 540 students, from fourteen different tribal communities covering nine tribal villages, each provided with free education from nursery to tenth standard. Interestingly there are 256 girls attending the school. The school boasts of a small hostel also. It is his visionary idea that has been the path breaker for the children in Pamohi.

He has started collaborating with industrial training institutes to increase the employability of the students. His focus is 'Learning for Earning'. He has also started the Parijat Tailoring and Embroidery Centre directed to make women self-dependant.

Uttam Teron was not computer literate, but he overcame this challenge by educating himself by going to a city cyber cafe and learning how to use the Internet. He has since used Skype to connect to people who are interested in contacting and working for this noble cause. His actions have resonated far and wide and today volunteers from the Czech Republic, the USA and Korea come to Parijat Academy to teach spoken English, arts, craft, etc. The school is mainly dependant on donations from various sources, and one such initiative from a non-resident Assamesse has helped in building a library for the school. Uttam Teron has been successful in mobilizing people who are interested in social work to contribute to his cause. He has overcome the barrier of distance through the Internet and now he interacts with students from Flinders University, South Australia, where twenty postgraduate students of various nationalities are getting to know about his work. He has addressed these students over Skype to talk about his journey and about the sustainable tribal practices in day-to-day life. His networking has helped to create a platform where this university has started an organization called South Australians Supporting Children and Women in Assam. His platforms have not only helped him in getting donations but also a free-flowing exchange of ideas on how they can grow and sustain.

The school now has twelve classrooms and twenty-three teachers. The payment of salaries requires a monthly expense of 70,000 rupees. Funding is one of the biggest challenges for the academy. It is through the donations of volunteers that he has been able to carry out the work.

His parents are happy that he has been the harbinger of change in his village and adjoining villages. According to Uttam, producing more Uttam Terons would make him twice as happy as receiving any award.

RAJANI PARANJPE

The process of thinking independently and in a unique manner originated from her home. Rajani Tai belonged to an old-fashioned, middle-class joint family where she had a lot to learn from her parents, grandparents and other elderly persons. The way they cared and sacrificed for the betterment of the family helped her find a soft corner within herself towards serving others. Rajani Tai had the dream to do a postgraduate programme in Marathi but because of the transferable nature of her husband's job she could not pursue her education further. During that period she was a complete housewife, involved in activities like looking after the family and raising her children. However, at the back of her mind the desire to study further was always persistent.

One day, by chance, she came across an article about a course in a newspaper which grabbed her attention. Fifteen years after her graduation, Rajani Tai decided to go back to school to get a master's degree in the social work sector. By that time she had three children, the eldest one studying in ninth grade and the youngest in first standard. In the very beginning of her journey, she realized that her fondness for research and the possession of an analytical mind would definitely help her go a long way.

After spending a few years in the field, she joined Nirmala Niketan, the college of social work in Mumbai as a faculty member. School social work was initiated by this college in a few Municipal Corporation Schools of Mumbai. The primary motive of this programme was to reduce the number of dropouts in schools and to improve the quality of education. Experience of working with dropout students clearly revealed that one of the major reasons behind the hike in the dropout rate was the prevailing circumstances of the parents. A fair example can be that if the parents are working, the children will have to bear all the responsibilities of the family. The day-to-day activities will include looking after younger siblings and a house that lacks security without even a single door; keeping track of the water supply at various tankers or public taps which can include any odd time of the day. This clearly means that these children cannot afford to stay away from home for nearly eight hours a day to attend a formal school. Hence this is a typical problem of nuclear family units, particularly of the migrant population residing in the city slums. Thus was generated the idea of taking education to these children at their doorsteps. Rajani said during the interview for this book, 'I often think that the future is like a big dense jungle where we are able to see only one step at a time but that does not mean that there is no road ahead. When you take one step you see the road for your next step and so on.'

The various exposures she had as a researcher and a teacher, and the kind of support she acquired from some of her students like Ms Bina Seth Lashkari, helped her invent the concept of the 'Doorstep School'. The Doorstep School is an initiative that has aimed at establishing 100 per cent literacy. Rajani Paranjpe founded the Doorstep School in 1987 with her ex-student Bina Lashkari. The Doorstep School has today become a 750+ member-strong organization which serves more than 30,000 underprivileged children at construction sites and urban slum communities in the cities of Mumbai and Pune in India each year.[4] The organization is named so because the education is provided to children wherever they are and the classes are scheduled right there. The targeted children are aged from three to eighteen. Currently, the number of students covered by this programme is around 50,000 in the Pune branch and approximately 12,000 in the Mumbai branch. The Doorstep School is funded by donations from individuals and organizations like Vibha foundations and several government and corporate companies.

When asked about the inspiration in her life to cultivate such innovative ideas, during an interview, Rajani Tai replied, 'I think inspiration is like a spark. Simple things or small steps are like fuel. Both are required to become successful in whatever you are doing.' She is aware of the cruel realities of life. She knows that there are domestic workers, hotel workers, and even there are children who work on docks, go to sea on fishing boats and stay in the deep blue sea for days. There are several children on the streets that are the major source of income to their parents and also there are migrant families such as construction labourers whose children need not necessarily be working but still can't attend school because of the nature of their parents' occupation.

She states, 'Educated people have not given a thought to the significance of universalization of education. We as a class look at our uneducated brothers as a hopeless case. This attitude needs to be changed. But changing it is a big challenge.' Despite these unfavourable circumstances, Rajani Tai has displayed significant interest and bravery to combat these issues.

She states that those traits which if inculcated within oneself can revolutionize the persistent thinking in a common man include patience, flexibility, willingness to initiate ideas, conviction, openness to learn, analytical thinking, perseverance, and above all a happy-go-lucky and positive attitude. She believes that instead of jumping to distinct conclusions, one should focus on one step at a time. This way the analysis is justified and the path becomes clearer. She also thinks that failures can bring greater glory as they make one stronger and adaptive. In short, Rajani Tai has proved that even if situations are inconsistent and adverse, with the willingness to bring about a change in the society coupled with a 'not giving up' attitude, one can sail the boat right through a tormenting storm.

VIRENDRA SINGH

Virendra Singh was born in the town of Anupshahar, Uttar Pradesh, in 1940. He was schooled in Aligarh Muslim University and completed his engineering in Punjab. After his engineering degree, he joined a textile industry, but he then moved to the USA to complete his master's in textile engineering. After his postgraduation, he joined DuPont and remained a part of it till his retirement. Soon after his retirement as South Asia Head of DuPont, Washington, he started working on his aspiring dream to serve his town. His prime concern was the education of girls in the rural sector. While the lack of education was a remarkable conundrum, the existence of the caste system and female foeticide in rural areas made women's lives even more miserable.

In 2000, he started Pardada Pardadi Educational Society (PPES) to improve the lives of girls in rural India. PPES is situated in Anupshahar, Uttar Pradesh, one among the least educated places. In 2011, almost 97 per cent of the students of PPES passed the UP board exam. This success was even furthered when in 2012, all the students of PPES in all grades passed, i.e. a stunning 100 pass percentage. PPES aims at educating girls and making them self-sustaining. It believes that education can free them from poverty and violence. Girls can graduate from school at an appropriate age after which they will be eligible for marriage. Apart from this, they will be capable to earn and hence can become financially independent. This will certainly make the girls aware of their self-worth and they can control their own lives.

There are different community programmes which PPES has set forth. They include toilet construction, and health and cataract camps. In 2008, PPES launched an initiative 'Rags to Pads'. The idea was to produce low-cost menstrual pads because most of the village women don't have access to sanitary pads. These women use rags which can lead to several infections and illnesses. This programme was also initiated keeping employment opportunities in mind. The machine was bought and the first lot of pads was sold. The materials used in the pads are biodegradable making them environment friendly.

When asked about the challenges he encountered, he replied, 'UP is both the worst governed and the most criminal state of India. One may have all the money in the world but if one is not willing to bribe, then it takes a minimum of four years to start even a very small primary school. Whereas my promise to myself was to start the same within three months (school is the first of the four steps one has to take to eliminate poverty systematically). Secondly, everybody in UP believes that if you are rich, then you must be corrupt and so, cheating a cheat is a fair game. Initially 80 per cent of the people cheated on us on all aspects possible. Thirdly, the girl child is the most neglected creature in this part of India. So, they all, especially politicians, suspected my intentions. Lastly, the government of UP uses the Indian legal system to prevent one from doing any good because that would further expose their indifference and inadequacy. They take pride in screwing you and then bragging about it— "See, I taught him a lesson! What does he think of himself, just because he has returned from USA?" So on. Anyway, we overcame all the difficulties and now all four verticals— education, health and hygiene, economic empowerment and community development—are operating and our energies are being directed towards expanding to more and more villages.'

When we asked him about the inspiration to initiate the process, he said, 'I was in the industry for thirty-eight years. I managed the businesses globally. I started the work, believing mainly in the idea that the only way to eliminate poverty was by adopting the hard core business approach. And I still believe in the same. Therefore, returning to my village and creating a model which would eliminate poverty was a business challenge for me. Because of my experience I was confident that I could do it, the only challenge was doing it in India and that too in Anupshahar, UP, the place where no industry, no power, no roads, no medical facilities and no running water exist. May be because of all these reasons it became more fun.' He adds, saying that the first and foremost hurdle is gaining the trust of the parents of the children. He is always questioned about his intention to promote only the education of the girl child. The villagers even doubt his intention to provide jobs to their daughters after school. The only way to convince these people is to help them with their queries with absolute perseverance.

Mr Singh believes that the encouragement that he receives is solely from the smiles of these little girls. The feeling that he can bring a difference in someone's life is precious. It is his passion to help others which motivates him inevitably. He defines an effective person as the one who discovers the inner talent and utilizes it to make a difference in the lives of other people. He adds, 'Successful people all over the world have certain common traits. They dream big! Like Gandhiji who fought for azadi, Sardar Patel who again fought for freedom, Tendulkar who turned out to be the best cricketer of the world and many more! They convert dreams into vision; a vision into a personal commitment. This commitment facilitates the generation of ideas; these ideas help to give the vision a practical shape. In my opinion anyone can dream and if they sincerely believe in their dream, they will get the ideas to actualize their dreams.'

Lessons of Effectiveness from Social Workers

The case studies reviewed here cover people who fit the definition of social work we stated in the beginning of the chapter: 'Social work practice has focused on meeting human needs and developing human potential. Human rights and social justice serve as the motivation and justification for social work action. In solidarity with those who are disadvantaged, the profession strives to alleviate poverty and to liberate vulnerable and oppressed people in order to promote social inclusion.'

Only two of the social workers presented here are professionally trained social workers (MSW). The rest of them are naturally evolved social workers whose activities fit the definition of social work. Six of them are working on educating the disadvantaged or those less privileged including street children, construction workers' children, migrating workers' children, poor children, girls, dropouts, etc. They are also up-skilling them in other cases. One of them was working with addicts, one on planting trees to make the earth liveable, another trying to solve the water problem through borewell recharge and other techniques, two of them are helping the destitute and widows by providing food and shelter, cremation and other facilities. Almost all of them have either registered societies, started other forms of NGOs or taken the help of established NGOs or institutions. Gagan Sethi has built a large number of associations and works on several fronts and nowadays focuses on institution building activities. All the cases covered here are very effective or super effective people because of the institutional base they have built to carry out their work. Most of them are heroes working for a cause which they believe to be their mission. To answer the question with which we began, we now list the characteristics of effective social workers:

1. Effective social workers are highly sensitive people. They are sensitive to the needs of others and have a high degree of empathy. They start with compassion coming out of the empathy to others and develop a commitment to serve them. They are either moved or touched by what they see around them, especially the suffering of people, or lack of care or opportunities, and they compare their status with those who do not have and decide to do something for them.

2. They take small steps to begin with and work to help those around them. Begin small and do what you can within the limitations you have but do it with devotion. Each one of them started with their own unique model of serving others. They have not learnt these lessons from any school but intuitively or from great leaders like Mahatma Gandhi. Gagan acknowledges Fr Heredero as his mentor in working for the weaker sections of society.

3. The small grows slowly bigger and bigger or larger and larger, resulting in more children enrolling in schools, more destitute people housed, or more people served, etc. If they don't succeed they seem to treat failures as challenges and rather than withdrawing they pursue their goals with more

rigour and determination. Perseverance and determination seem to characterize them.

4. They use their talent and the resources they have from early stages of their social or community work. As most of them come from ordinary families and are not necessarily well educated, their talent is their attitude of compassion and their desire to serve others.

5. Almost all of them face resistance from families in the beginning and also from neighbours and the community if they have to feed the poor, house the destitute or bring home the sick and ill. However they don't give up to demonstrate their point and have a knack of converting the resistant families to supportive families with their hard work and perseverance.

6. They start thinking big and have larger plans like making the country self-sufficient in water or making the earth a liveable place, or making the future secure for the future generations, or enabling every girl child to go to school, alleviating poverty, etc. From starting small, they graduate to becoming mission driven and having larger goals.

7. With larger goals taking over on successful implementation, they need to mobilize funds and therefore largely seek institutional help, start institutions or register NGOs. They expand and grow to serve others.

8. In all this work—integrity, commitment, honesty and transparency characterize their behaviour and governance style. Without these qualities they cannot grow and serve a larger number especially because funding needs value-driven people.

9. Most of them seem to be technologically savvy and take the help of the networks they have built. Without networking and support mobilization skills, they can't grow and achieve the mission goals.

10. In social work it may be necessary for everyone to grow into a super effective person as one cannot do without an institutional base. Registering an NGO or taking the help of an institution becomes a necessity. However, some may not let the institution grow out of their wings and may block the achievement of the very objectives with which they have started. They may not let others grow if others become more articulate than them and start getting media and national attention. They enjoy getting attention and this may prevent them from expanding.

Self Assessment Tool: How Effective Are You as a Social Worker?

Use a five-point scale for evaluating

5 = Very good/High, 4 = Good/High, 3 = Moderate, 2 = Low and 1 = Very low

How good are you as a social worker in terms of the following criteria? (ESW/EP)

☐ 1. Depth of knowledge in your areas of work (making children literate, education, health, drug addiction, girl child education, skill development, self-employment, etc.)

☐ 2. Breadth of knowledge in your area of work (extent of awareness of how others are doing, experiences, lessons, etc.)

☐ 3. Communication skills to convince and enrol people to use services you offer

☐ 4. Knowledge of the area, people, culture and habits and possible resistance to help

☐ 5. Ability to read, tour, visit other places and learn from the experiences of others on your own

☐   6. Creativity or originality of thinking in your area of work

☐   7. Working hard to ensure that you do justice to your beneficiaries through your work

☐   8. Passion and commitment to the cause you are trying to work for

☐   9. Taking pride in helping others

☐ 10. Respect for those whom you help or those who seek help

☐ 11. Presenting your work, philosophy and intent, etc., or publishing or disseminating your work and points of view to various agencies: government, NGOs, funding agencies, etc.

☐ 12. Offering interventions that are appropriate for the community you are serving

☐ 13. Extent to which you are value driven and known for your integrity and honesty in work

☐ 14. Promoting values like maintaining good character, honesty, integrity and search for truth as values for all

☐ 15. Setting an example for others in following values of social workers and living as a good teacher and role model

What is the breadth and depth of your reach in terms of the services you provide? (VESW/VEP)

☐   1. Reaching a large number of people or beneficiaries in terms of action and disseminating knowledge, ideas and points of view

☐   2. Studying and understanding means to benefit a large number of people at present or in the future

☐   3. Writing and publishing to be read by a large number of people in the country and outside to emulate your model

☐   4. Getting acknowledged for the work done

☐ 5. Promoting others to start your way of doing things or improved versions of your work

Established institutions or processes and systems that make your work and innovations and ideas available to many more people for future use (SESW/SEP)

☐ 1. Networking with many institutions to disseminate and participate in your work
☐ 2. Established at least one institution or agency that is doing well and is benefiting many people
☐ 3. A lot of activities are carried out by people in the institutions established
☐ 4. Philosophy, vision, mission, ideas and messages reach a large number of people through the institutions established
☐ 5. Many people are trained to carry on the work through the institutions established
☐ 6. The institution ensures that skills and teachings reach a large number of people and help in growth of knowledge

8 Other Professions

For this book we started with a view that effective people come from various sectors of life and different professions like teachers, doctors, actors, social workers, educational entrepreneurs, civil servants, lawyers, managers, chartered accountants, etc. We had to make some choices on the number of categories and people covered. Of them, the management profession is well researched and a lot of literature has appeared on this issue. I felt any effort to cover businessmen, entrepreneurs and professional managers would be unnecessary and a duplication of effort. For example, in the last decade a large number of books have appeared on Indian leaders including businessmen, scientists, reformers and nation builders. Combining all this and drawing from the available literature was adequate, I felt. In this chapter a few of the categories are combined. This book is not about various professions but about effective people: the issue is what makes them effective people? In this chapter some case studies of effective people from various other professions have been included to give a flavour of effectiveness in other professions. After a short review of what makes business leaders, wealth creators and professional managers effective, this chapter goes on to delineate the characteristics of bankers and a few nation builders that have contributed a lot to the building of India.

Businessmen and Wealth Creators

A lot is written about very effective and successful business persons. Their qualities have been adequately analysed in many books in the last decade and a half. There are a lot of writings and scientific explorations on them and quite a bit of information about them is public knowledge. In this book, some significant studies are summarized and no case studies are presented.

On the basis of his long years of experience and interaction with leaders and managers, Udai Pareek[1] (2002) emphasized that business leaders should be institution builders. They should focus their attention on the following eight roles: identity creation; enabling (resource creation); synergizing; balancing (conformity and creativity); linkage building; futuristic; impact-making; and creating super-ordination. The implication of Pareek's studies for leaders is to create institution-building capabilities of top-level managers and senior executives.

R.M. Lala's study of an analysis of Indian leaders of yesteryears has indicated thirteen qualities of leadership: communication, compassion, competence, courage, decision-making, humility, love, integrity, man-management, stamina, teamwork, training and vision (Lala, 1986).[2]

Srinivas Pandit[3] (2001) studied twenty-two Indian leaders from various fields. These included entrepreneurs like Bhavarlal Jain, Deepak Kanegaonkar, Ravi Khanna, Kiran Mazumdar Shaw, Ronnie Screwvala; entrepreneur-managers like H. Dhanrajgir, V. Kurien, Deepak Parekh; manager-entrepreneurs like N.R. Narayana Murthy, Ashok Soota, Pramod Chaudhuri; family entrepreneurs like B. Kelkar, R. Chitale; and, exceptional managers like Anu Aga, R. Mashelkar, etc. Each of them can be considered an effective business person and wealth creator (intellectual wealth included). The common traits he found among them include the following:

1. Commitment (drive, dedication, passion, obsession and zeal);
2. Persistence (doggedness, determination, hard work; insistence and tenacity);
3. Difference (distinctness, differentiation, innovativeness and talent);
4. Curiosity (creativity, clarity of thought and intelligence);
5. Persuasiveness (negotiation, influencing and presentation skills);
6. Risk-taking or entrepreneurship;
7. Focus (concentration, goal-orientation and centring);
8. Values (honesty, integrity, honouring commitment, truthfulness, etc.);
9. High energy (spiritedness and stamina);
10. Learning;
11. Humility (modesty and unpretentiousness);
12. Non-listening (firmness and not obstinacy).

S.N. Chary[4] (2002) studied seven Indian business leaders: Kiran Mazumdar Shaw, Azim Premji, N.R. Narayana Murthy, Venu Srinivasan, Deepak Parekh, Dr V. Kurien and Mukesh Ambani. The following emerged from his study:

1. They are passionately committed to their goals.
2. They are visionaries rewriting management principles—they are ahead of their time
3. They are missionaries of the world.
4. They have exalted goals and social concerns.
5. They had a mission and they acquired core competence, making us revisit the core competence theory.
6. They had a firm foundation of values (integrity, humility, compassion, honesty, customer service, etc., being some of these).

7. Simplicity and humility characterize most of them.
8. They share a love for people.
9. They all practice out-of-the-box thinking.

The qualities implied from various studies are in tune with the observations made in the earlier chapters. Only those who fulfil qualities of effective people have been chosen by the various authors. These effective business persons or wealth creators have been good at their business, created wealth, presumably exhibited values and ethics, developed others, and obviously built and expanded business. They are constantly under scrutiny from the media and under study by management researchers.

Professional Managers

Another category of professionals that I want to consider for this book are the professional managers. They are normally trained as Masters in Business Administration (MBA). Normally, companies recruit engineers and other graduates and train them through a series of short-term programmes over a period of time and they are also considered as professional managers. They are expected to follow the ethics of their profession though, interestingly, whether management has become a profession or not is being hotly debated. After reviewing a number of articles on professions we arrive at the following essential characteristics:

1. A body of well-developed knowledge with theory and amenable to practice
2. A body to educate and certify people to develop professional competencies through education and training (like in Law, Chartered Accountancy, Medicine, etc.)

3. A code of conduct
4. An agency or professional body to control the entry and exit and conduct of the professionals (Medical Council of India, Institute of Chartered Accountants, Bar Council, etc.)

Out of these four, management and social work fall short on two counts to qualify as a profession. It is evident that today management has not yet fully become a profession. But just as you can be a social worker without a master's in social work, those without an MBA can also become managers. However, there is a good body of knowledge and there are professional bodies and institutions like AICTE (All India Council for Technical Education) which prescribes some criteria for awarding degrees and carrying out management education though it is not a certifying body for managers. Hence management is treated like a profession. Lessons are available here again from scientific studies and hence no attempt is made to present case studies. The book, *100 Managers in Action*, and other such books offer enough case studies and hence I highlight the conclusions drawn from these studies here.

J.H. Zenger and Joseph Folkman,[5] (2003) on the basis of their study using 360 Degree Feedback data, of about 20,000 managers, assessed by over 2,00,000 assessors, using twenty different instruments, have identified several insights on leadership. Some of these remarkable insights are:

1. Great leaders make a huge difference as compared to merely good leaders.
2. The relationship between improved leadership and increased performance outcomes is neither precisely incremental nor linear.
3. Great leadership consists of processing several building blocks of capabilities, each complementing the other. These include: character, personal capability, a focus on results,

interpersonal skills and the ability to lead organizational change.

4. All competencies are not equal. Some differentiate good leaders from great leaders, while others do not.
5. Effective leaders have very varied personal styles. There is no single right way to lead.
6. The key to developing great leadership is to build strengths.
7. Powerful combinations produce exponential results. For example, focus on results and interpersonal skills is a powerful combination. Improving interpersonal skills may be the best way to improve technical skills.
8. Greatness is not brought about by the absence of weakness. Great leaders are not perceived as having major weaknesses. Fatal flaws must be fixed. These include: inability to learn from mistakes and develop new skills, being interpersonally inept, being closed to new ideas, failure to be accountable for results, and not taking initiative.
9. Leaders are made, not born. Leaders improve their leadership effectiveness through self-development. The organization, with the help of an immediate boss, provides significant assistance in developing leadership.
10. The quality of leadership in an organization seldom excels that of the person at the top.

From the study of this research on leadership using 360 Degree Feedback, the following implications can be drawn for building leadership competencies:

1. *Display high personal character.* Everything about great leadership radiates from character. Personal character improves the probability of exhibiting strong, interpersonal skills. Character is based on innate values and high self-awareness.

2. *Start small.* Do something now that has immediate impact. Small things lead to big things. Identify some quick and readily visible things.

3. *Excel at something.* Zenger and Folkman (2003) indicate that the impact of one perceived strength moves leaders to the 64th percentile. Three strengths move them to the 81st percentile. They also suggest that the candidate figures out what they are good at which moves them to the 90th percentile.

4. *Connect competencies and leverage combinations.* See the power of combinations. For example, focusing on results and interpersonal skills is a powerful combination.

5. *Use a non-linear approach to becoming a better leader.* Improving interpersonal skills may be the best way to improve technical skills.

6. *Build on your strengths.* Figure out what you do well and magnify it. It only takes strengths in a few areas to make an impact. Find what you do well and then figure out what combinations are required to be more effective.

7. *Remedy fatal flaws.* These include the inability to learn from mistakes and develop new skills, interpersonal ineptness, being closed to new ideas, failure to be accountable for results, and not taking initiative.

8. *Work on these fatal flaws fast and furiously.*

100 Managers Study

I[6] analysed the 360 Degree Feedback of over 8000 managers assessed by around 80,000 assessors across a fifteen year period. I identified the top scorers as highly influencing managers. The results of this study are described in a book I wrote called *100 Managers in Action*. The results have indicated the following as common characteristics of these managers who are effective as they impacted others and made a difference:

1. *They are hard core networkers*: They are spread all across on the Internet communities like LinkedIn, Facebook, etc. They could be seen on the boards of organizations, in social functions, conferences, quality meets, etc. They are accessible and people write to them often. This ability to network leverages their performance.

2. *They are great learners*: Carrying forth from the above point, these managers learn from each experience. They keep a mental note or write in a diary what they find interesting. Also, they apply these learnings elsewhere. They can replicate the learnings in a different scenario. They have marched head-on into certain situations which apparently led to an abyss.

3. *They are achievement driven and focus on building achievement and problem solving culture*: To put forth a view, which is primarily with an intention to improve the prevailing conditions which is completely opposite to the thinking of the audience is a mammoth task. Culture building is like painting nowhere without any colours.

4. *They want to live many lives*: These leaders want to share their own experience with others. They are teachers, mentors and role models. They want to expand their aura continuously.

5. *They are perseverant*: They implement systems and keep coming back to them for monitoring. They are process drivers and process owners. This trait forms an integral part of their leadership. They understand things have their own incubation time to take up shape and become cash cows.

6. *Early exhibition of leadership skills:* Most of them were either holding leadership roles as school monitor/prefect or as sports captain leading the team. They have known to guide, delegate, monitor responsibilities

7. *They are self-motivated*: As James Allen has put it in *As a Man Thinketh*—You are the master of your thought, you mould your own character, the maker and shaker of your condition, environment and destiny. Man is buffeted by circumstances as long as he believes himself to be the creative power and that he may command the hidden soil and seeds of his being out of which circumstances grow, he then becomes the rightful master of himself.

8. *They are aware about self*: They are deliberately conscious about themselves. Not only do they know their strengths, but also their weaknesses. Awareness about self and admitting to it are the first two steps towards improving self. Knowing the low points may also be an advantage. They teach you the art of doing things differently.

9. *They are open*: They like to talk about themselves. Leaving their egos behind, they talk freely about their lives and accept criticism.

10. *They build on strengths*: All the managers covered here have focused the most on their strengths. They have taken care of the weaknesses too. This particular attitude has made them even more successful. A general attitude of a person is to pay attention to only the weak areas. In this process, they attempt to see a magnified picture of their mistakes which definitely hampers high achievement and motivation. A more intelligent step is to utilize strengths to be even more effective.

11. *They follow up with the outside world*: The fact that they have well-formed opinions shows that they have their finger on the pulse of the market. Their actions reflect far-sightedness.

12. *They have family support*: Their families have been with them throughout. Many times, they have put the organization before families. Their wives and children have been supportive and not bitter about this.

These studies are good indicators of what makes managers effective. You will note that they are fairly self-explanatory, and so I make no attempt to further analyse the qualities of effective managers or businessmen.

Bankers

R.K. TALWAR

R.K. Talwar (1922–2002)[7] is considered an undisputed leader in banking. Raj Kumar Talwar, born in 1922, joined the Imperial Bank of India in Lahore in November 1943 as a probationary assistant, immediately after taking his MA degree in mathematics from Lahore University. He had an outstanding career at the bank. In 1961 he was Superintendent of Branches and Superintendent of Advances in the Bengal Circle of the State Bank of India and Inspector of Branches under Central Office. Later he worked in various circles including Bengal, Madras, Hyderabad, Bombay. On 1 February 1968 when he was appointed as one of the two managing directors of the State Bank, he became the youngest to adorn that office. Talwar became chairman of the State Bank of India on 1 March 1969. The youngest chairman ever, he gave a sense of direction and a new orientation to the bank as never before. Besides expanding the bank's business manifold by extending its reach, his missionary zeal saw the State Bank take several initiatives in the areas of innovative banking, rehabilitation of sick industries, credit plans for rural development, etc. He ensured simplification of procedures for financing of small-scale industries and launched new schemes for the benefit of smaller enterprises, small businessmen and agriculturists. He also put in place systems to ensure proper end use of bank funds besides comprehensive analysis of corporate balance sheets much before the Reserve Bank of India prescribed norms for credit analysis of large advances. It was again his rare vision and foresight that initiated the first ever organizational restructuring exercise of the State Bank in 1971, which withstood the test of time for well over three decades. A highly principled banker, Talwar was known for his values, integrity, dynamism and professionalism. All through his career, he gave his best to nurture a culture of openness, frankness and transparency in the bank and bitterly opposed arbitrary decisions. A man of exceptional attributes and indomitable spirit, with an abiding faith in the grace of the divine, and honesty and integrity as his guideposts, Talwar commanded respect both within and outside the bank. To him, principles dear to his heart were above all else and never was he ready to compromise with them. When he left the bank on 3 August 1976, he was only fifty-four. By then, hailed as one of the country's most distinguished bankers, Talwar had galvanized the bank by his vision, dynamism and dedication. His was undoubtedly the golden era of the State Bank. He decided to settle in Pondicherry but his connections with the corporate world did not cease as he served on boards of companies and headed the Industrial Development Bank of India for a couple of years in the late 1970s. He was by then more focused on spiritual matters. He lived a spartan life and was often seen moving around the town of Pondicherry on a bicycle. Talwar breathed his last on 23 April 2002 at the age of eighty. Talwar's name is closely linked with the issue of customer service as he was the chairman of the Committee on Customer Service (1975). Today whenever customer service related issues are discussed and debated, the far-reaching recommendations made by the Talwar Committee are often quoted.[8]

R.K. Talwar was considered as the trail-blazing chairman of the State Bank of India from 1969 until his abrupt departure in 1976, at the height of the Emergency. The following report from N. Vaghul (who is himself a great leader in the banking industry) as a part of the 5th R.K. Talwar memorial lecture delivered at the Indian Institute of Banking and Finance[9] speaks about the man.[10]

Mr Vaghul, who started his own distinguished banking career in SBI, recalls that a cement company to which the bank had given a loan became 'sick', with mounting losses. Seeing that the problem was mismanagement, the bank agreed to a restructuring package provided the company's promoter, also its chairman and CEO, made way for a professional. The promoter happened to be a friend of Sanjay Gandhi.[11]

Sanjay called the finance minister (who, though unnamed, was C. Subramaniam; Pranab Mukherjee was nominally under him as minister for revenue and banking), and asked him to direct the bank to waive the condition on change of management. The minister phoned Talwar, who called for the details of the case, satisfied himself, and informed the minister that the condition could not be waived. The minister summoned Talwar to Delhi and told him that he had instructions from 'the highest authority' in the country. Talwar stood his ground.

This was communicated to Sanjay, who called for Talwar. Talwar refused to meet him, saying he had no constitutional authority. Sanjay's response was swift: Sack Talwar.

This was easier ordered than done, because under the State Bank of India Act the chairman could not be removed without sufficient cause. So the minister offered Talwar a different assignment, to chair the proposed Banking Commission. Talwar said he would accept and could do that in addition to being the SBI chairman.

The minister looked unhappy, so Talwar observed that the minister seemed to be 'very particular' that Talwar should not continue as the bank chairman. The minister admitted that the problem was Talwar's lack of flexibility on the cement company issue, and said that if he did not resign, he would have to be dismissed. Talwar said he had no intention of resigning, and the minister could decide on dismissal.

As Mr Vaghul tells it, Sanjay next asked the Central Bureau of Investigation (CBI) to look for grounds on which Talwar could be dismissed. It turned out that Talwar had sent appeals to many businessmen, seeking donations for the Auroville project to which he was devoted. But no businessman was willing to testify that Talwar had spoken to him or tried to persuade him to make a donation. All that he had done was to forward an appeal signed by the prime minister and the secretary-general of the United Nations (U. Thant), recommending the Auroville project for support. The CBI was forced to close the case.

Sanjay now lost all patience, and told the minister to amend the SBI Act so that Talwar could be dismissed without stating the reason. With Opposition leaders in jail, Parliament rubber-stamped the Act's amendment in no time. The minister told Talwar one final time that if he did not resign he would be dismissed. Talwar remained defiant.

Finally, on 4 August 1976, Talwar was given thirteen months' leave and asked to hand over charge to the managing director of the bank. Even after arming itself with the required powers, the government could not bring itself to sack Talwar. Mr Vaghul records that there was hardly anyone to see off the SBI's greatest chairman that evening, so great was the atmosphere of fear at the time.

S. Parthasarathy, former managing director of SBI's Overseas Operations, reminisces that when human resource development was still relatively unknown management jargon, Talwar propagated the idea of human and social capital. He took a personal interest in officers and called them for discussions to encourage and develop their potential.[12]

K.V. KAMATH

K.V. Kamath[13] was CEO of ICICI Bank from 1996 to 2009. ICICI Bank is India's largest private sector bank with a global footprint, total assets of $102 billion, and 25 million customers worldwide with over 1500 branches. Kamath was awarded a Padma Bhushan by the Government of India, lifetime achievement award by the *Financial Express* and best bank award by NDTV. K.V. Kamath gets his entrepreneurial spirit from his father and the power of introspection and looking for solutions outside the ordinary from his mother. Both his parents have taught him to aim high and achieve a leadership position in whatever you do.

'The two years at IIMA helped him to develop his skills as a business leader of the future. He became famous for his sheer brilliance on campus. The tale of him submitting the written analysis of communication assignment well before the deadline and yet scoring the highest grade became nothing short of mythical as even the best of minds struggle with these assignments. His proficiency, diligence, and speed during those early years stood him in good stead when he was ready to take on the world of business.'[14] (Pota, 2010)

Kamath joined ICICI in 1971 in the project finance division. He worked as executive assistant to the chairman (S.S. Nadkarni), subsequently moved to general management positions, set up ICICI's strategic planning division and planned its diversification into the new areas of investment banking, venture capital and credit rating. He initiated the bank's computerization programme. Between 1988 and 1996 Kamath worked with the Asian Development Bank and a group in Indonesia and gained a lot of experience in other countries. He rejoined ICICI in 1996 as CEO. Kamath is a good example of a leadership engine. He created an environment that helped many people become CEOs in ICICI Bank or its outfits or outside.

Recently in 2015 he has been appointed as the chief of a $100 billion New Development Bank, established by the BRICS nations—Brazil, Russia, India, China and South Africa. He has also served as the chairman of Infosys Limited, the second-largest Indian IT services company, and as the non-executive chairman of ICICI Bank, India's largest private bank. Kamath also served as ICICI Bank's managing director and CEO from 1 May 1996 until his retirement from executive responsibilities on 30 April 2009. An alumnus of IIMA, he was also given the Outstanding IIMA Alumni Award in its golden jubilee year.

DR ANIL K. KHANDELWAL

Dr Anil K. Khandelwal retired as chairman and managing director of Bank of Baroda in April 2008, after bringing it to a leadership position in the banking industry. He has a glittering academic career and over three decades of banking experience. A chemical engineer with an MBA and a degree in law, he also holds a doctoral degree in management. He is also a Fellow of the Indian Institute of Banking and Finance. Dr Khandelwal maintains that banking happened to him by accident. He graduated in chemical engineering. In 1970, he went to Jaipur with his uncle who was a publisher. He saw a Bank of Baroda advertisement looking for probationary officers. He took the test out of curiosity and totally forgot about it later. When he was visiting Hyderabad for a book exhibition, he got a telegram informing him of an interview in Indore for the PO's position at Bank of Baroda. He was reluctant but his uncle forced him to go. In 1976, he resigned and joined Bank of Rajasthan. In 1980 he came back and worked for over a decade at the Bank of Baroda Staff College. He then shifted to BOB, Mumbai deputy general manager personnel and then was posted as zonal manager of the Meerut Zone where he successfully managed the bank's operations. He later became its executive director and in 2004, he joined Dena Bank as a chairman and executive director. Dr Anil Khandelwal took over as chairman of Bank of Baroda in March 2005, and has brought about deep changes in several areas, particularly branding, leadership and retail banking. During his tenure at Dena Bank he had successfully piloted the turnaround of the bank. Prior to this he was the executive

director at Bank of Baroda since 2000. Dr Khandelwal, besides
being an astute banker, has also been closely associated with
the HRD movement in the country and is one of the founder
members of the National HRD Network. He authored the first
book on HRD in banks. He was selected as HRD consultant
by the United Nations to work on a project for the Presidential
Commission on Banking, Tanzania. In recognition of his
application of HRD interventions in business situations, he was
awarded the coveted National Award of 'Best HRD Chief' by
the National HRD Network. The Conference of Intellectuals
awarded him the Great Son of the Soil Award. He has also been
the recipient of the Grid Leadership Award for Excellence in
Corporate Management in 2004.

Khandelwal is known for many innovations in Bank of
Baroda including creating a sense of pride and identity among
employees through innovations and taking them close to the
customers. He increased the number of ATMs from 158 to about
1100 in two years and got 1700 branches to do 90 per cent of their
business online. He introduced 8 a.m. to 8 p.m. banking in over
510 locations; introduced twenty-four hour human banking in
nine branches with three shifts a point, rarely used by any bank
in the world. He maintained a rigorous communication strategy
with employees; increased the customer base from 25 million
to 33 million; opened twelve new offices in new countries and
new locations to increase foreign presence from fifty-seven
to seventy-one locations, and increased international business
(contributes to 20 per cent of business and 30 per cent profits).
He boosted the business level from 1,24,733 crores in 2005 to
nearly 2,50,000 crores when he retired in 2008.

Subsequently in 2011, Khandelwal led the Committee on
Human Resources for the banking industry, popularly known as
the Khandelwal Committee, perhaps one of the few committees in
banking whose recommendations were accepted almost in toto.[15]

Scientists and Nation Builders

There are certain professionals in various sectors including science and technology, space, nuclear power, dairying (white revolution), and agriculture (green revolution) who have contributed a great deal to the building of our nation. It is important to know their lives and understand how they have become effective contributors to nation building. Nation builders for the purposes of this book consist of only those professionals that have contributed to the building of the nation through science, technology, culture, systems and processes, global image, human resources development, employment, quality of life, GDP and other economic parameters. These may include professionals from various fields. Politicians are excluded for a variety of reasons.

The names of professionals who contributed are many. Prominent among them could be scientists like C.V. Raman, M. Visweswarayya, Dr Homi Bhabha, Vikram Sarabhai, C.N.R. Rao, Abdul Kalam, Dr M. S. Swaminathan; technology persons like Sam Pitroda and so on; institution builders like Vergehese Kurien (white revolution), Ravi Matthai (management education); social workers like Mother Teresa; wealth creators like N.R. Narayana Murthy, Azim Premji, Kumar Birla, J.R.D. Tata, Kiran Mazumdar Shah; social reformers and workers like Anu Aga, Bunker Roy, Aruna Roy.

HOMI BHABHA
Homi Bhabha is known as the father of the Indian Space Programme. He was the founding director of two well-known research institutions, namely the Tata Institute of Fundamental Research (TIFR) and the Trombay Atomic Energy Establishment. He was born in a prominent industrial Parsi family and joined Caius College, Cambridge University

in 1927. He died in a plane crash in 1966 while heading to
Vienna to attend a meeting of the International Atomic Energy
Agency. 'Bhabha gained international prominence after deriving
a correct expression for the probability of scattering positrons
by electrons, a process now known as Bhabha scattering. His
major contribution included his work on Compton scattering,
R-process, and furthermore the advancement of nuclear physics.
He did further research to describe how primary cosmic rays
from outer space interact with the upper atmosphere to produce
particles observed at the ground level. Bhabha later concluded
that observations of the properties of such particles would lead to
the straightforward experimental verification of Albert Einstein's
theory of relativity. He is credited with formulating India's
strategy in the field of nuclear power to focus on extracting
power from the country's vast thorium reserves rather than its
meagre uranium reserves.'[16]

SALIM ALI

Salim Ali (1896–1987)[17], known as the 'birdman of India',
was among the first Indians to conduct systematic bird surveys
across the country. This passionate biker and Padma Vibhushan
awardee was a key figure behind the Bombay Natural History
Society (BNHS). He was born in a Sulaimani Bohra Muslim
family of Bombay and passed the matriculation exam of Bombay
University in 1913 with great difficulty. Salim Ali discovered
an opportunity to conduct systematic bird surveys of the
princely states that included Hyderabad, Cochin, Travancore,
Gwalior, Indore and Bhopal with the sponsorship of the rulers
of those states. Later on he was very influential in ensuring the
survival of the BNHS and managed to save the then 100-year
old institution by writing to the then Prime Minister Pandit
Nehru for financial help. He helped in the establishment of
an economic ornithology unit within the Indian Council for
Agricultural Research.

VERGHESE KURIEN

It was more than sixty years ago that Dr Verghese Kurien came to Anand, a small town in Gujarat, after completing a graduate programme in the United States, intending to soon leave its dust and heat behind. But drawn by the power of an idea—milk producers cooperating to build a better life—he stayed on.

When Dr Kurien arrived in Anand, there was a fledgling dairy cooperative that had been born during the Independence movement. The chairman of that cooperative, Tribhuvandasbhai Patel, was a man of extraordinary wisdom, ability and integrity. He drew the young Verghese Kurien into his vision of dairy farming transformed by cooperation, by people pooling their resources to achieve together what they could never accomplish alone. He quickly saw in the young man talent, intelligence and energy, and together they were a team that over time transformed millions of lives.

The success of this cooperative drew attention in an Indian dairy scenario that was marked by stagnating domestic production and growing imports. In 1964, Prime Minister Lal Bahadur Shastri visited Anand to inaugurate the cooperative's cattle feed plant. He spent a night in the village and learnt the secret of Anand's success: cooperation. He created the National Dairy Development Board (NDDB) to replicate the spirit of Anand throughout India and asked Dr Kurien to be its first chairman. Kurien accepted on the condition that the headquarters remain in Anand, close to the cooperative, which was the model, and its members.

Promoting and establishing close to 1,50,000 village cooperatives, with about 15 million members, and leading India to become the world's largest milk producer was no mean feat. They are an ever growing testimony to the dream that Dr Kurien pursued, a dream that continued as long as he lived and remains as an eloquent memorial to him for years to come.

It was Dr Kurien's single-minded determination against odds that would have overwhelmed a lesser mortal and the vision that he steadfastly strove to achieve that helped make this possible. It was the quality of leadership he provided that enabled NDDB to impact the lives of so many millions.

Dr Amrita Patel who worked for long years was groomed as Dr Kurien's successor and had taken over as chairperson of NDDB in 1998. She had the following to say on Dr Kurien: 'He strode like a Titan across the bureaucratic barriers and obstacles that at every stage of NDDB's history could have brought it to its knees. Undaunted, he stood steadfast against the machinations of those who beheld his achievement with envy and were affronted by the sheer tenacity of the man. By his example, he taught us to act with courage when faced with those who oppose the interests of our nation and its farmers. The sense of professionalism, integrity and his constant search for excellence in everything that he did, set a shining example for those who followed him to live up to. He taught us that in order to succeed our integrity must be beyond reproach, for those who oppose cannot successfully defeat an honest man. He had an extraordinary ability to convert threats into opportunities—never letting an opportunity pass him by that could be of advantage to the organization or those it served.

'At a personal level, it has indeed been a great privilege, and one given to very, very few, to have worked so closely and for so many years with such a great man. Every moment of my working life with him was a learning experience. He was demanding, set very high standards, had his own unique style of training and believed that there was no better way of helping people develop than by giving them greater and bigger responsibilities to shoulder. May his vision continue to guide all those who work with and for farmers and farmer-owned institutions.'[18]

C.N.R. RAO

Dr C.N.R. Rao is one of the world's foremost solid state and materials chemists. He has contributed to the development of the field for over five decades. Dr Rao was born in Bangalore in 1934 in a Kannada family to Hanumantha Nagesa Rao and Nagamma Nagesa Rao. He was an only child and did not attend elementary school but was home-schooled by his mother, who was particularly skilled in arithmetic and Hindu literature. He entered middle school in 1940, at age six. Although he was the youngest in his class, he used to tutor his classmates in mathematics and English. He attended Acharya Patashala high school in Basavanagudi, Bangalore, which made a lasting influence on his interest in chemistry.

He initially thought of joining the Indian Institute of Science (IISc) for a diploma or a postgraduate degree in chemical engineering, but a teacher persuaded him to attend Banaras Hindu University. He obtained a master's in chemistry from BHU in 1953. In 1953, he was granted a scholarship for PhD in IIT Kharagpur. But four foreign universities, MIT, Penn State, Columbia and Purdue also offered him financial support and he chose Purdue. He completed his PhD in chemistry in 1958, in two years and nine months, at age twenty-four. Dr Rao returned to Bangalore in 1959 to join IISc as a lecturer. He started his own research with six PhD students. After three years he got a permanent appointment in the Department of Chemistry at IIT Kanpur. The director immediately appointed him as head of the department. He worked there from 1963 to 1976. In 1964, he was elected as a fellow of the Indian Academy of Sciences. In 1976 he returned to IISc to set up a solid state and structural chemistry unit. He became director of IISc from 1984 to 1994. He has also been a visiting professor at Purdue University, the University of Oxford and the University of Cambridge.

Rao is currently the National Research Professor, Linus Pauling Research Professor, and Honorary President of Jawaharlal Nehru Centre for Advanced Scientific Research, Bangalore, which he founded in 1989. He was appointed chair of the Scientific Advisory Council to the Indian Prime Minister in January 2005, a position which he had occupied earlier during 1985–89. He is also the director of the International Centre for Materials Science (ICMS).

On 16 November 2013, the Government of India conferred the Bharat Ratna upon him, the highest civilian award in India, making him the third scientist after C.V. Raman and A.P.J. Abdul Kalam to receive the award.[19]

C.N.R. Rao also received Japan's highest civilian award for promoting academic interchange and mutual understanding in science and technology between the two countries. He was presented with the 'Order of the Rising Sun, Gold and Silver Star' by Japanese ambassador to India Takeshi Yagi in the presence of senior officials of the department of science and technology, which Rao has helped shape over the years.[20]

A.P.J. ABDUL KALAM[21]

Dr A.P.J. Abdul Kalam was the 11th President of India, professor, author, scientist, aerospace engineer, and above all a nation builder. Dr Kalam was born on 15 October 1931 in a Tamil Muslim family at Rameswaram, located in Tamil Nadu. He came from a poor background and started working at an early age to supplement his family's income. After completing school, Kalam distributed newspapers in order to financially contribute to his father's income. In his school years, he had average grades, but was described as a bright and hard-working student who had a strong desire to learn and spend hours on his studies, especially mathematics.

'I inherited honesty and self-discipline from my father; from my mother, I inherited faith in goodness and deep kindness as did my three brothers and sisters.'[22]

Kalam set a target of interacting with 1,00,000 students during the two years after his resignation from the post of scientific adviser in 1999. In his own words, 'I feel comfortable in the company of young people, particularly high school students. Henceforth, I intend to share with them experiences, helping them to ignite their imagination and preparing them to work for a developed India for which the road map is already available.' He continued to interact with students during his term as President and also during his post-presidency period as a visiting professor at IIMA and IIM Indore. He died while giving a lecture at IIM Shillong. His books, including *Wings of Fire*, *India 2020: A Vision for the New Millennium*, *My Journey* and *Ignited Minds: Unleashing the Power within India*, have become household names in India and among Indian nationals abroad.

What Made Him Effective?

Having a goal in life: From supporting his family at a tender age, being the first graduate in his family, to becoming a scientist and later the President of India. All these shows that Dr Kalam always had well-defined goals in life that he strived to achieve.
Creating turning points in life that change your life for good: Graduation from MIT; his initiatives like vision 2020, India 2020; his books that have created a tremendous impact on the people of India, especially the youth.

Recognizing strengths and leveraging them: He emphasized on self-reliance in defence systems by progressing multiple development tasks and mission projects. Thus as a scientist he utilized his strengths and leveraged them for the betterment of his nation.

Managing difficult times: In his interview with *The Hindu*, he remembers 'staring into the pit of despair' when he failed to make it as an IAF pilot and how he pulled himself up and rose to become the man who headed India's missile programme and occupied the highest office in the country.

Strong values: Humility, integrity, humility, spirituality—these are the qualities Dr Kalam portrayed in his entire life through his conduct and preaching. Be it his books or his visits to schools and colleges, the former President says that true nation building is not made by political rhetoric alone but should be backed 'by the power of sacrifice, toil and virtue'. He was an ideal secular Indian and read the Quran and Bhagavad Gita daily with equal devotion.

Being compassionate and having an integrative mind: 'When grand plans for scientific and defence technologies are made, do the people in power think about the sacrifices the people in the laboratories and fields have to make?' he wrote in his book, *My Journey*. These lines shows the compassionate nature of Dr Kalam.

I was fortunate to meet Dr Kalam a few times as my colleague Anil Gupta used to invite him to teach a course at IIMA and, thanks to Anil, I even had tea with the great visionary a couple of times. One of the meetings was specially requested by me when Ravi Kanth Reddy, president of NHRDN Hyderabad, told me that he accepted to inaugurate the HRD Network conference at Hyderabad. I had been struggling hard all the time to get NHRDN (which I founded but left for others to lead) to focus on nation building. I made a PowerPoint presentation, met Dr Kalam that evening along with Anil, and shared my desire to get NHRDN to focus on education and other development issues of concern. He took my PPT. I actually think he did not require any PPT from me as development was like an eternal flame in his heart. Ravi Kanth surprised me when the conference began. Earlier, the

Hyderabad chapter had given me an award for my contributions to HRD. At that time I was out of the country so they did not present it to me. Ravi Kanth Reddy had kept the award to be handed over to me by Dr Kalam during the conference. This was kept as a secret. Dr Kalam gave an excellent speech. He did not have to use the PPT I shared with him as his book on 2020 had all the points on HRD. While handing over the award Dr Kalam whispered to me, 'I hope I covered all the points you mentioned.' Probably no one understood what he was whispering. But it was nice of him to remember me and my points.

It is worth mentioning here that there are a large number of people who work for the country with a high degree of commitment in many organizations such as ISRO, NDDB, CSIR and ICAR, and laboratories and universities like the agricultural universities with devotion and commitment. They are highly purpose driven and what inspires them is the science and curiosity to discover and the determination to know the unknown. In my view, all such people are effective people as they are living with purpose to discover and use their talent for the welfare of the nation and society. In the recently successful landing on the moon, many ISRO scientists who contributed are effective scientists as they enjoy their work. The author had the privilege of working with some of them in leadership development programmes. Their talent is their education, skills, commitment, hard work and a continuous desire to learn. The tools given at the end of this chapter may be useful for self-assessment as an effective leader or scientist.

Checklist for Effective Scientists and Others in National Institutions of Research and Action

1. I carry out my work well and deliver results on time and with quality.

2. I view team members as valuable resources and give them space and encouragement to try new ideas and approaches.

3. In managing my own mission, goals or projects, I operate from an overall and integrated perspective, not being influenced by the limited or partial view of project management.

4. I manage stress and distress by remaining calm and composed.

5. I put the right amount of pressure and drive achievement in juniors and others.

6. I pay adequate attention to values, culture and norms of the institution.

7. I assign work in ways that makes my juniors and others take responsibility.

8. I encourage others to come up with ideas and solutions and develop a sense of ownership rather than imposing my own ideas and decisions on them.

9. I listen attentively to others in discussions, meetings, presentations, class sessions, etc.

10. I analyse issues and problems in projects and goals extensively from all possible angles.

11. I articulate well and present my views clearly and persuasively in discussions and meetings.

12. I show openness, accept the opinions and views of others and respect them.

13. I come up with innovative solutions to problems and issues.

14. I take initiative, volunteer and undertake new activities.

15. I think positively and present myself and my institution well to others.

16. I show openness to learning new methods and techniques, and I am open to change.

17. I influence the group and try my best to take the group along.

18. I always work for group goals and I am willing to sacrifice individual goals for the larger interest of the group.

19. I help others when they are down.
20. I show interpersonal sensitivity and interpersonal competence.
21. I show a high degree of personal energy and passion in whatever I undertake.
22. I acknowledge and appreciate others when they have done something well.
23. I am a good and effective team player.
24. In team meetings, I make good contributions, demonstrates positive behaviour and help the team reach effective conclusions.
25. I am able to raise dissenting views or perspectives in a constructive and timely manner.
26. I actively seek feedback.
27. I am able to effectively network with people from different backgrounds, functions and levels in the group or organization.
28. I am able to deal effectively with conflicts.
29. I share my knowledge and expertise with others freely.
30. I invest in understanding ways of working effectively with people from diverse departments, disciplines and background.
31. I think I motivate people through my energy and enthusiasm.
32. I am a keen learner and I constantly seek new ideas and better ways of doings things.
33. I invest time and effort in guiding, developing and mentoring subordinates and other juniors.
34. Instead of suppressing differences, I manage the conflicts by letting interpersonal differences emerge, followed by discussion and resolution.
35. I maintain a good character with ethics and values.
36. I maintain a high degree of integrity in financial matters.
37. I maintain a high degree of professional integrity in all my work and dealings.

38. I take risks to the required extent, neither being excessive nor being too safe.
39. I manage stressful situations well and maintain balance.
40. I am able to balance work and personal life with hobbies and other healthy activities.

Youth in Education and Early Careers

The big lesson for me is that the way you act and work as student or as a young person lays foundation for you to do big things. This section is meant to help the youth get inspired and pave their path to be effective.

India is a young country, with the median age being around twenty-nine and about 6000 million people in the age group of eighteen to thirty years. A great demographic shift is expected in subsequent decades. For India to be what it aspires to be in the next couple of decades or by the time we complete a century post-Independence, it is important for these millions of youth to be effective. As I defined earlier in this book, an effective person is constantly discovering their own strengths or talent (knowledge, skills, attitudes, values, etc.) and applying them for the good of others. I have explained in the rest of the book what it means to be an effective doctor, teacher, educational entrepreneur, civil servant, banker, scientist, social worker and even an actor and given several case studies based on personal interviews or data from social media.

Youth today—irrespective of their current status as students, employed, job seekers, job creators like start-up founders and first jobbers—are likely to play a critical role in building our nation and society. They were born in totally different context from the 1960s–80s. Today's world is filled with technological developments and the nature of work is changing rapidly. As Abhijit Bhaduri observes in his book, *Career 3.0*, we are moving away from stable jobs to a world where specific skills become critical for work. The skills needed to be successful as an employee will be different from self-employment and yet many aspire to be self-employed. We have to navigate in a world where there is work but fewer jobs. The degree or pedigree of the educational institution will become less important than the ability to learn and teach. India will become a talent pool for the world.

This opportunity for people to benefit from all developments across the world can be thrown out of the window if we don't have our youth becoming effective, irrespective of the setting they are in, whether a student in a college or university, unemployed, self-employed or employed, everyone has to learn to be effective. India, with more than 62 per cent of its population in the working age group (fifteen to fifty-nine years) and over 54 per cent below twenty-five years old, boasts a demographic dividend. The economic trigger for growth occurs when the working-age population surpasses the dependent population, a scenario India currently enjoys.

Youth constitute a vital social capital for economic growth anywhere in the world. The Indian government recognizes that the current youth population is an abundant asset and offers immense leverage in terms of skilled labour, entrepreneurship, innovation and knowledge to accelerate the developmental needs of the country. Keeping with the vision and intent of the National Youth Policy (NYP) 2021 to 'unlock the potential of the youth to advance India'.

To be effective means to use one's talent. To use talent one should be aware of what one has. Ironically, for discovering talent one has to use their talent or keep trying to use it. In using your talent to benefit others, you are also discovering and contributing to your own growth. Therefore, we need everyone to be effective, for their own good or for the good of the society.

To communicate to people that they can be effective as some effective persons we know, I am documenting case studies in this book and drawing qualities that make everyone people effective.

SHREYAS HARISH

Reflecting on, documenting and sharing his learnings with others seems to be Shreyas Harish's mission, which he established at a very young age. He did his B.Tech at IIT Madras between 2013 and 2018 in computer science and engineering. He was elected as cultural affairs secretary at IIT on his own merit at a time when getting such positions required political connections. During his tenure as cultural affairs secretary, Chennai saw a number of problems, from floods due to torrential rains disrupting life to the death of a popular chief minister which threw the city out of gear and a number of other issues. In spite of all the issues, he worked to remove all cumulative losses of the cultural society of IIT and enabled it to make surplus to take care of itself for next few years. Shreyas also authored two books while at IIT and IIMA. He worked for a couple of years with Reckitt as a trainee in sales and marketing and, in a short period of time, rose at an unusual speed to manager GTM, heading national sales automation. While at IIMA, he participated intensely in learning from every session he attended and kept documenting his learnings and reflections. His love for learning, combined with his documentation and dissemination, resulted in another book, *Freshly Minted MBA: Essentials for First Time Managers*. Shreyas believes that learning enriches one's life. He considers learning fun as it excites him all the time. He is a strong believer in relearning to learn more. He enjoys learning new things, reflecting about what he learnt and examining the learnings from different lenses. Shreyas is also involved in a not-for-profit organization called Artma Foundation (a charitable trust).

DIVYA RAGHAVENDRA RAO
Who Started a Restaurant Chain Inspired by a Lack of Indian Brands?

Divya Rao was born into a lower-middle-class family with barely ₹1000 as monthly pocket money in early years. She became a CA at twenty-one and went to IIM Ahmedabad to pursue an MBA in finance. While at IIM Ahmedabad, Divya had detailed case studies on McDonald's, KFC and Starbucks and how they became successful. When one of her professors remarked that Indians weren't good at running such food chains and that there were no world-class food chain from India, it triggered her to introduce traditional South Indian food to the entire globe. Along with Raghavendra Rao, who had previous experience in the food industry, she started a roadside cart in Seshadripuram that was the beginning of Rameswaram chain of hotels—a big success now.

AKASH SHARMA
Twenty-two patents at twenty-three years of age.

Akarsh comes from a small town in Himachal Pradesh and became interested in sustainability and the environment inspired by his beautiful surroundings. While pursuing his B.Tech in mechanical engineering, Akarsh encountered the problem of his car windscreen getting dirty while driving in the hills. He developed a water-wiper system that sensed the water that fell on the windshield and got collected via the vanes and passed it through a semipermeable layer which helped filter the dirt from it with pressure. Hence, the water got collected and could be reused. He patented the same. He currently holds twenty-two design and utility patents, with eleven of them granted by the Indian Patent Office. He is also deeply involved in sports and adventure activities and serves as a Special Olympics skiing coach, where trained individuals with different cognitive abilities engage in this exhilarating sport. He frequently indulges in trekking, hiking, swimming and football, which has held a special place since he was seven years old. As a small-town individual, he always sought exposure and new experiences, and these challenges have been the crucible that shaped the person he is today. He teaches others on patenting.

Many times people say that age is a number. I like to maintain that age is not a number but a great resource. Every number or age brings with it a lot of things. If you are young, you have innocence and your mind is like a blank slate. A lot can be written on it. In the olden days people spent a lot of time writing the three Rs on it (reading, writing and arithmetic). The enormity of the mind got to be known with passage of time. Today's young minds, within three to four years of their birth, can handle all gadgets like the iPad, mobile, computer; control room gadgets with remotes; search various channels on the TV; and understand and master video games. A few years later, they even create new games, etc. This indicates that young minds have tremendous potential. So, the younger you are, the smarter you are in learning. You can learn anything and everything. Your energy, inquisitiveness, initiative, risk-taking ability, etc. are all resources when you are growing up. When you get older your experience and the wisdom gained from becomes a resource. As a student, your ability to participate in multiple activities and learn multiple skills are exemplified in the stories of students. Some of them even started innovations and are making a difference. It is important to encourage your innovative and risk-taking behaviour and experimental attitudes. If you kill them and incorporate only one idea in your mind set—like seeking employment and focusing on one job, career or skill—you may be missing out on many. This does not mean you shouldn't focus but you should be willing to explore.

STREET CAUSE

Street Cause is an NGO and it envisions to be a student-run NGO in India to create sustainable impact in thirty cities by 2030. They build socially conscious leaders who will be torch bearers for the future, uplifting the lives of the underprivileged. Started by Akhilesh Juka Reddy in 2009 when he was a student, it has executed over 15,000 projects impacting over 3 million people. With divisions in various colleges, all work is done by volunteers who commit their time for various causes. Street Cause gets young students to commit two years of their time (www.streetcause.org). In the view of the author, every volunteer working with Street Cause is an effective person.

India is a country that offers scope for effectiveness of everyone. Each one has to just discover something (s)he can use for others. Many of the effective youth spend their time simultaneously in more than one activity: knowledge acquisition in the classroom or outside the class, using various sources of learning, participating in sports, music and dramatics, trying out various other activities and exploring the world and their talent. They see constraints as challenges and take inspiration from teachers, seniors, parents and accomplished people and influence themselves by reading stories and lives of other effective people.

The following tools may help you explore more of yourself and set yourself on the path of effectiveness.

How Effective Are You as a Student?

1. I take every lecture seriously and try to learn from my teachers even if some feel the sessions are boring.

2. I listen attentively in class and try to learn from each session.
3. I carry out all assignments given to me seriously and with commitment.
4. I listen actively in the class and ask questions if I have any.
5. I clarify and discuss issues with teachers and learn from them.
6. I engage in debates and discussions on academic topics and try to learn from other students.
7. I carry out all reading assignments with devotion.
8. I read all suggested readings for class sessions.
9. I go well prepared for each of my sessions.
10. I participate in at least one or more of the sports, cultural activities, clubs and other forums at the institutions.
11. I like to play an active role in the non-academic forums, clubs and other avenues to explore my talent.
12. I help other students in sharing the knowledge I have.
13. I encourage my fellow students to take active part in areas of their strength.
14. I use some of my time to help others in society.
15. I enjoy activities involving helping other people in society.
16. I enjoy helping my classmates and juniors in building up.
17. I share my learning material and learning experiences with others.
18. I try my best to put up a good academic performance.
19. I give my best in extracurricular activities to build my personality.
20. I like to test myself in various situations.

How Effective Are You in Your First Job?

1. I took my induction programme seriously and learnt a lot from my initial years at work.

2. I went well prepared for my first job.
3. I learnt a lot about my organization even before I took up the job, from various sources like annual reports, internet, others who worked at the company and social media.
4. I used my time well in my first job to learn from my seniors.
5. I used my time to learn about various functions and departments in the organization.
6. I took initiative and created many sources of learning in the first year of job.
7. I am always curious to learn about other people, jobs, work and events.
8. I seek information from my seniors to get clarity of their expectations and try to meet them.
9. I take a lot of initiative to seek work rather than waiting for my boss to assign work for me.
10. I try my best to deliver results expected from me.
11. There is never time wasted at my job.
12. I use organizational opportunities to learn and build myself.
13. I keep helping others in my organization in learning.
14. I assist my juniors in learning and making an impact.
15. I get involved in socials service and other activities in my company even if I am not asked.
16. I take initiative to promote learning among other colleagues.
17. I participate actively in community and team-building activities.
18. I try my best to look for opportunities to use my talent in my job.

What Makes People from Different Categories Effective?

We can draw the following conclusions from the analysis and stories presented above:

1. Effective people are firstly good in their own field. All the scientists, bankers, wealth creators and nation builders indicate this. Scientists have excelled in their field and have done research and made discoveries that have wider application for the society at large or the country they live in. Bankers have done their job extremely well. Businessmen have created the wealth for the bankers. Professional managers have managed their work and impacted people around them.

2. Each of them generally leveraged what they are good at. When they faced failures they took them as challenges and learnt from them.

3. They seem to follow ethics and are known to be people who are high on integrity and values. They follow their professional ethics.

4. They are passionate about their work. They are highly perseverant. They do not give up even in the event of failure.

5. They are continuous learners and in many cases, good networkers. They write papers and publicize about their work, philosophy, vision, passion and outlook.

6. They develop others. They invest in building intellectual capital for the country.

7. They are hard-working and this is because of their high commitment and passion.

8. They are institution builders. Where they need not build their own institutions they contribute to the institutions given to them and take them to new heights.

9. They leave behind a legacy for others to enjoy the fruits of their labour besides being an example to be emulated.

10. They are role models and normally super effective people.

9 Discover Your Inner Talent

(Effective People Think Differently)

We have presented various case studies so far of effective people from different professions. Wherever possible we have highlighted their thoughts, philosophy, talent, how they have discovered it and applied it and multiplied their service to others using their talent. The next few chapters are intended to draw lessons across all professions. In these sections, I like to take lessons from the lives of various people we have covered so far. The focus hereafter is going to be on the qualities that cut across all professions and backgrounds, that make these professionals effective, very effective or super effective. An attempt will be made where possible to highlight ways of developing or transforming oneself to be a more effective person.

The first lesson that emerges from the various case studies and from various professions is that all these people perceived and responded differently to some of the common experiences we all have. They experienced the world around them a little differently and thought differently than most. Such a differentiated experience can be cultivated by heightening your sensitivities to yourself and your strengths. The following are the simple steps which will be highlighted in the chapter that follows:

1. Evaluate your strengths. Find out what you are good at

2. Keep trying out different activities to discover more of your strengths
3. Once you choose an activity, stick to it and give it enough time
4. Specialize in something and cultivate it to the Nth degree
5. Remember you can never do it alone. Always take help form others and acknowledge that help
6. Think differently

1. The first lesson we draw on from effective people flows from our starting definition of effective people

'Anyone who discovers inner talent, uses it and makes a difference in the lives of other people by benefiting them can be considered an effective person.'

We found in Part 1 that all effective persons, irrespective of the profession they are in, recognize and use their talent. A few of them do it very consciously—they first acquire competence and then start using it as in the case of doctors and professors. A few others start acting with whatever talent they have and without formally acquiring competence like in the case of many social workers who were just educated enough to start running education classes for children. These kinds of people eventually recognize their talent after undertaking some activities. In both cases, as they progress, they make efforts to develop, multiply and expand their talent. The medical profession has well-defined distinctions in terms of specializations. All the doctors whom we have reviewed are known for their specialization: M.C. Modi as an ophthalmologist, Mukesh Chawla as a gastroenterologist, Dr Trehan, Devi Shetty, Pratap Reddy and Ramakant Panda as cardiologists and heart surgeons. As they grew older and gained experience, they further specialized and started researching and inventing their own interventions and technologies ending up as super specialized doctors. Effective people start with their strengths and keep expanding on them and keep discovering more and more of their strengths vertically within their discipline and horizontally in other areas that help them spread their discipline or specialization. So they grow vertically and also horizontally. Those who grow horizontally spread themselves into other areas like management to acquire new skills to manage large entities. All of the doctors who have become famous also spread themselves horizontally to become managers of hospitals, leaders, entrepreneurs and popular speakers and interventionists. The same can be found among professors. A good example is Deepak Chopra who is an alternative medicine advocate and a promoter of popular forms of spirituality. Through his books and videos, he has become one of the best-known figures in the holistic-health movement. All the professors are specialists in their fields and pick up one or more aspects of their areas of interest to build on them. Anil Gupta as an agricultural scientist found it easy to identify innovations at grass-roots levels and spread them to a variety of other fields. He subsequently started working with schools, artisans, farmers and other innovators and also spread himself and his work to other countries. Shantha Sinha aligned her work with what she teaches as a part of political science but spread her work to action, focusing on democratized development that goes beyond her discipline. She focused on mobilizing communities to participate in educating children and protecting child rights. In social action perhaps the disciplinary boundaries disappear. This is well demonstrated in the case of Trilochan Sastry. He was a professor of operations management but he turned his attention to societal issues like political corruption and democratic values. He has also moved from political issues to developing self-help cooperative structures in villages. The knowledge he uses in villages is in alignment with what he teaches as a part of 'operations management'. Extending operations management to village farmers perhaps gives birth to a new area of specialization. Khandwalla and Ramachandran stuck to their fields and went deeper and deeper to gain complete mastery over their subject. Ramachandran is still a specialist in entrepreneurship and family business, while Khandwalla as an organizational theorist has gone into a variety of related areas from structuring organizations to government and creative society. Pillai remained a crusader of value-based education and his self-discovery was more as an institution builder and promoter of value-based leadership education. Even in the case of film actors, this theme seems to apply—as actors mature, they widen their repertoire to include different kinds of roles. Anupam Kher played the role of a sixty-year-old father when he was young in the film *Saaransh* and later moved to play a variety of roles. Kangana as she got successful is becoming bolder to experiment. So did Bachchan and others. Aamir Khan lent himself to social issues. A lot of actors diversify from films to television and culture and so on. We can draw the following lessons about identifying talent and strengthening it:

1. Find out at an early stage or age what you are good at.
2. Use it as an anchor and start activities or work which use that talent.
3. Keep building on it and gather expertise until you almost perfect it.
4. As you go along, specialize and go deeper or alternately diversify as you get the opportunities.
5. Don't give up your original strengths. As you diversify or go deeper into your field, you will build additional strengths. Weave these newly discovered strengths into the old ones and keep expanding your talent.
6. It is at this stage, when you have succeeded and demonstrated enough, that you can build institutions or help institutions to use your talent and magnify your services.

To summarize: Recognize your own talent. Use it. Develop it through practice and perseverance. Keep learning and multiplying and developing your talent. Multiply it to the Nth degree. Expand and grow vertically and horizontally as opportunities come and maximize your impact.

2.   Evaluate your strengths. Find out what you are good at
From the various professions all effective people are effective in their contexts. The context is their profession or occupation. The profession may be medical, law, social work, business, management, acting, teaching, etc. There are contexts within contexts. You have to make choices all the time. Some are lucky to make these choices at an early stage. Others keep discovering them at every stage. Kaza Gandhi did not know when he was young that he would go on to found Truth Labs one day and that stopping crime was going to be his life goal. It came perhaps around the time of his retirement. The same is true for Samuel Paul. Nor did Samuel Paul. It was only in the early nineties that he discovered the Bangalore scorecard and started the Public Affairs Centre (PAC). Though he decided to be a doctor at an early age, Dr Devi Shetty could not have dreamt that he would go on to establish the world-famous Naryayana Hrudayalaya. Everything has a small beginning. But it is up to us to discover that initial seed that we have that goes on to grow and yield fruit that will help many. Ragi (who I will talk about in detail in Chapter 10) kept trying her skills at everything—from Ayurveda to the rice business to politics. She had only one ambition early on in life— to educate her son and later it grew into being of some service to someone. Bachchan established himself as a great actor early on in his life but wanted to try out his hand in politics. When he failed at that, he tried to start his own company ABCL. That did not work out either and finally he settled down to what he was good at. We have in each profession examples of people who have

constantly made efforts to discover what they are good at and ultimately settle down with that discovery. They then gain success through multiplying that talent. Chetan Bhagat discovered that he was talented at writing only after his first book was published and got good reviews; even when many publishers refused to publish his work, he continued to write and his books became popular year after year and were made into films. He then started writing columns in newspapers and film scripts. He has now become a significant stimulator of thought. In a lecture, which I had the opportunity to attend at IIMA in 2014, Bhagat said that he is still trying to figure out what to do next and is now searching for what he could be good at after writing many books.

3. Keep trying different activities to discover more of your strengths

3.1. **Use your time to express your talent**: There is no substitute for initiative, hard work and more work. It is only the hard work that gets you to do different things to finally discover what you are good at. In my own case my search for what I am good at began from early childhood and went on till around 1980 (when I was thirty-three years old) by which time my competencies were reasonably well tested in different areas. I put on different hats, though rather unconsciously. I forayed into institution building—starting two departments of psychology at Andhra University and Udaipur University; started the Education and Training Department at NIHAE; made a few futile attempts to start a body called Young Applied Behavioural Scientists at NIHAE when a group of us were not invited to be a part of the ICSSR-sponsored conference in 1971; started the Education Systems Unit at IIMA; initiated 'Endeavour' an international body for researching entrepreneurship based in Malaysia and NERDA Malaysia. I became a researcher, a consultant and an executive (General Manager HRD at BEML in 1978–79) at a young age. I followed the suggestions of others who were well-wishers. I did not have any clear-set ideas. You are guided by others and you need good guides. However, you need a lot of action and implementation which needs some hard work, willingness to face difficulties and optimism. Following the suggestion of Fr Gordon to try to get admitted to RECM as a village boy who never went beyond the nearby town of Vijayawada, I had to travel all the way to Mysore alone without reservation while changing three trains. When I was admitted to the RCEM I had to travel unreserved from Mysore to Waltair changing trains and meet the registrar and get the marks sheet, etc. Today it appears to be insignificant but in those days for me as a village boy who mostly spoke Telugu it was a great adventure. Then Prafullachandra Dave encouraged me to try psychology at Osmania; here again I needed to foray into uncharted waters and give the field a shot. A sense of optimism and a desire to try are necessary to explore your talent and what you're good at. Often enough opportunities present themselves and it is up to us to grab them and convert them into turning points. Some people are fortunate to realize their talents and make choices at an early stage of their life as they are born in well-to-do and well-educated families—they are born with a golden spoon. When you are born into a poor family, getting a job becomes all important, and the opportunity to work with great people comes as a bonus. Once such an opportunity comes your way, you focus your attention on doing a good job and impressing the people you look up to. That is the way you build your career. Today, choices have to be made at an early stage. If you have parents who are rich enough you will perhaps get into an international school, a public school or a residential school with a high fee, and your future is taken care of largely with the education you get. Hard work is the only option. If you don't work hard and try yourself in a variety of tasks you will remain where you are. Among all my classmates from my village Akunuru in Andhra Pradesh, only three of us are said to have brought some good name to the village: Kaza Gandhi who started Truth Labs, M.V. Reddy who retired as a high court judge and headed land reforms in AP and me.

3.2. Hard work and commitment: At the Andhra University where I started my career, I established myself as a committed teacher in the six months I spent there. We had no classrooms and the head of psychology and parapsychology (carved out of the department of philosophy) was also the head of library science department. Therefore, we got a room in the library where we used to conduct classes. Every day early in the morning I would walk to the library and stay till late in the evening. In fact that time at AU is often recounted as exemplars of devotion and hard work. Stories of how students in chemistry labs spent days and nights there are still talked about. As a fresher from the Osmania University psychology department I had all knowledge of psychology experiments by heart. In fact at Osmania, I still remember the public exhibition we conducted on all the tests and experiments we did in the psychology laboratories. It was a two- or three-day exhibition to the public and we explained to people all our experiments, like how we measured reaction time with an equipment, how we used the tachistoscope to study subliminal perception, etc. So I could order equipment, and fix all of it up. I had set up the experimental psychology lab in a room of the convocation theatre of AU. The students were my friends. When I left at the end of January there were still two months left for the year to complete. I used to send notes from Delhi to help them to complete the courses I started. At NIHAE where I worked, my day would begin at 6.30 a.m. and would only end at 10.30 p.m. I had nothing else to do. It is this that led to the start of a new journal called *Indian Behavioural Science Abstracts* (IBSA). One day Dr Pareek mentioned that he had an idea of starting an abstract service as most research scholars in behavioural science didn't have ready access to journals. Delhi has so many libraries and the various journals in behavioural science were scattered among them. He desired to get the articles from these journals abstracted, classified and published every quarter. He just had to mention an idea like this. I jumped on it and got a letter of introduction from him to various libraries and started visiting and summarizing the articles. In a month's time I visited Delhi University, IIPA, IIT, NCERT, the Institute of Economic Growth and other national institutions and prepared 247 abstracts. It required another three months to finish the first issue, which Dr Pareek himself completed. The IBSA was out in two months. Dr Pareek made me the associate editor, and the Behavioural Science Centre located in Manasayan published it. Impressed by my work, Dr Udai Pareek recommended me to be appointed for the post of assistant professor of education and training within a year of my joining and subsequently also made me the head of the project when he left NIHAE. By the time I reached Udaipur University, where we were setting up a psychology department, I was married and also had a little boy, Raju. Out of the respect I had for Fr Gordon who influenced my career and work, we decided to call my son Gordon Raju, although we never formalized it. My hard work continued, and I enjoyed my work. My experience at AU helped in setting up an Applied Psychology Department at Udaipur.

Dr Pareek had moved to Udaipur as director of the School of Basic Sciences and Humanities (SBSH). I was already an assistant professor in NIHAE. In a health or medical institute, an assistant professor is considered to be higher than a lecturer and equivalent to a reader in a university. Udai Pareek asked me if I was willing to shift to Udaipur to start the psychology department at a lecturer level, one level lower than my current position, as he did not have any sanctioned post for a reader or associate professor. Without thinking twice I agreed to be considered. I did not apply as I may have been found to be ineligible due to the higher post I was already occupying. I was taken in and they were nice enough to match my basic salary at NIHAE. Udaipur University gave me an opportunity to complete our first book: *Handbook of Psychological and Social Instruments*. The students were also involved in this project. We collected the various questionnaires and other tests developed across the country until then with the help of an ICSSR project. IBSA continued as well as my teaching for almost twenty hours a week to master's students.

Working hard and using every minute of your time is very important. When you are young you are often advised that since youth never comes back, you have the freedom to do whatever you want to do and enjoy life. For me my work was my enjoyment and I did a variety of things related to my profession which laid good foundations for my subsequent growth. The objective in life at a young age should be to do a good job and perhaps to do a number of jobs if they come your way. That is the only way to explore what you are good at. By working hard and doing a number of things you create more and more opportunities for making a choice. It is the hard work that has taught me and helped me explore the specialist in me in various fields:

as a researcher, an author, an institution builder, in fields like psychometrics, behavioural science abstracts, etc. The later part of my career was left to be discovered only in IIMA. All the people we covered in the first eight chapters of this book are hard workers from early days. None of them were lazy and as a result they expressed themselves in studies, work and new initiatives. It is hard work and utilization of talent that pays in the long run.

3.3. Create dots early in life which may become turning points: We have to create our own turning points by doing something different and doing things differently. In the first chapter I mentioned how different opportunities were converted into turning points in my life. I started creating turning points myself. Every project I worked on was picked out due to my interest or choice. Some of the biggest turning points I created for myself were to accept the L&T Chair and start the Centre for HRD at XLRI. It was difficult to leave IIMA ten years after I joined it in 1983, uprooting the family, disrupting my children's education, etc. But I could not imagine the name of HRD being diluted by an unknown person as L&T professor. Another turning point was to start the National HRD Network in 1985. Yet another one was to start the Academy of HRD five years after we started NHRDN to pursue its mission. A subsequent turning point was when I decided to leave IIMA after getting my twenty-year service medal in 1993. I felt that I was doing the same thing again and again and wanted to take up newer challenges. I had just finished a Commonwealth secretariat assignment of HRD for Commonwealth countries in 1992 and had good exposure to national-level issues. I did not know what I wanted to do but I knew I had to do something different and something more. For several months after I left IIMA I went on discovering what I should do while helping AHRD to stabilize. It was only after two years that I decided to set up my own company—T.V. Rao Learning Systems Pvt. Ltd. Even today I don't know if that was the right thing to do. You can never predict what could have happened if you did not turn another way, and continued to travel on the line you had started along. You can only conjecture. Everyone has such turning points in life. If you look at the lives of people like Paul, Gandhi, Dr Shetty, Dr Trehan, Shantha Sinha and Anupam Kher, you will find many turning points where they had chosen to take a turn rather than remain on the same path. So to be effective we need to create turning points in our life.

4. Stick to your choices like a leech

At IIMA I was working on many issues. I was taken as a member of the Organizational Behaviour (OB) area. Simultaneously, I was to work with the Education Systems group. I did a project with IIMA as soon as I joined on evaluating the entrepreneurial development programmes, and even developed and started teaching a course on entrepreneurship (LEM). I had started my career a few years before with NIHAE and the health institute with the ministry of health, and had also written a book, *Behavioural Science Research in Population*. So I had five clear areas of work: health and population, entrepreneurship, education, HRD and OB. I continued to work in all five areas. Later, I became the chairman of the Public Systems group which added the requirement that I had to work with government systems extending my areas of work from five to six. The director one day called me and advised me that I should focus on one or at best two areas and not spread myself so thin. I tried to convince him by saying that as a behavioural scientist I was applying my knowledge to any sector of interest. For example, HRD is a part of BS and it has no sectoral boundaries. He was viewing it from his sectoral angle while I was learning from all sectors. He appreciated the point I assume as he never tried to insist on it again. I continued to work in all areas and I think that is the reason I have a perspective on HRD as well as OB which is different from many. I have devoted the rest of my life to apply OB and HRD concepts and learn from different sectors.

Our life provides us with many settings. All settings are opportunities. Once you choose your area of work you should keep trying to apply it to many others, one after the other. You should remain focused and at the same time dissipate or spread yourself to a variety of settings. Balancing is your job; self-awareness and a clear understanding of what you are doing are also essential. Once you are clear nothing should stop you. Bachchan got a lot by working on a variety roles: from *Anand* to *Zanzeer*, to *Deewar* to *Waqt*, *Nishabdh*, *Paa*, *Black*, *Piku*, *Cheeni Kum*. 'Kutch nahi dekha toh kuch nahi dekha' (If you have not seen 'Kutch', a desert area in Gujarat, you have seen nothing, from an ad campaign on Gujarat) is altogether different from his role as the *Kaun Banega Crorepati* host, 'Computer mahashay lock the option D'. But the thing that is common is that he is an actor and he is applying acting to all these differing roles. So is Anupam Kher in different roles from *Saaransh* to *A Wednesday* or *Wake Up Sid,* and Shah Rukh Khan from *Darr* to *Dilwale Dulhaniya Lejayange* and *Pardes* to *Swades* or 'My name is Khan and I am not a terrorist.' You need to make up your mind about your talent and keep applying it to different settings to develop it.

5. Specialize in something and cultivate your skills to the Nth degree

Once I was flying from Mumbai to Chennai, and I began talking to the people sitting next to me. They started a conversation and mentioned to me that they were both returning from their consultants in Mumbai who were helping them in reviewing the performance management system. They were curious to know my views on their system once they discovered my name and identity. Apparently they had read my books. I asked them a few questions about their current system. The main problem with most appraisal systems is their overemphasis on ratings and efforts to eliminate subjectivity. They are largely communication and implementation problems. I mentioned the same and suggested what an ideal solution should be. It is my nature to share my knowledge with anyone and everyone. On listening to me for a few minutes one of them remarked, 'Sir, our consultants took six months of interviews and presentations to come to the recommendations you have so simply summarized.' I was not surprised as I had worked with over 200 organizations and done similar studies. It does not require a long time to figure out what is wrong and what needs to be done. Experiences sharpen your skills and enhance your diagnostic as well as problem-solving skills in any field.

Specialization is not an enigma. Any activity which you keep working on and developing new skills in over a period of time leads to specialization. It is said that famous surgeons like Trehan, Panda and others have gained so much expertise in cardiac surgery that they can do any surgery with ease. The same is true with professors, educationists, actors, managers and so on. Gandhi specialized in forensic diagnostics and solutions, Paul eventually in measuring public satisfaction, Shantha Sinha with educating children, Ramachandran in family business and entrepreneurship. Specialization makes you effective in your field. It builds self-confidence and enhances your ability to serve a larger number of people. It also helps you get motivated to multiply your talent. Through specialization, your circle of influence increases. Specialization makes you a master of your field if you pursue it to the Nth degree. This is what was done by doctors, professors, social workers and everyone we covered. For film actors the specialization takes the shape of versatility. As a specialist one also sees meaning in extending one self and services to other sectors. For example, heart surgeons after some time may extend their healthcare services to eye care and then to poverty alleviation and so on.

6. You can never do it alone. Always take the help of others and acknowledge their service

Institutions can never be built by any one person alone. Interventions also cannot be successful beyond a point if they are only made by one person. In every activity we need the support of others. Shanthi Ranganathan had determination to set up a facility to treat addicts after her husband's death. She was assisted by many counsellors, family members, doctors, government agencies and so on. Finally, when children had to be educated, she needed teachers and other grass-roots workers to help her.

Though NHRDN was conceptualized and founded by me, it was built with the help of many persons. Fr Abraham was the secretary and used to edit the newsletter and I personally guided its contents and format. Chandrasekar was constantly implementing all the ideas we conceptualized in KLMDC in Chennai. K.K. Verma provided academic support. Later, M.R.R. Nair provided a variety of support and Udai Pareek institutionalized the body. Subsequently, many chapter presidents and secretaries made a success out of it.

7. Think differently

Effective people do all that we have talked about so far but with a difference. The intention is not to create personal wealth but community service. All the people who we have covered in this book think differently than most others in their comparable positions. They put their own self-growth as a tool for service and not for self-aggrandizement. That is what makes them effective. They are driven by commitment to a larger cause which gives them the determination, energy and passion to learn and disseminate and multiply their competencies. Some of them exhibit such competencies from early childhood like in the case of many of the social workers we covered. Some others acquire the service motivation only after they have acquired sufficient wealth and security for themselves.

In order to be effective we have to learn to think differently. Our approach to life has to be different. Mother Teresa once said when we give alms to the poor we should not think that we are doing them a favour. By accepting what we have given they have done a favour to us. This is what thinking differently means. When we serve others and enjoy it we are doing a favour to ourselves. We have to learn to enjoy our service and make it a habit and even a part of our inner motivation. This is what Udai Pareek has called as Extension Motivation—an inner desire to extend oneself to others or to live for the sake of larger goals or substitute one's goals with larger goals. So be extension motivated rather than motivated to accomplish only power and wealth.

The following questions may help you to introspect and plan to become more effective:

1. What are my strengths?
2. What are my core strengths in terms of
    a. knowledge
    b. attitudes, traits and/or qualities
    c. skills and skill sets
3. What am I good at according to my family members?
4. What are some of the strengths others have pointed out to me?

5. Am I doing enough to cultivate and utilize my strengths? What more should I do to use them?

6. What can I do to discover more of my strengths? Which ones do I pick up to develop deeply?

7. What are the related areas where I can explore and grow horizontally?

8. How is my reading habit? What books should I read to cultivate my strengths and get inspired?

9. What are the various sources of learning I am using? Can I expand to other areas?

10. Do I keep talking about my ideas, interests and views to others so that they can readily view what I am good at?

11. Do I seek feedback periodically from my friends, family members, and others to discover more of my strengths as they see them?

12. Do I keep experimenting with new things or new methods of doing things to discover more?

13. Am I risk averse that I don't want to try anything new?

14. Have I failed any time? How do I take failures? How can I learn to celebrate failures if necessary?

15. Do I give up easily? Who are the people who can get real benefit from my talent?

16. What are some of the small steps I can take to use my talent for the benefit of others? Which of my talents will be of use to others? And for whom?

10 Stretch Your Talent

Raghavamma (Ragi), a beautiful young girl, was born in 1930 in a village in south India. Her father was a woodcutter and toddy tapper. When she was young everyone in the village admired her beauty. She had offers to join films which was a taboo in those days. There was a rich young man Krishnamurthy (Krishna) in the village who was very handsome. He was from an upper caste. Raghavamma's father used to take her to the fields for work. Krishnamurthy was educated and rich. The beautiful young girl and the handsome young boy met in the village, liked each other and became fond of each other. They belonged to different communities, one from a upper caste and the other from a slightly lower caste, and the village had strong caste biases. Murthy and Raghavamma decided to secretly get married by running away from home. When Ragi became pregnant and was about to have her baby, the rich villagers from Krishna's community in the village got together and managed to recall Krishna to the village. They also got him married to another rich girl from their community. Krishna couldn't do anything and Ragi was helpless. She returned to the village and started living with her father. She gave birth to a male child. Some of the village folk suggested that Ragi go to court and get a part of the property due to her from Krishna. Ragi decided to bring up her son all by herself and refused to pick up any legal battle. Krishna and his new wife had a child. They were afraid that Ragi would someday take them to court. Krishna transferred all his property to his wife's name to escape any legal liability. This did not give him peace and he always had a fear that there may be a legal battle. He sold all the property in the village and migrated to another state to escape legal battles which Ragi never intended to take up. He started doing business but none of his efforts worked out.

Thirty years later . . . Ragi was a determined girl. She led local women to form a team and collectively worked in the fields. She tried to put up a toddy shop and a small vegetable store in the village. It did not give her much of an income. As her son grew up she wanted to educate him and had big dreams for him. She did not know what he would become but she decided to make something of him. She learnt about Ayurvedic medicines from a baba and started treating people. She had a good practice but it did not pay much. She shifted from Ayurveda to business. She became a businesswoman for some time. She would go to all the nearby villages and collect paddy, get it milled and sell the rice to wholesale rice merchants in nearby small towns. She earned enough to educate her son. Her son studied well and ultimately took up a government job. He slowly advanced in his career and became a highly respected and reasonably high-salaried professional manager. He participated in a lot of social activities and became very popular in his profession. He wanted to construct a house for his mother in the state capital. While in the process of construction, the builder took money from her son and ran away. The architect contracted to supervise the work threw up his hands in surrender. Unable to complete the work and feeling cheated, her son called Ragi to complete the project. Not knowing the language and not knowing how to read and write, Ragi landed up in the state capital. She went to the architect, got the address of the absconding contractor, met his family members, explained her situation and got the brother of the absconding contractor to complete the work. She managed to get the house completed with all her initiative and determination. She started living in the house and slowly introduced herself to the local politicians. She became friendly with them and got their admiration for her contacts with farmers in the villages. Ragi did not know how to read and write but she listened to the radio regularly and watched television and came to know all the politicians by name. She collected all the local taxi and auto drivers and poor people and got them to fight for their rights. Ragi had by now become a popular woman in the state capital and also known to most politicians. She could go to anyone. She knew the chief minister, leaders of the Opposition and others by name and had access to them. She was elected as the general secretary of the State Mahila Sabha. She directed other staff, brought the issues of poor people to their notice and participated in formulating the agenda for the poor. She died at sixty-five while serving as general secretary.

Krishna went from town to town buying and selling property and in the process lost a good part of it while his brothers from the same village multiplied their property in business. Ultimately, he started working as an insurance agent and settled in one of the south Indian towns to provide education for his two children. He died at eighty, and refused to be taken care of by his children as they did not agree with the way he led his life.

This story from the village has many lessons. One of them is that we are all born talented. However, the circumstances and the surroundings in which we are born are different. If we are fortunate to have the right circumstances we may grow up to become famous scientists, doctors, artists, musicians, managers, CEOs, ministers, institution builders and so on. Ragi was a talented woman like every one of us. She did not have the right circumstances but as life took her through different settings, she tested herself in these settings and became what she could and also gave her son a good future. The first set of circumstances was that she was born in a poor family which had a hand-to-mouth existence. Her parents could not afford to send her to school. Also her parents never thought of it as she was born in an age when sending the girl child to school was not considered a virtue by the society. As she couldn't carry out the family occupation as a girl, she was made to do unskilled or semi-skilled labour. When driven to a corner, with a determination to educate her son and not wanting to be left behind, she started trying her hand at different things. The small grocery store did not work out, Ayurveda also did not give her enough money but the paddy business gave her a decent income to educate her son. She was doing well but what helped her most was her ability to network with farmers and rice merchants. She also had courage and used her initiative. So she kept trying different things. It was only when she went to Hyderabad and came in contact with various politicians and started working with them that she discovered her skills: initiative, drive, high activity level, empathy for the poor and commitment to improve their welfare. She also had a special ability to speak to and convince the politicians. Popular opinion was that if she was educated she Could have easily become a Cabinet minister if not the CM. She had all the qualities needed to lead and help the poor. The circumstances in which she was placed—to be in the capital city, to have free time, to live in her own house gifted by her son, all helped her create new circumstances and platforms to apply her skills. You discover your talent only when you apply it in new settings. Ragi rose to the occasion and succeeded. If she weren't held back by the circumstances of her birth perhaps she would have had an altogether different life. But we have no choice of the family and circumstances into which we are born. She tried hard to change or influence her future circumstances. If she had had a privileged background, she may not have risen to do great things. The only way to discover our talent and multiply it is by constantly making efforts to create new settings for ourselves to test and magnify our talents. Ragi did not do it by choice. A set of circumstances pushed her to bring out her hidden talent. The lesson to be learnt here is not to keep waiting for a chance to take charge of our life. Success needs initiative. Take initiative and test yourself out by creating different sets of circumstances for yourself.

Many of the cases reviewed in the first eight chapters give insights into how effective people changed their circumstances or created settings or platforms for trying themselves out.

Amitabh Bachchan tried politics and set up ABCL and discovered that he was not cut out for them. He tried television and found that it was a good fit for his talent. Before Aamir Khan tried *Satyameva Jayate*, he would have had no way to know that he could be a great TV anchor and social crusader. Among the doctors, Dr Trehan, who did not have a roof over his head when his parents came to Delhi from Lahore in 1952, kept on changing his circumstances and kept creating new opportunities for himself until he finally settled down with his new venture in Gurgaon. So did Dr Devi Shetty who resolved to be a doctor on seeing his father's sufferings. He was further influenced by his fifth-grade teacher telling the class that a South African surgeon had just performed the world's first heart transplant. In shifting from Birla to Manipal Hospital, to starting his own hospital, and from starting hospitals in different cities and spreading into other specialties like eye care, Dr Pratap Reddy kept on creating new circumstances for his Apollo group, taking it from one city to another, and then to other countries. He was discouraged when he started up in Chennai. But his determination and perseverance have taken him to success. He spread his talent and is now benefiting thousands of people across the world. Paul was a professor and a World Bank consultant. He created circumstances to concert the difficulties he was facing in living in Bangalore to develop a scorecard that helped a number of governments. Trilochan Sastry has a doctorate from MIT and had little to do with starting farmers' cooperatives or getting politicians to declare their assets and criminal records. He tested himself by doing things which were closer to his heart. Kiran Sethi created new circumstances by starting a school when she did not like the education her son was receiving. After starting the school, her success with various projects got her to foray into other aspects of making the lives of children better. She extended her design capabilities to food and even started a restaurant. Shantha converted her experience of working with landless labourers and children into a movement and started creating settings to help them. Every single social worker mentioned in chapter 7 has shown initiative and created settings for using their talent and benefiting others.

The lessons are:
- Never be satisfied with the talent you discovered in your current settings.
- Take initiative to create new settings to apply your talent and discover new talent.

That is what will make you an effective person and a more effective person.
- There is never an end to discovering new talent.
- You are the master of your life and the creator of settings wherever you are.

1. Self-awareness starts with experimenting with new settings

Self-management involves discovering your inner potential or talent, putting it to use, spreading it to fields that you have not tried before, multiplying it or developing it by stretching it horizontally and vertically, and benefiting yourself and others. In this process, we are likely to be more and more effective if we are able to make others feel that we matter in helping them lead their lives better. Self-management starts with enhancing our self-awareness. Self-awareness should keep changing with new discoveries about ourselves, our strengths and weaknesses or talent.

There is a Chinese saying, 'If you know the enemy and know yourself you need not fear the results of a hundred battles.' If a person knows himself, it becomes easy for him to work according to his strengths and weaknesses. Effective people take some time out to self-assess their strengths and weaknesses. On the basis of the results, they design the strategy to achieve their goals. Everybody has their own strengths. Effective people recognize this and put their strengths to effective use. Also, identifying and understanding their vulnerabilities helps them to manage and correct them to turn them into their strengths. That is why successful start-ups have leadership roles divided as per the strengths of effective people.

Laxmi Gautam is one brave soul who took the initiative to give the old widows of Vrindavan all their basic necessities. These abandoned women often come to Vrindavan to leave their soul in the hands of their God so that they can be in peace. They are not accepted by their families and the government is also not doing anything for them. She gives them her personal attention. She has been in the city since her childhood and this adds to her strength. She is well acquainted with the processes and the people of the city. She helps them attain all the facilities they need. She started cremating the bodies when she found them lying on the road. Many people opposed her as in Hindu religion women don't go to the cremation ground but she asked them if she will not cremate them then who will. She has shown courage which the families of the destitute widows, hospitals and government officials have not shown and has proved herself to be a winner.

When Nirmala Kaldangaonkar decided to start an initiative for the benefit of farmers, she wanted to do good for them, but she wasn't sure how to go about it. She introspected and decided to use the acumen she acquired from her education and the experience that she got from her stint with Akhil Bharatiya Vidyarthi Parishad. As she had studied biology and done some social work earlier she decided to use that knowledge to start vermicompost preparation to provide low-cost manure to farmers. For her, family support is her biggest strength. Her husband helps her in designing the vermicompost system using his engineering skills while her children help her in administrative work. She has shown that a person should know her strength to make an effective use of it.

It is a good quality to analyse oneself to know where one stands and work on your weaknesses while leveraging your strengths for your use. Rajesh Kumar is a middle-class man who has a general store in Delhi. He had to drop out from college due to his financial condition. He decided to help underprivileged kids to get into school. He understood that he didn't have the money to start a new venture but what he had was his dream to help the underprivileged and use whatever knowledge he had acquired in school. He is working on the motto 'shiksha daan maha daan (there is no great gift than education)' and teaching around sixty underprivileged kids to prepare them to get admission into government schools.

Desire to be educated, and independence characterize Manjula Shroff's journey from a conservative royal family in Orissa to being a change agent in Ahmedabad. Manjula Shroff sees herself more as an entrepreneur, and not as an educationist. She knew that education was her only salvation and way to know the world better. She has been pragmatic and aware of the limitations on her career due to her family values. Taking small steps, she did her studies in Delhi where she even acted as a computer trainer to her teachers. She has made her choices by carefully understanding her strong points. As an administrator and entrepreneur, she values the importance of trust and respect. This comes from the fact that she places herself in the shoes of her subordinates. Her ability to remain detached, rational and objective through a humanitarian approach is reflected in the work that she has done for the earthquake victims. She values her ability to persevere and get the work done. Seeing the contemporary education level in Gujarat with respect to institutions like IIM, NID, she started the Delhi Public School, knowing education was something that was close to her heart and she could use her strategic and managerial abilities to improve the situation.

2. Keep enhancing your self-awareness all the time

An effective person is one who has a high degree of self-awareness. Such awareness is characterized by good insight into one's own strengths and weaknesses. In addition, effective individuals are constantly searching for opportunities to test themselves in new situations, gain more insights into their own personality, improve upon their strengths and overcome their weaknesses.

Every individual's personality and psychological world (attitudes, values, habits, knowledge, abilities, etc.) can be considered as consisting of four parts in terms of their self-awareness and the awareness of others. One simple model for self-awareness, which is used widely, is the Johari Window[1] (Luft and Ingham, 1973), see figure on page 237. In this model, there are two main dimensions for understanding the self: those aspects of a person's talent (knowledge, traits, skills, styles, values, attitudes, etc.) that are known to them (self) and those aspects of their talent that are known to those with whom they interact (others). All four dimensions are explained in detail.

	Known to self: Talent individual is aware of	Unknown to self: Talent individual is not aware of
Known to others: Talent others are aware of	Open Self Public Self	Blind Spots
Unknown to others: Talent others are not aware of	Private World Hidden Part of Self	Dark Arena— Unknown

Figure: A schematic representation of the Johari Window

Every individual's talent and personality (attitudes, values, habits, abilities, competencies, etc.) can be considered as consisting of four parts in terms of their self-awareness and awareness of others. These include the following:

i) An 'open' or a 'public' personality and talent which consists of those aspects that the individual is aware of (known to self) and which others around them are aware of: Most of the time when we interact our talent is observed by others and we are also aware. For example, some people high on technical know-how are aware of their technical knowledge and all others around also have noticed the same. This is the open part or publicly known and acknowledged talent of the individual.

ii) A 'hidden' or a 'private' part (his knowledge, attitudes, strengths, etc.) which only the individual is aware of and which others are not aware of: There are a number of things we have done in our life and it is all registered in our inner self or mind or brain. However others at a given point of time may not be aware of these things. For example, a newly joined senior doctor in a hospital knows the kind of patients he or she has dealt with and the situations where he or she had met with many successes while those around him may not be aware of all the difficult cases the doctor has resolved. Always, we have more knowledge and awareness of our talent than those around us.

iii) A 'blind' part which the individual is not aware of, but others are aware of: Many times we may not even know our strengths until someone notices them and tells us about them. For example, an accounts manager who was always shy of communicating in English developed a perception that he lacks communication skills and that he is not very articulate, until he participated in a 360 Degree Feedback when he was told that he was more articulate and communicative compared to other accounts managers they came across. Similarly, our studies have shown that about a third of primary school teachers were not aware of their classroom styles until they were told by observers about the extent to which they are directive and lecturing types more than non-directive and encouraging types.[2]

iv) A 'dark' or 'hidden' part which neither the individual nor others are aware of: This is because you have not exposed yourself to all types of situations. In our lifetime we can test ourselves only in limited settings. When we take up a new task sometimes we ourselves may be surprised to discover how well we have done it. For example, many social workers did not know that they could be institution builders until they got down to it. Hence the only way we can discover our talent is by continuously doing things that we have not done before and testing ourselves in situations we have not been in before.

If 100 points have to be assigned to all four parts together, for most people the first three parts may get less than 10 points and the 'dark' or 'unexplored' part may get over 90 points. This is because in our lifetime we do not get enough opportunities to discover our own strengths, our potential and abilities. Every choice we make in our education, profession, career, etc. helps us to explore and discover only a small part of our talents, at the same time narrowing the scope or closing the doors to discover many other parts. Thus the day one chose to be a medical doctor one closed the doors or at least narrowed the scope to discover the architect, the engineer, the philosopher in oneself, and innumerable other talents. Similarly, in choosing to be in marketing or sales jobs one has closed the doors to discover a number of other talents which may have surfaced in other jobs.

If the remaining 10 points are to be distributed, an effective individual is one who has a large part of these points assigned to the first two parts, i.e. the 'open' part and the 'private part', as both these constitute a high degree of self-awareness.

3. Discover your blind spots and work on them

A blind spot is a dark or hidden part which neither the individual nor the others are aware of. This is because we never get an opportunity to try ourselves out and discover what we are capable of. During our entire lifetime we may get an opportunity to discover only a small part of our potential.

* Having a large area of blind spot impedes effectiveness
* Discovering more of the dark arena helps bring out latent talent
* A high degree of awareness of one's strengths, weaknesses and qualities helps in making conscious choices and enhances effectiveness

- Blind spots can be reduced by seeking feedback from others, accepting it, reflecting on it and using it to improve
- A high degree of 'private world' could mean non-availability of your talents to others, as others are not aware of your strengths. You may need to enhance your communication and let others know your competencies
- Dark arena can be reduced by undertaking new tasks, and activities, exploring new methods of working, experimenting, job rotation, etc. A high action orientation, experimental and risk-taking attitudes are needed. Proaction and initiative are the most important prerequisites
- Leaders, effective managers and effective people constantly explore their dark arena and attempt to reduce blind spots
- 360 Degree Feedback is one of the effective tools to reduce blind spots, put to use hidden talents and capabilities and initiate actions to discover new areas or competencies

I have described many cases in my book *100 Managers in Action*[3] on how different people who went through a 360 Degree Feedback experience have started doing things they have not done before to enhance their effectiveness. For example, G.V. Prasad, vice chairman and CEO of Dr Reddy's Laboratories discovered his entrepreneurial skills and strategic thinking as strengths and leveraged this by training others to multiply his talent. He also worked on listening and impatience as his weak areas and enhanced his impact further. Ashok Agarwal who went through 360 Degree Feedback acknowledges that he changed his working style and interaction pattern with his colleagues after a 360 tool that sensitized him to the nature of impact his style has on others. Sometimes you may see that what others perceive as your weakness is your strength. That realization helps one to use the so-called weaknesses as strategic advantages with a controlled expression. For example, dynamic people are sometimes perceived as too aggressive and even manipulative. If you discover some such feedback, you need to work on continuing to be dynamic but avoiding occasions that can be perceived negatively as manipulative. G.V. Prasad, for example, found that his impatience is hurting some people but if he gives it up he can't take his company forward. Similarly, after a 360 Degree Feedback, Shivender Singh, CEO of Fortis who was suggested as impatient and that he needed to slow down, shared with his colleagues that he did not want to become more patient and expected his colleagues to change to catch up with his pace. Thus one may accept some weaknesses as a part of oneself and continue with the positive effects of such weaknesses, and at the same time reduce the side effects or negative effects.

4. Exhibit other qualities of personal effectiveness

It matters very little whether you are an extrovert or an introvert, whether you are reserved or the socializing type, whether you are a feeling type or intuitive type, etc. It is important to be aware of what your qualities are and how they affect you and contribute to the outcome of your actions. In other words, self-awareness is an important component of effectiveness. In addition to a high degree of self-awareness and continuously striving to enhance self-awareness, certain qualities contribute immensely to personal and managerial effectiveness. These include:

1. Action/exploratory orientation
2. Self-disclosure
3. Receptivity to feedback
4. Interpersonal sensitivity
5. Self-confidence
6. Internality and inner directedness
7. Trustworthiness

8. Inner core values like honesty, sincerity, truthfulness, etc.
9. Goal-orientation
10. Drive and passion (passion for results, innovations, achievement, etc.)

Action/exploratory orientation: A person who takes initiative to keep experimenting with themselves in new situations, is action-oriented, is not afraid to make mistakes, can take risks, is restless in their work, has high activity levels, and likes variety and change is likely to discover more and more of their potential. They are constantly applying themselves and doing things. Such a person may be called an action-oriented explorer. It is such explorers who can discover more and more of their talents and benefit themselves and their organizations.

Self-disclosure: People who communicate to others about themselves rather freely, who are frank and open, who express their views, opinions, knowledge and feelings freely, who share their knowledge and personal experiences with others (including subordinates, colleagues and bosses) can be considered as the self-disclosing type. These people constantly communicate with others and make an impact on them. This communication or self-disclosure helps in generating data and such an individual has more of an open and public self than private self. Without an optimal amount of self-disclosure we deny an opportunity for others to know us and for ourselves to get appropriate feedback. Low scorers are private individuals who may have difficulty discovering themselves fully. At least it is difficult for them to see themselves fully through the eyes of others and also they make limited impact on others.

Receptivity to feedback: Those who seek feedback constantly or periodically and try to find out about the impact they and their behaviour is having on others, those who take criticism sportily, examine themselves and their behaviour and try to learn from such feedback, and those who value what others say about them, their actions, behaviour, etc. are good learners from feedback. They are likely to develop themselves more and become more effective in the process. Those who are not willing to listen to the views, opinions and feedback from others, and those who become defensive and are closed to feedback are likely to develop less. Receptivity to feedback is therefore an essential element of managerial effectiveness and growth.

Perceptiveness: Those who are sensitive to the cues and non-verbal communications of others, those who are perceptive of the impact of their behaviour on others and therefore are sensitive in not saying and doing things which may turn to be out of place, those who are sensitive to the needs and feelings of others, and those who make an effort to understand the other person or group before saying anything can be called as perceptive individuals. Such individuals are likely to utilize their time properly and make an impact on others. This results in making the individual effective in most managerial settings.

Self-confidence: This refers to the self-concept or self-worth an individual carries with them all the time. A confident person is able to accomplish a number of things. Self-confidence enables an individual to make use of their strengths, and to be more open to feedback and experimentation. Self-confidence puts a glow on an individual's personality and makes them attempt to do things and also take risks. There is an 'approach orientation' in confident people and an 'avoidance orientation' in less confident people.

Internality and inner directedness: This relates to the tendency to do things out of one's own initiative and direction rather than merely doing them to comply with others or due to role expectations by others. An inner directed person is dictated by their inner self and is likely to put more of their talents to use.

Trustworthiness: Trustworthiness or reliability and sincerity are hallmarks of effective people. They honour their promises and make statements, which they always mean. Trustworthiness enhances the reliability of a person and creates a healthy society. It enhances confidence and both the inner and outer image of a person.

Inner core values like honesty, sincerity and truthfulness: It is these values that give direction to life and also a sense of joy. They are essential for creating a healthy society, and a healthy society is essential for healthy living.

Goal-orientation: A goal-oriented person is clear about what they want to do, where to put their efforts and consequently reduces wastage of time. Goal-oriented people are likely to remain focused. If one knows what one wants to achieve, one has already come half way in achieving the same. Most people don't know what they want to achieve and as a result remain unfocused and waste a good part of their lives.

Drive and passion: This includes passion for results, innovation, achievement, etc. While being goal-oriented gives direction, drive gives intensity. It saves time and enhances the value of life. A person with drive and passion can achieve the same things in less time as compared to the person with less drive and passion. In other words they have more time available to do other things.

These are just a few qualities and attitudes that make an effective person. These are by no means exhaustive. There may be many more. Qualities like emotional intelligence, emotional maturity, psychosocial maturity, etc. also contribute to effectiveness.

5. Manage yourself through discovering more and more of your talent and emotional self-control

Arising out of our educational system is the belief that personality development is a one-time effort; that it can be achieved through something like a crash course. However, there are no quick fixes in personal growth. The first step is to know yourself. The key is self-awareness: being alive to one's being, one's thoughts, behaviour and motivation, through a constant process of introspection, and it is a lifelong commitment.

In Daniel Goleman's *Working with Emotional Intelligence*, emotional intelligence does not merely mean 'being nice', but at times would rather mean bluntly confronting someone with an uncomfortable but consequential truth they have been avoiding. It means managing feelings so that they are expressed appropriately and effectively, and enabling people to work together smoothly towards their common goals.

The conditions for 'personal effectiveness' in any given setting, as highlighted above point towards an increasing need for:

→ SELF-AWARENESS: One of the basic emotional skills involves being able to recognize different feelings and giving a name to them. Equally important is to be aware of the relationship between thoughts, feelings and actions.

Specifically, it concerns:
• Emotional awareness: recognizing one's emotions and their effects

- Accurate self-assessment: knowing one's strengths and limits
- Self-confidence: a strong sense of one's self-worth and capabilities (Goleman, 1998)[4]

→ EMPATHY: Getting the measure of a situation and being able to act appropriately requires an understanding of the feelings of others. Sensitivity/empathy helps us to share each other's concerns and goals and walk together towards a common goal of well-being instead of confronting and colliding all the time (Goleman, 1998).

→ ABILITY TO EXPRESS EMOTIONS: The ability to identify emotions in one's physical stages, feelings and thought; the ability to identify the emotions of others, in designs and works of art, etc. through language, sound, appearance and behaviour; the ability to express emotions and needs related to those feelings; the ability to discriminate between accurate and inaccurate or honest and dishonest expressions of feeling (Singh, 2001).[5]

→ ABILITY TO REGULATE EMOTIONS: This refers to the ability to be open to feelings, both pleasant and unpleasant; to engage or detect from an emotion, depending upon its judged utility; to monitor emotions in relation to themselves and others, such as recognizing how clear, typical, influential or reasonable they are; to manage their own emotions as well as those of others by moderating negative emotions and enhancing positive ones; to build rapport with various segments of society and create a network of people (Singh, 2001).

One precondition for personal effectiveness is better self-awareness. But only understanding one's self does not make a person effective.

Peter Drucker says in his article on managing self (*Harvard Business Review*, 1999)[6] to build a life of excellence one should ask oneself the following questions:

1. What are my strengths? Know what you are good at. A person can perform *only* from strengths. One cannot build performance on weaknesses. Feedback analysis is the only way to identify your strengths. Write down expected outcomes for your key decisions and actions. Work to improve your strengths. Avoid intellectual arrogance— acquire skills as required. Remedy bad habits; have no lack of manners. Know what *not* to do—identify incompetence areas and avoid them. This is also what we teach in our 360 Degree Feedback workshops.[7]

2. How do I perform? As any personality trait—*How* a person performs is a given, just as *what* a person is good at or not good at. A reader prefers reading reports before meetings, discussions (e.g. US President Kennedy). A listener likes facing it, and talking the matter out aloud instead of reading and writing (e.g. US President Roosevelt). A reader cannot fully become a listener—and vice versa. An extrovert acts with little thought and an introvert thinks a lot and has difficulty being decisive.

3. How do I learn? A person may learn by reading, writing, doing, talking, listening, or any combination thereof. One must always employ the methods that work. Do not try to change yourself (too much)— instead, work harder to improve the way you perform.

4. What are my values? One's personal value system should be aligned and compatible with that of the organization's. The typical conflicts one needs to resolve all the time are: Organization's commitment to new vs. old (practices, employees, products, processes, etc.); incremental changes or risky 'breakthroughs'; short-term results vs. long-term goals; quality vs. quantity, growth vs. sustenance and openness vs. secrecy; close monitoring vs. trusting, etc. Value conflicts can be disastrous and should be understood and dealt with sooner rather than later.

5. Where do I belong? What is your aptitude? Cooking, painting, service to people, engineering, mathematics, music, etc. If you have an aptitude for one thing, you shouldn't be wasting your time on something else. These are known at an early stage of life in the initial ten years. Highly gifted people discover early where they belong, or where they do *not* belong and start making wise choices. Successful careers develop when people discover their strengths, their method of work, and their values and make choices aligned with these. Knowing where one belongs can transform an ordinary person—hard-working and competent but otherwise mediocre—into an outstanding performer.

6. What should I contribute? Given my strengths, methods and values, what is 'the' great contribution to what needs to be done? What results have to be achieved to make a difference? As most performance management systems say, set extended and challenging goals and work to achieve them. Demonstrate visible and measurable outcomes in the short term.

7. Responsibility of relationships: Bosses are neither the 'title' on the organization chart, nor the 'function'—to adapt to what makes the boss more *effective* is the secret of 'managing the boss'. Working relationships are as much based on people as on work—co-workers are just as human and individual as you are. Taking the responsibility of communicating how you perform reduces personality conflicts. Organizations are built on trust between people—not necessarily meaning that they like each other—but that they *understand* one another.

Many of these lessons, like those drawn by Peter Drucker, have also been demonstrated by Indian managers as described in my book *100 Managers in Action*.[8]

6. Develop your talent

Talent development means acquisition of new competencies or application of old competencies to enhance impact every time. These competencies may be in terms of knowledge, attitudes, values and skills. They may be in technical areas, in management areas, in human relation areas or in conceptual and visionary thinking. As technologies, environments, profiles of organizations and profiles of people keep changing, organizations are continuously faced with new challenges. Employees in supervisory and managerial positions need to face these challenges much more than those at lower levels. To face the challenges of the changing nature of jobs, to contribute one's best to the organization and to pave the way for career growth, supervisors and managers need to keep acquiring and sharpening their competencies. Thus 'competency development' on a continuous basis is a 'necessity'. Most people do not recognize this and take their own development for granted. Every job provides learning opportunities for an interested individual. However, these learning opportunities may go unnoticed or unutilized if the individual is not learning. Organizations can be viewed as excellent learning communities for those interested in development.

Talent needs to be developed vertically and horizontally. Vertical expansion of talent comes from its repeated use to gain more and more experience and to become skilled, and it signifies the depth of knowledge or expertise in a skill. For example, the doctors who take longer periods of time for diagnosis and interventions (like conducting a heart surgery) as they gain experience become experts in carrying out the same procedure flawlessly and in a shorter period of time. Vertical development of talent is discovering it in the same field. Horizontal development involves developing talent in other regions or areas one has not worked in before. For example, doctors could extend their talent to be managers and administrators or institution builders. Or they may try out their talent in new regions and cultures they have not worked in earlier.

The test given at the end of this chapter helps you to examine the extent to which you have the first four of these attitudes (exploring or experimenting; openness or willingness to share and disclose; receptivity to feedback; and sensitivity to others) required to explore your talent, reduce your blind spots and get the best out of life. The first part of the test gives you a score for your aptitude to take initiative and act, or create settings for testing your effectiveness. The second score for self-disclosure gives an idea of the extent to which you communicate to others your own views, ideas, feelings, accomplishments, strengths, etc. and create options for yourself to make an impact. When you open up to others, you are creating opportunities for others to use your talent. If Ragi did not communicate her contacts with farmers and the poor, the politicians would have shown very little interest in her talent. She used her networking skills to gain more ground. That is exactly what most others in earlier chapters have done, be it civil servants, social workers, doctors, professors, etc.

The Personal Effectiveness Questionnaire[9]
(*Reproduced with modifications from* Managers Who Make a Difference *by T.V. Rao, IIMA Books, Random House*)

Rate yourself on each statement using the following five-point rating scale:

0 = Not at all characteristic of you, you normally do this ('0' to less than 10 per cent)

1 = **Not characteristic of you and you may do this rarely (less than 25 per cent)**

2 = **somewhat characteristic of you and you do this sometimes (50 per cent)**

3 = **fairly characteristic of you and you may do this most of the time (around 75 per cent)**

4 = **highly characteristic of you and you do this almost always (90 per cent and above)**

□ 1. I am always involved in some activity or the other and find it very difficult to have any free time

□ 2. I express myself openly without inhibitions

□ 3. I go out of the way to seek feedback on the impact of my actions on others

□ 4. I am very sensitive to the feelings of others

□ 5. I spend a lot of my time gathering information about something or the other

□ 6. I have no inhibitions in talking about myself even with strangers

□ 7. I make it a point to seek feedback about myself from my seniors and others

□ 8. I can easily make out if a person with whom I am talking is not interested in what I am saying

□ 9. I keep trying out new methods and work practices wherever possible or needed

□ 10. I voluntarily share information about myself to others easily

□ 11. I make it a point to seek feedback from my colleagues

□ 12. I am very sensitive to the moods of my colleagues

□ 13. I like to take new initiatives and play leadership roles at my workplace

□ 14. In the company of strangers I can be counted upon to speak freely

☐ 15. I actively seek feedback from my subordinates

☐ 16. I am very sensitive to the feelings of my boss

☐ 17. I like to do different things and have variety in my work

☐ 18. I express my disagreements without any inhibition to my superiors

☐ 19. I keep trying to find out how my behaviour is being perceived by others with whom I have been interacting

☐ 20. I am very sensitive to feelings, even of strangers

☐ 21. I am not happy if I am not involved in some activity or the other all the time

☐ 22. I express my views and opinions freely with my colleagues

☐ 23. If someone criticizes me I take it seriously, reflect about it and change where required

☐ 24. I am very perceptive of the non-verbal messages given by others in conversations

☐ 25. I do a lot of things in my job without being afraid of making mistakes

☐ 26. I express my feelings even if they are not likely to be acceptable to others

☐ 27. I value what people have to say about my habits, style, behaviour, etc.

☐ 28. I rarely find myself in situations where others have misunderstood what I said

☐ 29. I am ready to take risks and innovate by doing new things or working in new ways

☐ 30. I express my feelings frankly and openly, even if they are likely to hurt others

☐ 31. I am highly receptive when a colleague shares his views and opinions about me

☐ 32. I am quite perceptive in assessing the positive or negative feelings of others

☐ 33. I prefer to keep myself engaged in some activity or the other, all the time

☐ 34. I volunteer and give feedback to others even if I am not asked

☐ 35. When someone gives feedback to me I receive it without hesitation

☐ 36. My judgement of people is mostly accurate (example: open-minded or close-minded, cooperative or uncooperative, etc.)

☐ 37. I prefer to test myself in various new situations and do not hesitate to take up new activities

☐ 38. I am quite diplomatic in contradicting others if I sense that it is not likely to be acceptable to the other person

☐ 39. I think and reflect seriously about the feedback others give me

☐ 40. More often than not I can judge the integrity or character of others correctly

Understanding the Personal Effectiveness Test

Each one of us is born with tremendous potential to do a number of things. In our lifetime we are not likely to realize even a small part of it. However, some people discover and apply more of their potential, while a few others may not be able to discover even a small part of it. The reason for our underperformance is that we are not fully aware of our inner resources, hidden potential and inability to utilize resources. This lack of awareness about our inner resources affects our effectiveness. Our potential to perform is immense but the major hindrance is lack of self-knowledge. Thus in order to be effective we need to know more about ourselves, and build upon our weak areas. This test will help you to know about yourself in the various dimensions

of personal effectiveness. Scores above thirty are high, while
below twenty can be considered low. A high score on all four
facets makes you the ideal manager. A low score will indicate
the areas you have to work on.

Use the scoring sheet to record your responses

Name or code...

Item No.	Item No.	Item No.	Item No.
1------	2------	3-------	4-------
5------	6------	7-------	8-------
9------	10------	11------	12------
13------	14------	15------	16------
17------	18------	19------	20------
21------	22------	23------	24------
25------	26------	27------	28------
29------	30------	31------	32------
33------	34------	35-------	36-------
37------	38------	39-------	40-------
Total	**Total**	**Total**	**Total**
Exploratory Orientation	**Self-Disclosure**	**Receptivity to Feedback**	**Sensitivity**

11 Values Are the Core Drivers

Values

The great scientist Albert Einstein once said, 'Try not to become a man of success, but rather try to become a man of value.' He also said: 'Possessions, outward success, publicity, luxury—to me these have always been contemptible. I believe that a simple and unassuming manner of life is best for everyone, best for both the body and the mind.'

The power of values arises from the fact that they help us transcend ourselves. Values are what we consider valuable. Placing any ideal of perfection above our own personal convenience and interests expands our personality and opens it to wider and higher influences. The pursuit of higher values is the pursuit of spiritual Truth. The expression of higher values is to bring Truth down into one's life. A value is a belief, a mission or a philosophy that is meaningful. Whether we are consciously aware of them or not, every individual has a core set of personal values. Values can range from the commonplace, such as the belief in hard work and punctuality, to the more psychological, such as self-reliance, concern for others and harmony of purpose.' (Human Science)[1]

The effective people from various professions we covered follow the values articulated by their respective professions.

There is a code of conduct for doctors, social workers, professors, teachers and all other professions. Those who are effective pay special attention to the values and code of conduct promoted by their profession. The super effective people seem to not only follow their values and set a personal example but also promote the values in their respective institutions.

Honesty, integrity and character are the most cherished values of effective people. Zenger and Folkman in their study of 80,000 managers on what made them extraordinary leaders state that everything about leadership emanates from character. Honesty and integrity, which are the core of character, give rise to good interpersonal competence and many other associated virtues. Very effective and super effective people are highly self-aware. They honour their commitments. They do not make promises they cannot keep. They are also transparent in terms of speaking their mind and not saying things that they don't mean. Integrity is integration of thought with words and actions. People with integrity and character make very effective and super effective people. Hence it is essential we train ourselves to strive for higher integrity and character.

As mentioned earlier the mission of the social work profession is rooted in a set of core values: 'service', 'social justice', 'dignity and worth of the person', 'importance of human relationships', 'integrity' and 'competence'. The dozen and more of the social workers mentioned earlier personify these values. Their entire work depends on their value system.

The medical profession's code of ethics emphasizes the following: service to humanity is primary and financial gain is a subordinate consideration; a physician should be an upright person, pure in character, and should be diligent in caring for the sick; they should be modest, sober, patient, prompt in discharging their duty without anxiety; the personal financial interests of a physician should not conflict with the medical interests of patients; utmost punctuality should be observed in making themselves available for consultations.

Professors are teachers and the teaching profession has certain values. These are reasonably well accepted and include: Human worth indicated by the treatment of every person as a being of inherent worth and respected regardless of gender, sexual orientation, outward appearance, age, religion, social status, origins, opinions, skills or achievements. Truthfulness indicated by constant guidance to learners, frank discussion and a search for the truth. Honesty to oneself and to others, and mutual respect in all interactions with other people form part of the foundation of a teacher's work as does fairness which is promotion of equality and impartiality and the avoidance of discrimination and favouritism.[2]

Practice Values

These values are well expresed and followed by many reviewed in the early chapters.

Professor Pillai says SCMLD's entire education system is based on and aims at values. Values of honesty, integrity, commitment, transparency and purpose-driven actions with tenacious execution shape success. Eagerness to learn, being flexible, adapting to change and most importantly the courage of conviction at all times enable us to grow and enrich ourselves by our experiences. A sense of responsibility and accountability can be infused only by enforcing discipline from early years in life in the family and educational institutions. Therefore at SCMLD, there is caring, compassion, giving, listening, and freedom. But indiscipline, being lazy or casual, giving excuses, etc. are not accepted. Errors and mistakes are acceptable, but not subterfuge and stealth.

Srinivas Pandit's analysis of successful businessmen from India indicates values like integrity, honesty, truthfulness and honouring commitment. This was further confirmed by Chary's study of seven modern Indian leaders from industry. They had a firm foundation of values, integrity, humility, compassion, honesty, customer service, etc.

A highly principled banker, Talwar was known for his values, integrity, dynamism and professionalism.

Dr Kalam stands for qualities like humility, integrity and spirituality. Dr Kalam portrayed these virtues his entire life through his conduct and preaching, be it in his books, or his visits to schools and colleges. The late President said that true nation building is not made by political rhetoric alone but should be backed 'by the power of sacrifice, toil and virtue'.

Generally, family plays an important role in imbibing the good moral values and ethics in the person. One such example is Captain Indraani Singh who despite having fame and money always remained close to her roots. She always wanted to do something to uplift the underprivileged children. She gives credit to her humble upbringing by her parents for her compassion towards others. The value to treat others equally with compassion and empathy was imbibed in her at a tender age. Due to these values, as a kid she felt distress after watching other kids on the street and decided to help them in whatever way she could. A good value system shows the right path, and acts as a source of strength to effective people to keep moving forward towards their goals.

Renu Singh gives credit for her inclination towards social work to her grandmother, Late Kuntala Devi. Her grandmother was a freedom fighter and a social activist. From her she developed an interest in social work. She considers her grandmother her first mentor. Her father was an educationist and from him she realized the importance of education. It is this value system which gave her the courage, at the age of fifteen, to stand for a small girl against a rowdy crowd. At that small age when she decided to be a social worker to work for oppressed women, her grandmother supported her and gave her the moral backing. By watching her family work for the country and countrymen she imbibed those values. She considers activism as an act of patriotism. For her good values coupled with integrity and high character have given her endurance and the inner power to sustain and prosper.

D.J. Pandian has contributed to the society in every way possible. He has even gone beyond his duty as an IAS officer for the betterment of the people. What could possibly drive a person to go beyond his responsibility to help others? The answer can be found in his upbringing. His father was a freedom fighter. He devoted his life to the upliftment of the poor and the downtrodden of the village and its surrounding hamlets. His services were focused on the needs of the deprived and the unfortunate at the grass-roots level. He didn't even care for his polio-affected legs while helping others. He was a role model for Mr Pandian. Mr Pandian has acquired a high need for affiliation from his mother and great patriotism from his father. His love for his family and for social justice has been very strong and consistent. That is visible from the fact that he encouraged his brother to establish a charitable society, the Navajeevan Educational and Welfare Society, with the objective of service to the poor, imparting education, medical relief, and public utilities, and creating scientific awareness.

The entire Calorex Foundation's approach to education is based on values as promoted by Manjula Shroff. K.K. Nair at AMA attributes his ability to get cooperation from so many people to build the institute to his honesty and integrity.

Inderjit Khanna emphasizes the values mentioned in India's 11th plan document which the civil servant should be mandated to reflect on and follow, which are, objectivity, integrity, neutrality, dedication to public service, transparency, exemplary conduct, accessibility and efficiency. No doubt, each value is important and necessary, but it is only the sum total of these values which will make a difference.

There are many people who acknowledge the values they have learnt from celebrities.[3] For example, there are people who acknowledge that the following are the qualities they grasped from Tendulkar:

Humility—No matter how famous you become, don't ever let success get to your head nor let failure pin you down. Stay humble and keep working towards your goal.

To err is human, learn from your mistakes—Everyone knows about the famous Sydney test incident where Sachin refused to play the cover drive which fetched him tons of runs throughout his career and he then went on to score a superb double hundred with hardly any runs on the off side. It is important for every one of us to learn from the mistakes that we have committed.

Respect your guru—Sir Ramakant Acherekar has played a significant role in Sachin's life and even after achieving so much, he never forgets his first guru and considers him one of the most important people in his life.

Stay hungry, stay foolish—Choose whatever career path you are interested in, take success in your stride and don't let anything stop you. Always stay hungry and keep growing.

Self -confidence—'People may throw stones at you but it is up to you to convert them into milestones.' This particular quote is reminiscent of Sachin Ramesh Tendulkar's confidence. He always had belief in his own abilities, and that kept him going even during bad days.

Always recognize the importance your close ones played in your life—
During his farewell speech, he spent a good chunk of time
recognizing the people behind the scenes (his brother, his
wife, family and friends) who kept him going for twenty-four
years. One should never ignore the importance one's family
and friends play in one's success.

*Some people have learnt the following from Bachhan—*Apparently
it was not all a bed of roses for the Shahenshah of Bollywood
the first time he stepped into the city of opportunity. Every
film-maker he approached found him too tall and dark to be
exposed in a film. In fact he even tried to work for All India
Radio trying to utilize his attribute of a deep baritone voice but
he failed there too. Even when Bachchan did manage to bag
a National Award for his role in the film *Saat Hindustani* his
path to glory was still not a smooth one. After doing several
voice-overs and small roles, he bagged a role in the critically
acclaimed *Anand* and after that there was no turning back. It
was a new dawn in his career. Although Amitabh Bachchan is
an experienced professional in his field, he believes that learning
is an ongoing process. He's worked with junior co-stars and
directors half his age, but he's never reported to throw tantrums
or push his weight around on set or otherwise. A director's
actor, he tells us that one must be eager to learn through life.
(Saumyya Mishra acknowledges this.)[4]

*Rahul Dravid—*There are many lessons one can learn from his life.
One of them is: 'He never forgot from where he started and knows
how to use his skills and talent to serve—whether it is nation or his
childhood club.' (Piyush Mahajan acknowledges this.)[5]

The following are a few of the qualities of Rajinikanth
acknowledged by Sonali Walia in a similar article—[6]

1. *He is spiritual and goes to the Himalayas after every film.*
2. *When his films don't do well he returns the money to distributors from his own pocket.*
3. *He never makes anyone wait for him and reaches shoots before time.*
4. *Prefers driving his own car.*
5. *Looks up to his mentor K. Balachandra who gave him his first breaks.*
6. *Reads a lot on science, spirituality, politics and culture.*
7. *He treats everyone around him with respect.*

Extension Motivation and Extension Value

The concept of extension motivation simply means a need or a desire to extend oneself or the ego to others and relate to a larger group and its goals. It means a motivation for helping others, and working for larger goals that benefit larger groups or society. It also means an ability to sacrifice one's own comforts and desires for the sake of others. It is this powerful motivation that has led many great people to make sacrifices for the good of the larger community. All great preachers and saints have led a simple life and taught people to lead a simple life. Mahatma Gandhi said earth provides enough to satisfy every man's needs, but not every man's greed—it elucidates that the nature earth has enough resources and means to meet the basic requirements of a person but it can't serve their endless greed. Here he also implied that people should help the needy of the society. Dr Pareek proposed that it is extension motivation that causes any given society to develop. 'A super-ordinate goal probably arouses this motive. Such goals may therefore be important not only in developing harmony but also in sustained motivation of people in development.'[7]

Narayanan Krishnan,[8] a bright young award-winning chef of a five-star hotel group, was shortlisted for an elite job in

Switzerland. But he gave that up for the service of humanity. With the unconditional support of his team members, till now he has already served more than 1.2 million meals including breakfast, lunch and dinner to India's numerous homeless ones who were mostly elderly people abandoned by their families and who often fell prey to unending miseriy and abuse. Narayanan Krishnan is a good example of sacrificing one's career for the sake of larger goals that help others.

Super-ordinate Goals[9]

Super-ordinate goals are not ordinary goals. They are meant to serve a larger principle. In creating and working towards these goals, a person derives satisfaction from the feeling that they are existing for a cause. Perhaps they were born for that. As one starts doing good work, others begin to appreciate them. With every good deed the person gets more power, appreciation and recognition and this has a tremendous force. Take the example of Sarath Babu, the IIMA graduate who decided to set up his own 'idli factory' immediately after his studies at IIMA instead of taking up a high paid, secure job. He has become a success story and a role model for many management graduates to emulate. Recently he narrated an incident about a troubled young girl who was about to end her life. She came across Sarath Babu's story and was so inspired by his achievements that she decided to live and make something of herself. It is incidents of this kind that help build one's determination to work for super-ordinate goals even though they may be weak at first.

Super-ordinate goals give individuals a high sense of efficacy. Mahatma Gandhi worked for an independent India adhering strictly to the principle of non-violence. This was the driving force that enabled him to make several sacrifices and it was this ability to make sacrifices, not seeking power for himself and leading a simple, immaterial life that made him the greatest leader on earth. He derived his values from his family and what he read when he was young. He was most influenced by the stories of Harishchandra and Shravana Pitrubhakti Natak. He experienced the power of ahimsa in the way his father reacted to his confession that he stole.

Dr V. Kurien is another example of a super-ordinate goal achiever. He worked single-mindedly to make India self-sufficient in milk production and was the architect of Operation Flood, the world's largest dairy development programme. Mr Narayana Murthy of Infosys started with a long-term goal of liberating information technology and generating wealth to be distributed among a large number of those who work for Infosys. After creating Wipro, Azim Premji started devoting his time to nation building and has been promoting education in rural India. They are all examples of super-ordinate goal seekers.

I consider this very appropriate in today's circumstances when both India, at a macro level and at a micro level, and the world at large are witnessing certain events that threaten mankind. These events include scams that have shaken the very basic fabric of a country, unethical and irresponsible dealings by some of the corporate sector leaders who sacrificed basic values and the long-term interests of the company or the country for immediate financial gains. Incidents like these result in confusion in the minds of people and loss of faith in professionals and professionalism. In my view the reason the scams and unethical activities like insider trading, fudging of accounts, etc. take place is essentially because of greed and selfishness. This greed and selfishness is obviously on the increase. Extension motivation and extension values are antidotes to such diseases. They work as antidotes to cure and even prevent selfishness and unethical exploitation of others for the short-term gains of a few.

In this context I must mention that a long-term friend and colleague of Dr Pareek and the author, Dr Prayag Mehta, has been doing a lot of work on similar lines. Dr Mehta's conceptualization of 'Social Achievement and Development Motivation' are particularly relevant to note here (Mehta, 1994 and 1995). Prayag Mehta has observed in his book *Social Achievement* that the pace of development has been slow. 'Studies emphasize the importance of organization, participation and motivation along with public action for achieving such development goals. People are motivated by the need for social achievement and for acting on the environment for obtaining better quality of life and work.' (p. 1, Mehta, 1994). I am not going into details but Prayag Mehta's writings are of great significance in promoting development motivation particularly among government agencies and agents and social achievement among the poor. In both these concepts Dr Pareek's extension motivation, seem to play a part, though Prayag Mehta's concepts go far beyond a single motive and have great implications for development interventions.

To give a few examples, persons who lived with extension values and motivation include Mahatma Gandhi, Mother Teresa and in recent times Dr Abdul Kalam. Many other doctors, professors and civil servants demonstrate extension values. All social workers, especially those that do not have any professional qualifications in social work but have undertaken social work, demonstrate extension value. See the box below:

Extension Motivated Leaders

We all know a little bit about Mother Teresa. One incident that is narrated often is when Mother Teresa went to a baker for bread for her orphan children. The story goes that as she raised her arms, the baker just spat on her hand. Then Mother Teresa told him, 'I would keep this for me, but give me some bread for my children,' while holding out her other hand. At that moment, the baker realized Mother Teresa's gentleness and become one of the main bread donors for her orphanage. She started Nirmala Bhavan to look after orphans and the disabled, and now it has spread throughout India. All her life she worked for the poor and destitute.

Mahatma Gandhi lived a simple life and worked for the country following non-violent principles. When Mahatma Gandhi was travelling on a train one of his sandals slipped off on to the track, and he could not have picked it up; so he promptly threw the second one also on to the track. When asked why he did that, apparently he answered that when someone finds the first sandal, the second one will help him to have both and use them. That is reflective of extension attitude.

Dr Kalam took up academic pursuits as professor, technology and societal transformation at Anna University, Chennai from November 2001 and was involved in teaching and research tasks. Above all he took up a mission to ignite the young minds for national development by meeting high school students across the country. Dr Kalam was an extremely simple man. He remained a bachelor throughout his life. He was a strict vegetarian and teetotaller. He was a workaholic who knew no holidays in the seven-day week. He worked eighteen hours a day. He was fond of music and spent his leisure hours practising the lute and the veena. He was a great lover of books. He was a voracious reader of both the Bhagavad Gita and Quran. Dr Kalam famously said, 'For great men, religion is a way of making friends; small people make religion a fighting tool.' Dr Kalam died as a teacher while lecturing at the Indian Institute of Management Shillong in July 2015. He always wanted to be remembered as a teacher and made igniting the minds of the young his mission.

Ela Bhatt has been working towards making women economically independent through the Self-Employed Women's Association (SEWA) which was born in December 1971. She is widely recognized as one of the world's most remarkable pioneers and entrepreneurial forces in grass-roots development. Known as the 'gentle revolutionary', she has dedicated her life to improving the lives of India's poorest and most oppressed women workers, with Gandhian thinking as her source of guidance.

All our super effective people exhibit extension motivation and values, extending themselves and their talent to the society at large. They come from every profession. Among those involved in social service, the many unsung heroes included in this book personify extension value.

If I analyse the people behind the scams, insider trading, fudging of accounts or cheating the public, they largely come from those who were born in early independent India—in the 1940s and 1950s, and perhaps a few born in the 1960s. I believe those born around that time were born in an independent yet insecure India. They had high aspirations and a few of them perhaps did not have the patience to put in hard work. As an outcome of this, they started resorting to short cuts. They were perhaps born in a 'subsidy' country, a country of reservations, and a country where the government was supposed to 'give' rather than 'take'. Their ambitions resulted in greed out of which they indulged in unethical activities. Such greed is not the property of some but unfortunately many. If this greed characterizes the youngest and upcoming generations (Gen Y or Gen Z) then the country has no great future. To prevent this epidemic from breaking out, we need a strong medicine. Extension motivation is not only a good medicine to cure but also a great medicine to prevent. We need to inculcate the same right from childhood, through schools, colleges, education and corporate training programmes.

I would also like to propose the term 'extension value' to be added to our list of desirable values for an effective person.

Extension value is the extent to which the individual values thoughts, words or talks and activities that extend beyond themselves or their competencies and resources, and makes them available to the people, especially the needy in the society.

After India gained independence we created our own models of development. There was a need to build people and make them capable of higher productivity and economic development in all fields. People needed to value education and schooling. Farmers needed to use better agricultural practices. All those living in villages without access to medical facilities needed to be educated to prevent the spread of diseases. The Government of India thought of various programmes aimed at developing people in all walks of life: farmers, unemployed people, labourers, rural and urban poor, and citizens in general. They started a lot of community development programmes and created new roles called 'extension workers'. Their job was to extend the knowledge available from science, and technological discoveries, and extend it to people who needed it in every section of the society. There were education extension officers to work with and motivate parents to educate their children; agriculture extension workers to educate farmers to use improved farm practices and produce more; health extension workers to educate people to use better health and family welfare practices. They were appointed at village block and district levels and this was continued for several decades. However, it has not worked as it was intended to because the people who were appointed to do this job were hired as employees and many of them lacked extension values. They were more target driven than value driven. As a result they were more occupied with filling records and drawing their salaries than bringing change. Real change comes when a person trying to help you is doing so out of a value and not because they are paid to do it. That is illustrated in all the cases of self-initiated social workers we discussed in chapter 7. They were all people with extension values. They were touched by human misery of different kinds. It is the lack of this value in those employed to serve the nation that has kept India from developing. Consider the fact that India was one of the lowest in the UNDP's Human Development Index and has not improved much in the last twenty-five years. This is because most of those who work for development lack extension values. Those who have them either leave the service like Kejriwal, Jayaprakash Narayan and Aruna Roy or set up their own foundations to serve the poor. Extension motivation and extension values are necessary for nation building. All those covered in chapter 8 demonstrate this value to a large extent.

I had an opportunity to study how the Family Planning Health Assistants and Block Health Extension Educators function in two of the primary health centres in Uttar Pradesh as a part of the World Bank project with IIMA. I accompanied a few of them and observed them very closely. In one case the BEE (Block Extension Educator) goes to visit a carpenter working outside the village and the conversations goes like this:[10]

BEE: What is your name?
Carpenter: Gives his name (coughing and looking very weak but working).
BEE: How many children do you have?
Carpenter: Three.
BEE: You look very old and sick. You should not have produced three children. If you don't use Nirodh (condom) you are likely to produce more children and your health will be further spoiled. So I will give you Nirodh and you should use it.
Carpenter: Sir, I am suffering from TB. You see I am very weak. I have been given a lot of medicines by the doctor and I am taking so many of them. I am sick and tired of having these medicines. I can't have any more, sir. Please excuse me.
BEE: No no! You must use Nirodh. It is good for you and your health.
Carpenter: No sir I can't have any more medicines.
(This utterly insensitive conversation continues for another few minutes until the BEE moves on to another potential target client to fulfil his family planning targets without a genuine concern for the welfare of the people or extension value.)

Lessons for the future of developing effective people all around for nation building:

- We must create an extension culture in India where (a) people value sacrificing their own conveniences for the sake of others and the larger goals; (b) they are willing to sacrifice short-term gains for long-term good; and (c) they become considerate about future generations, and leave the planet for the safety and healthy living of future generations.
- We need to make policies that are driven by extension motivation and culture.
- Extension values and the related family of values should be promoted and taught in schools, colleges and families everywhere.
- Extension motivation and value-based films and stories that promote the work done by social reformers and others should be made available to the public at large. Some industry groups are already making efforts in this direction.
- The corporate sector should be genuinely motivated by concern for the welfare of the larger society and undertake CSR activities out of genuine concern and values rather than as a business strategy.
- The government and various ministries must make policies that truly reflect concern for the welfare of the society and long-term thinking rather than short-term goals. Maybe, for example, the finance ministry ought to look at the extent to which tax laws are promoting development of the country rather than merely increasing tax collections in a particular year to meet immediate needs. Other governance systems should be made extension friendly.
- Award ceremonies to felicitate those who help others to be organized.

- Extension motivation and extension value to become a core value of the country and the education system.
- Recruitment for teaching, health and other social service professions will be based on extension value.
- Scholarships shall be instituted for those exhibiting extension motivation.

How Value Driven Are You?
(Self-assessment)

Integrity

People with integrity speak the truth and make promises only when they believe that they can keep their promises. Are you a person with high integrity?

Rate yourself on each statement using the following rating scale

5 = Almost always (90 per cent)
4 = Most of the time (70 to 80 per cent)
3 = Normally (50 to 60 per cent of the time)
2 = Occasionally (30 to 40 per cent)
1 = Rarely (10 to 20 per cent)
0 = Never

Integrity

- ☐ 1. I make promises in my eagerness to help others but am not able to implement them
- ☐ 2. I don't make promises or commitments I can't keep
- ☐ 3. I value my time
- ☐ 4. I value the time of others and make sure never to be a late for my appointments

- [ ] 5. I stick to time schedules once they are set
- [ ] 6. Many times I am not able to help reschedule appointments with others
- [ ] 7. I make only those promises I can keep
- [ ] 8. If I agree to do something I can always be counted on to carry it out
- [ ] 9. I am very transparent
- [ ] 10. I speak the truth even though it may make the other person feel uncomfortable
- [ ] 11. I say what I am thinking. My thoughts and commitments are fully aligned
- [ ] 12. My verbal commitments and statements and my actions are totally aligned

Honesty

- [ ] 1. I maintain the highest degree of financial honesty
- [ ] 2. I never cheat others
- [ ] 3. I don't tell lies
- [ ] 4. I try to set an example for others in my behaviour
- [ ] 5. I am honest in my dealings with customers, suppliers and all others I deal with
- [ ] 6. I am a value-driven person

Equality and respect for others

- [ ] 1. I respect all individuals irrespective of their community
- [ ] 2. I respect all people irrespective of their religious background
- [ ] 3. I respect all people irrespective of their political affiliations
- [ ] 4. I respect all people irrespective of their gender
- [ ] 5. I respect all people irrespective of their social status

☐ 6. I give opportunity for others to express their viewpoint
☐ 7. I listen carefully to others in case of controversies

Valuing seniors mentors and teachers

☐ 1. I value my teachers
☐ 2. I value my parents
☐ 3. I value what young people have to say
☐ 4. I value my mentors
☐ 5. I value whatever elders and more experienced people
       have to say

Crediting others

☐ 1. I don't wish to own anything that does not belong to me
☐ 2. I acknowledge what is due to others
☐ 3. I don't take credit for the work of others
☐ 4. I give due credit to others when their inputs become a
       part of my work or accomplishments

Value for learning

☐ 1. I keep reading books
☐ 2. I learn a lot from films, television and other media
☐ 3. I read magazines and newspapers to update myself
☐ 4. I listen carefully to others and try to learn from them
☐ 5. I believe that there is a lot to learn from each other
☐ 6. I use the Internet and other mechanisms to learn
☐ 7. I am a constant and restless learner. I can't sleep until I
       learn about any issue that starts bothering me

*'We hang on to our values, even if they seem at times tarnished and
worn; even if, as a nation and in our own lives, we have betrayed*

them more often that we care to remember. What else is there to guide us? Those values are our inheritance, what makes us who we are as a people. And although we recognize that they are subject to challenge, can be poked and prodded and debunked and turned inside out by intellectuals and cultural critics, they have proven to be both surprisingly durable and surprisingly constant across classes, and races, and faiths, and generations. We can make claims on their behalf, so long as we understand that our values must be tested against fact and experience, so long as we recall that they demand deeds and not just words.'

—Barack Obama, *The Audacity of Hope: Thoughts on Reclaiming the American Dream*

12 Be Compassionate

Effective people think differently. Their thinking differently starts from an early age. As they start searching for their internal resources or talent, they have in mind, besides their own survival and growth, a desire to be of use to others. In some cases where they are born in well-to-do families this desire to serve others becomes a propelling need. In Maslow's need hierarchy, it is the fourth order needs called as self-esteem needs which appears after the basic needs—security, love and belonging—are fulfilled. They are called as ego needs or even self-actualization needs, a level above self-actualization. Self-actualization is the need to do what you are born to do or what is fulfilling to you.

The ability to rightly perceive what is there in someone else's mind is called compassion. The desire to free someone else of their sufferings or to ease their pain with one's own kindness is an essential trait to be imbibed within oneself. Effective people remain compassionate about others. They can relate to the pain of others as if they are themselves suffering. For them, everyone is equal. They are devoid of selfish desires and remain concerned about the well-being of others. They believe that investing in someone else's happiness will make them even happier. Their generosity helps them love others selflessly and thus feel for them. They extend their helping hands to those who lack basic facilities and whose lives can truly be bettered via some help from others. This helps them to stand out in the crowd and also bestows them with a lot of hopes and blessings from the unattended ones.

What propels them to start many development activities or welfare services is their compassion. Compassion seems to be a motivation that is almost nurtured from early childhood and sometimes even gives the appearance of an in-born quality. For example, my daughter Kritika is very compassionate to animals and birds from childhood. If she sees a bird or a squirrel anywhere lying injured she would get it home and feed it and make sure to leave it only after it regains health. Many children develop such compassion from birth. Others are taught by their parents. Yet some others develop this from their past experiences and tough and difficult times they had as children, etc. Thus the sources of compassion seem to be many but once it germinates in you it is difficult to contain. Many cases of social workers we outlined earlier indicate the same.

Compassion of Effective People

From the various professions we reviewed earlier the following could be noted:

Jadav Payeng says that he got his passion for preserving nature and providing shelter to dying animals from his community called the Mishing tribe, which literally means 'worthy man'. In earlier times their livelihood largely depended on forest plants and agriculture.

For Virendra Singh who lived long years in the US the compassion was always there, but it only came out after he was totally secure, having lived his life until retirement.

The compassion to serve the needy and underprivileged section of the society led Dr Bhushan Punani to join the Blind People's Association (BPA). He left a lucrative career in industry on completion of his management degree from the Indian Institute of Management in 1979 and joined the Blind People's Association. He is one of the first professional managers to join an organization for the disabled. He has been associated with BPA for twenty-seven years and during this period BPA has grown from a small organization to one of the largest and fastest growing organizations in Asia. BPA trains students in basic social skills, such as speech (if they are able), reading and rudimentary maths–however, it uses different methods depending on the type of disability. As the students grow they are placed in different departments that favour the particular skills in which the student had shown interest. After training them in their respective fields, the students are employed in different companies according to their skill set.

Such instances can be found on Madurai roads where one man Narayanan Krishnan, alone with his strength and compassion, has saved hundreds of lives. Seeing his own people lying on the roads with no food or shelter inspired him to do something for them. He sacrificed his job and personal life and started helping them. He provided them with their basic needs and he is very generous and selfless in his activity. He is satisfied with the little comfort he can afford for himself. The force behind his selfless motive is his determination and his strong belief in never giving up. He believes that any barrier can be overcome by passion. One should have compassion and should try to do what little they can do to help others. He wants that everyone should experience the joy of giving because helping one another will make the world a better place to live.

A similar trait can be seen in Mr T. Raja. His love for people made him rescue the lives of many homeless ones. He was their only hope; he couldn't abandon them. He has been through a miserable life and so he knows the pain which they feel. He helps them in all manners he can. When he started his noble work, he didn't have any money with him. All he had was love and empathy for those in need. His own parents and wife used to scold him. His neighbours used to criticize him but he was certain about his step. Slowly people started recognizing his work and helped him. He is satisfied with whatever he does to help the needy. He takes care of all the destitute with utmost patience and compassion. He and his family live in the same campus with all the occupants. The happy and contented faces of these people after recovery boost him to continue walking down this path.

The life story of Mr A. Muruganantham is another example of how compassion towards others can drive a person to do wonders. He decided to make low-cost sanitary pads by himself after finding out that his wife used unhygienic methods to take care of her menstrual flow. He got no support from anyone as this is a topic which is still considered to be a social taboo. Even adult medical practitioners are hesitant to talk about it. He came to know that all women in the village were using unhygienic methods. Empathy and compassion are the qualities which drove him to continue his research even after he received no cooperation from the target beneficiaries. He had to face social boycott but that didn't deter him from pursuing his research. His concern regarding the health of the women of rural India led him to visit several laboratories and he succeeded in making the low-cost sanitary pads. He even shared the whole process of developing a low-cost pad in several open forums so that women all over the world could become its beneficiaries. What he has done is nothing short of a miracle.

How Does Compassion Develop?

Compassion comes out of empathy. Empathy is the ability to put yourself into the shoes of others. It is experiencing the feelings and the state of mind the way the other person experiences things.

I believe compassion can be developed. When you experience what the other person experiences some time in your life you start feeling empathetic. When you meet a friend who is going through marital adjustment problems and shares with you their problems, you feel sorry about it and you sympathize. Unless you yourself have gone through this you do not experience the pain, anxiety, remorse, anger, frustration, helplessness and such other feelings of the other person. The death of a person close to your friend elicits sympathy until you experience it yourself. If you experience it, then your feelings to the other person when they share it with you can be empathetic. You don't merely feel sorry but something more, and that something more has empathy in it.

Imagine that a close friend of yours reports that his wife is suffering from cancer. What do you feel? If he is a close friend you feel sad and unhappy and want to help him at that time. On discovering you can do nothing about it, you will perhaps keep quiet. Your eyes and ears may be open to hear how such patients are cured, and in case you come across some such miracles reported, etc. you will immediately call up that friend and pass this information on to him. You will at best imagine the suffering the person or his wife may be going through due to chemotherapy, becoming weak, losing hair, etc. The stories you hear may get you to be a little scared and perhaps you will rush to a hospital to get yourself tested or your family members tested to ensure that there is no possibility of cancer. However, you don't know what the other person or his wife is experiencing. They have to live the rest of their life with it. All kinds of apprehensions, fears and possibilities may be going through their minds. They may be preparing themselves for the ultimate truth or they may be fighting with hope against all hopes. I know several cancer patients who lived with hope and miraculously survived and lived longer, happily and normally. Every cure appears to be a miracle. Some of them may become more charitable after they come out of it, and some others even if they are not able to come out of it.

Different people react in different ways. A compassionate person perhaps thinks big and may want to do something to alleviate the hardship of all those who are suffering. They may take up something big for their cause. Others may do this even without going through it themselves. Some may want to start a hospital for cancer if they can afford it. Others may want to become a doctor to discover ways of curing cancer. Another person may be interested in starting a spiritual group to attain a peaceful existence for the rest of their lives. Another may want to write stories of people who were cured of cancer or a collection of tips to make them feel good. The path they choose is different but the end goal is the same; the source of their doing whatever they choose to do is compassion. Compassion is not charity. It may lead to sacrifice and may even lead to egoistic sacrifice—to feel proud and good about what one has done.

Devi Shetty saw his father suffer and experienced empathy for all those whose parents suffer. Late Dr G. Venkataswamy, the founder-chairman of the world famous Arvind Eye Care Hospitals, believed that we can all serve humanity in our normal professional lives by being more generous and less selfish in what we do. His compassion has led to the establishment of a system that gives sight to millions of people across the world. In the year ending March 2015, 3.5 million outpatients were treated and over 401,000 surgeries were performed in these hospitals. Dr V. Kurien's empathy for farmers and the rural masses led him to work for the farmers and the poor. Mother Teresa's empathy for the downtrodden got her to devote her life to the old and destitute. When empathy is extended from a single individual to many others it results in compassion. Compassion results in commitment to a cause and it is commitment that makes people missionaries. These are people with super-ordinate goals and they can be called as super effective people.

Can Compassion Be Cultivated?

Compassion can be cultivated in many ways. Sometimes when people experience or study people who live in poverty, or suffer because they belong to disadvantaged backgrounds, they become compassionate. Life experiences can make one more compassionate. A visit to an orphanage or an old age home or a blind men's house could make you more compassionate. It is with this view schools and colleges organize social work camps and visits to such places.

As mentioned earlier, while working with the government of Rajasthan in the Jawaja project, as a part of the team, I toured around the state along with Ravi Matthai and Udai Pareek and discovered that the parents who couldn't afford to send their children to schools beyond fifth standard found the education system to be totally irrelevant—it did not help the child to do any productive work. We decided to demonstrate how education can be linked to economic activity by up-skilling some weavers, leather workers and farmers. We started tomato cooperatives, weaver-skill development activities, etc. I was due for my promotion at that time. I was called by the promotion committee and was given a piece of advice by one of the members of the committee that I should not be spending my time doing social work. He mentioned that IIMA is a management school and not a school of social work. The same person who gave me feedback later wrote a book on social development, highlighting the activities of various leaders across the world who changed the lives of others. I think it is after this experience of touring around the world and reviewing how such action research formed the basis of various social development programmes the person himself initiated a number of action-based activities. So the lesson is if you want to empathize, create experiences directly or indirectly similar to the one that you would like to empathize with.

Job rotation is a good method to create empathy and through it teamwork. When you ask the finance manager to manage production and vice versa or the HR manager to manage finance and vice versa their empathy for each other goes up.

Role reversal is also a good technique. Those of you who have seen the movie *Waqt* will understand the technique well. Role reversal is consciously playing the role you are in conflict with and defending the role. For example, a mother-in-law and daughter-in-law can play this technique for a few hours to enhance their empathy for each other. Ask the daughter-in-law to act like the mother-in-law. She has to live, feel, think, speak and act like her mother-in-law. Same way with the mother-in-law. Try it for a day. By night, the household will have a completely different atmosphere.

Spend time with the people with whom you like to empathize. Read books about them. Give talks on them. These are methods of developing empathy.

Professor need to be highly empathetic. They should, at all times, put themselves in the shoes of the students. When a bright student asks a question they should lift themselves up to a higher level and when a less bright student asks a question they should change their frame of reference. If they do not, it results in impatience or causes the student to feel smart or dumb. It does not help. A doctor needs to be empathetic.

Make Your Service Available to Others

Compassion is good for people. It drives one towards super-ordinate goals and helps develop a pride in the person. Life becomes meaningful when we start getting involved in activities that are of service to others. Our talent is a God-given gift. Teachers, doctors, lawyers, professors, social workers and many others who have chosen a profession are making products and services available to others. These are meant to make life easy and healthy to live. All services are meant for a larger cause. However, we need to recognize their utility and affordability for the less privileged. As the medical profession says, service is more important than making money. However, many doctors argue that they spent a lot of money to become doctors and they have to recover the same before they can become compassionate. The hospitals, particularly the commercially set up ones, say that they can't treat patients who don't pay the fee in advance for if the fee is a substantial amount sometimes the patient can't afford to pay later. A medical college refuses to admit a bright but poor student if they can't pay the fee. Many institutions have come up to aid such poor people. However, unless we become compassionate and take decisions on the spot when required, life will become difficult in the future for all.

We need to build a compassionate society and our life expectancy and economic growth are likely to go up if we can do that. We need to recognize the relationship between the two.

The best way is to start cultivating compassion. Everyone should offer free services at some point of time in their life and move from being greedy to servicing the needy. We should promote reading of life histories of great people who have worked with compassion. Dr M.C. Modi, the ophthalmologist in Karnataka, and Devi Shetty are good examples of compassion resulting in making many more full and better lives.

How do we develop compassion? As explained earlier, methods like job rotation and role reversal help. The best way to develop it is by showing it or practising it and experiencing the benefits. Some suggested activities include:

* Begin with small charities
* Participate in movements like 'Give India', 'Organ Donation', 'Teach India', etc.

- Watch movies that deal with compassion
- Watch television serials that deal with compassion
- Write stories and case studies
- Use Facebook and other social media to share stories of compassion
- Visit orphanages and old age homes. Start teaching in a school
- Work with an NGO
- Work in another department
- Volunteer to do your colleague's work when you find out that they are stressed
- Volunteer to teach something that you are good at in a school

Measuring Empathy and Compassion

'Sympathetic pity and concern for the sufferings or misfortunes of others', is the Oxford English Dictionary's definition of compassion. It is, therefore, intrinsically hard to gauge scientifically.[1]

Lesley Baillie,[2] principal lecturer on clinical skills development in the faculty of health and social care at London's Southbank University, is completely opposed to the idea of trying to develop measurements for compassion for these very reasons. 'How do you measure a light touch, silence or an important phone call? It is situation—and individual-specific. There is a risk that if you try to turn compassion into a check list it will become less than it really is and how meaningful is that?' she asked.

Dr Fran Grace[3] (Founder, Inner Pathway; professor of Religious Studies, University of Redlands) has been teaching compassion for over ten years at Red Island University. She reports the following in an interesting web article on measuring the immeasurable:

For 10 years, I've been teaching a college course called Compassion. We study the lives of the great exemplars of compassion: Gandhi, Nelson Mandela, The Dalai Lama, Viktor Frankl, and Mother Teresa . . . Students put the compassion teachings into practice. When they study Gandhi, one homework assignment is to live nonviolently for 24 hours . . . From Mother Teresa, they practice her principle to 'do small things with great love' at their community service site . . . From the Dalai Lama, they learn the practice of tonglen meditation, breathing in the suffering of others and breathing out compassion . . .

The study of compassion changes the people who study it. As the axiom goes: 'We become what we think about . . . not to let our mechanics get in the way of our metanoia . . . To study compassion is easy. To become it is a wholly different matter.'

However, attempts have been made to measure compassion. One such attempt has been made after years of research, and a fifty-item compassion tool has been developed by W. David Hoisington.[4] The items in the tool cover compassionate actions. An illustrative list of activities covered in the tool include the following:

- Communicating what you consider as helpful to the other person irrespective of how the person may react
- Pausing before reacting when you are irritated and trying to understand the other person's perspective
- Trying to visualize the details of sufferings of the other person almost as if it had happened to you
- Trying to make a difference in the lives of others
- Getting a compliment from others that it is easy to share their problems with you

- Using humour to make people feel better when they are troubled
- Planning in detail to help others in distress
- Complimenting by physical gestures like a hug or a pat
- Feeling connected to animals and plants
- Engaging in acts of kindness
- Reading, writing or talking about compassion
- Providing information to others that helps
- Feeling good while helping someone
- Getting moved by injustice done to others

David Hoisington maintains that, 'Compassion is an important characteristic for people in the human service sector; yet measuring it has been a difficult task. Most measurement devices have focused on the self-reporting of compassionate feelings and associated attitudes. In addition, these tools start with the premise that compassion is a singular phenomenon.' The CMT, Compassion Measurement Tool, is based on the 'Theory of Compassion Development' which proposes that there is a spectrum of compassion phenomena. The CMT focuses on actions, not feelings or attitudes. The CMT is on the Internet so people can take the test and automatically receive their score.[5]

We have a long way to go in compassion

The act of giving is an indicator of empathy and compassion. The Charities Aid Foundation (CAF) uses a 'World Giving Index' every year and ranks various countries on the extent to which they give. This index is a good indicator of compassion at a national level. When individuals are compassionate the nation gets ranked as a 'giving' nation. The World Giving Index is based on an average of three measures of giving behaviour:

percentage of people donating money to charity, volunteering their time, and helping a stranger.[6] In the 2014 study India was ranked 69 out of 135 countries indexed in the art of giving. Myanmar topped the list followed by USA, Canada, Iceland, New Zealand, Australia, Malaysia, UK, Sri Lanka, Trinidad, Bhutan, Netherlands, etc.

A more recently released ranking on the World Giving Index indicates that India ranks 106 out of 145 countries on this index.[7] India emerged as the last among eight countries included from South Asia in the survey, though in absolute numbers a large number of people (many millions) in India seemed to have helped strangers, donated money and volunteered for a good cause. The report also observed that the proportion of 'helpers' has dropped substantially over the last few years.

The alumni donations to colleges and educational institutions are a good indicator of this low giving index. While many institutions in the USA are financed largely by alumni, Indian institutions of higher education find it difficult to get any substantial donations from them. There are of course a few individuals who donate huge amounts for their alma mater. In a country where power is largely derived from the acts of 'giving' as observed by scholars like David McClelland in his book *Power the Inner Experience*,[8] there could be a lot more charity and compassion. The power of giving needs to be encouraged. The training programmes on extension motivation organized by the Indian Society for Applied Behavioural Science (ISABS) need to be conducted on a large scale to help people become more effective by practising the art of giving.[2]

We have developed a simple questionnaire at the end. It is more for reflection than any measurement.

The Compassion Questionnaire: How Compassionate Are You?

People with compassion are charitable, generous, empathetic and driven by extension drive and passion to help.

To find out how compassionate you are, use the point scale below and rate yourself

5 = Almost always (90 per cent)
4 = Most of the time (70 to 80 per cent)
3 = Normally, (50 to 60 per cent of the time)
2 = Occasionally (30 to 40 per cent)
1 = Rarely (10 to 20 per cent)
0 = Never

☐ 1. I often think about how lucky I am to have whatever I have

☐ 2. I see a lot of poverty around

☐ 3. I readily give small donations for old people homes or for Save the Child and such other social causes

☐ 4. I am willing to sponsor small costs for educating

☐ 5. I feel happy if the government sets aside a part of its earnings to take care of the poor and destitute

☐ 6. I feel happy if the rich in our country set aside a part of their earnings to take care of the poor and destitute

☐ 7. I feel happy that many NGOs are doing good work to support the needy

☐ 8. I am willing to donate liberally to take care of the poor and the needy

☐ 9. I liberally donate clothes, money, food, etc. to the needy

☐ 10. My heartbeats go up whenever I see a person starving and without food

☐ 11. I feel bad about old people left by their children without care

☐ 12. When I interact with people I am able to see their point of view without any difficulty

☐ 13. When in conflict I can appreciate the other person's point of view easily and change my stance

☐ 14. I can shift my frame of reference and accept that of the other person when in a heated debate

☐ 15. I can see through the games people play to amass wealth

☐ 16. I am considered a very sensitive person

☐ 17. I feel easily upset when I find anyone getting exploited

☐ 18. I help others in emergencies by being there with them and helping them: floods, earthquake, riots, etc.

☐ 19. In watching movies I identify easily with various characters helping others

☐ 20. I feel very bad and unhappy to see birds being hurt on kite flying days

☐ 21. I take care if I see a bird or animal is hurt or injured

☐ 22. I feed birds and animals

☐ 23. I appreciate those who plant trees and water them frequently

☐ 24. Compassionate people are my heroes

13 Live with Purpose

In my earlier book *Managers Who Make a Difference* I classified managers into four categories: Doers, achievers, visionaries and missionaries. I have defined the four categories as follows:

1. **Doers:** These are managers who get things done. Though they are not extraordinary, they are necessary in the work place. They do routine jobs. They take life as it comes. They may not have ambitions, but they work hard enough to sustain their jobs and progress at a normal rate in the organization. Without them the company may not be able to run. However, if they leave, another manager will fill their position. The 'doer managers' can be further classified into 'committed doers' and 'shirkers'. Shirkers try to find short cuts and try to do much less than what they are expected to do. We do not deal with them in this book. The 'doer managers' are sincere and hard-working managers.

2. **Achievers**: These managers do more than what they are required to do. Many of them are outstanding. Achievers are smart managers and they work hard and get things done fast. They are noticed in the corporation and considered as assets. They have career ambitions but do not have a mission or purpose in life beyond that. They are willing to move to any company that pays them a higher salary or uses

their competencies better. They are career managers. If luck favours them they may become CEOs at a relatively young age.

3. **Visionaries or entrepreneurs**: Visionaries are leaders. They are restless, creative, and they think big. They have long-term goals. They want to make an impact on the organization and are largely driven by creation of wealth for themselves and others around them. Thus, they make a lasting mark on society. These managers are found in various fields—government, social services, industry, trade and commerce. They are often entrepreneurs and empire builders. Personal wealth is often their distinguishing trait. Deepak Parekh, Kumar Mangalam Birla, Narayana Murthy, Kiran Mazumdar-Shaw, Venu Srinivasan, Anil Khandelwal, Shiv Nadar, Azim Premji, Sunil Mittal, Vijay Mallya, A.M. Naik, Mukesh Ambani, Anil Ambani, and many IIM graduates like Sharath Babu all fit into this group.

4. **Missionaries**: The fourth type of manager is mission driven. Their goals are not personal but more social and community related. They are highly driven by their goals, and there is an element of sacrifice involved in what they do. Mahatma Gandhi, Mother Teresa, Dr Verghese Kurien, A.P.J. Abdul Kalam, Ila Bhatt, Kiran Bedi and Vikram Sarabhai are all examples of missionaries. Type 3 managers may also qualify to be in this category the moment they focus single-mindedly on social objectives rather than empire building. One such example is Narayana Murthy. As managers, our goal might usually stop at type 3—after all, the visionary is the archetypal manager and not all of us want to change society. However, all of us have missionary elements in our nature and it is important we acknowledge type 4 as the ultimate kind of manager.

A recurring issue that keeps cropping up is who among these four classes of managers could be called as effective people. For the definition adopted here for this book it is quite possible a hard-working person who discovers hard work as their core talent and uses the hard work for the benefit of others is an effective person. So are the achievers or visionaries and missionaries. It is quite likely that we find an increasingly large number of people who are effective as we go up from one category to another. Almost all the IIM graduates covered by Rashmi Bansal in her first book *Stay Hungry Stay Foolish* are effective people. Each one of them has benefited many people. They are either in category 2 (achievers) or category 3 (visionaries) or category 4 (missionaries). Sanjiv Bikchandani who started naukri.com, Shantanu Prakash who started Educomp; Vinayak Chatterjee of Feedback Ventures; Ashank Desai of Mastek; R. Subramanian of Subhiksha fame; Narendra Murkumbi of Renuka Sugars; Chander Baljee of Royal Orchid Hotels; Madan Mohanka of Tega Industries; Sunil Honda of Eklavya Foundation; Vardan Kabra of Fountainhead School; Deep Kalra of makemytrip. com; Rasheesh Shah of Edelweiss Capital; Nirmal Jain of India Infoline; Vikran Talwar of EXL Service; K. Raghavendra Rao of Orchid Pharma; Jerry Rao of Mphasis; Shivaraman Duggal of ICRI; Shankar Maruvada of Marketics; Ruby Ashraf of Precious Formals; Deepta Rangarajan of IRIS; Cyrus Driver of Calorie Care; Venkat Krishnan of GiveIndia; Anand Halve of Chlorophyll; S.B. Dangayach of Sintex; Vijay Mahajan of Basix; are all successful people. Most of them created wealth for themselves and in the process for many others. By our definition they are effective achievers. They have achieved something in life. Of them some are even visionaries and missionaries.

If we look at their purpose many interesting things emerge: Almost all of them thought differently and their purpose was to do something different. They went on discovering newer and newer ways to do things. For example, Vijay Mahajan symbolizes this growth. He first worked with institutions that support farmers and then started Pradan, a body to assist and professionalize NGOs so that they can be run efficiently and effectively. As Pradan grew so did Vijay and soon he felt that he needed to do something different. He ended up starting Basix, a bank to develop and finance self-help groups. We find all of them always had a sense of purpose and the purpose was to try something different, something new and they chose the path many others had not chosen. Some of them are very successful entrepreneurs providing employment to many others and contributing to the economy of the country. Interestingly, rarely we find people starting to create personal wealth.

Sanjiv Bhikchandani says, 'If you are starting a business to make money, don't do it' (p. 17, Rashmi Bansal, *Stay Hungry Stay Foolish*: 2008, CIIE: IIMA). Raghavendra Rao says, 'Choose a goal and focus on it. It can be in the area of a product, service or knowledge. Longevity in the field is important. Combine reason with intuition. If there is a tie go with intuition. Think either big or niche. Doing what many others do won't take you anywhere.' (p. 191, Bansal, 2008). Venkat Krishnan of GiveIndia worked with a newspaper, a television channel and as principal of a school before he started GiveIndia, and he dreams of starting other ventures in the course of time (p. 283, Bansal, 2008).

Effective people always have a sense of purpose. It could be as broad as doing something different or as specific as starting a school with a difference. They inspire others with their purpose and mobilize support for the same. That is what is revealed in most of the stories we have discussed in this book. Some of them have great vision and others start with a small beginning and develop it into a great vision. All great people have started small and with a sense of purpose.

Effective people are visionaries

The ability to think about the future in a planned way, with wisdom and intelligence is known as having a vision. People who exhibit this ability are called visionaries. Visionary people have big aspirations; they dream big and see the larger picture. They take incremental steps to attain their goal. Visionaries are ordinary people who encounter challenges like anyone else; what separates them is that they commit themselves to finding solutions for the problem. They have long-term goals and are creative in their approach. They make a long-lasting impact on the society. Visionaries make things happen and are involved in transforming the status quo in the society. They develop a vision and articulate the vision to all. Visionaries inspire people to do challenging work by instilling in them a sense of purpose. Communicating and reiterating the vision from time to time is what visionaries do, and they ensure through their actions time and again that their vision is something not to be compromised with. Everybody needs to abide by the vision. These people generally find opportunities in adverse situations and create something substantial for the society out of nothing. They always look to better themselves and the systems through continuous learning.

Dr Abdul Kalam epitomized a visionary leader. Not only a visionary scientist who had made significant contributions to bolstering India's defence capabilities, he was an astute leader when it came to social development too. Dr Kalam's vision communicated through his books gives a model to government on development. He stressed the importance of education and knowledge and whenever he got the time he addressed the youth, prompting them to think big and achieve big. He reiterated the need to overcome challenges by quoting instances when he himself had done so. He lived by the secular principles that bind the country together and wherever he went he stressed the importance of compassion and love for the poor.

If Dr Devi Prasad Shetty's vision comes true, most Indians will have access to quality healthcare. Dr Shetty thinks that the cost of healthcare in India can come down by 50 per cent in the next 5–10 years, and this will be forced on the hospitals by the government if service providers do not get their act together. Dr Shetty is also setting up 'medical cities' in other parts of the country and his vision over the next five years is that his company will increase its number of beds to 30,000, making it the largest private-hospital group in India and giving it more bargaining power when it negotiates with suppliers, thus driving down costs further. His vision comes from his experience and command in his field. He pioneered the low-cost treatment model. His belief was in a combination of economies of scale and specialization that can radically reduce the cost of heart surgery. A sliding scale of fees is used for operations so that richer customers subsidize poorer ones. He thinks that the volume will be generated by the poor who cannot afford the current treatment cost, but will soon have a smart card with health insurance provided by government. He has taken significant steps to better the medical process. He has established video and Internet links with hospitals in India, Africa and Malaysia so that his surgeons can give expert advice to less experienced colleagues. He also sends 'clinics on wheels' to nearby rural hospitals to test for heart disease. Shetty's unique low-cost insurance programme, Yeshasvini, is estimated to be the world's cheapest comprehensive health insurance scheme which covers 4 million people who pay a premium of Rs 10 per month. He always says, 'There is no point in an innovation or a magic pill that is not affordable.'

Another such individual who exhibits these traits is Amitabh Shah. YUVA Unstoppable, the platform started by Amitabh

Shah, works on a simple, easy to implement model of dedicating two hours a week, in any of the projects. Not limiting himself to any particular sphere, his work is diversified into various fields like children education, digital literacy, cleanliness awareness and assisting the government in reducing accidents. He has inspired people through his work, and it is because of his commitment for the cause that his organization has spread its wings to forty cities across India. Like any true visionary he doesn't limit himself, but has a larger goal of implementing his model across the world. His vision is to instil a sense of purpose among the youth through being a partner with government in social development.

A visionary is also someone who uses creative ways to achieve his overall goal. When you talk about creativity in a visionary leader, the combination itself can be sustainable, effective and successful. Balaji Sampath, an IIT pass-out and also a fellow from the University of Maryland, has made learning easy. His creative ways make difficult subjects like science, and mathematics easy to comprehend. India as a country has a high student dropout rate in schools. This number swells once students ascend to higher classes, where the archaic ways of teaching science subjects makes clearing these subjects look like an insurmountable task. His unique approach, focusing on the poor and rural children, has created zeal in the students' minds to learn, to grow. His work has inspired many to take up science as their career. His efforts have helped students to come out of poverty and be self-sustainable. Balaji communicates his vision of improving the education system, not only among students, but also among his fellow volunteers. Like a true leader he reiterates the vision and motivates, whenever anyone gets demoralized due to lack of progress in their work. He is open to suggestions from the stakeholders to improve the systems in place.

Effective people are goal oriented

A person without a goal is like a ship without a compass. It is very important to have a direction in life. Setting goals is the first step in turning the invisible into the visible. The goal is a dream that a person wants to achieve, which he strives for day in and day out. When it comes to effective people, they set their goals and work towards achieving them. As Confucius said, 'When it is obvious that the goals cannot be reached, don't adjust the goals, adjust the action steps.' These people are determined to achieve their goals but also look for different opportunities to reach their goals and keep moving towards their goals. These people generally have additional responsibility to give direction to their followers. A big goal is further divided into small goals; which are simpler to achieve, easier to monitor. That is why it is said that a good plan is half the success.

Goal orientation is reflected in almost every single case we covered in the first few chapters. To mention a few: Uttam Teron's goal in life was to ensure that everyone in his village became enlightened by the lamp of knowledge. As he started out to fulfil his goal, the beginning was difficult. Irrespective of thinking about his personal comforts, with him being eligible for any government service, he started his school in a cowshed with just four students. After achieving success in his endeavour with 546 students from tribal families coming to his school, he has scaled up his dreams. His goal now is to help the youth be financially strong. Rajani Paranjpe completed her urge to be a postgraduate after fifteen years of marriage. Despite of some adverse circumstances in her initiative she never gave up and showed her full commitment to provide continuous education.

Dilip Banerjee's goal was to improve the implementation of government benefits and schemes through better understanding of the schemes by local institutions. He ensured that people were more involved in the schemes, thus enabling better and effective implementation of schemes.

In the case of Virendra Singh, his goal of educating girls was always clear to him from the time he left India, and he kept reminiscing about it while he was with DuPont for long years. He is now expanding his ideas to more villages.

For Renu Singh, founder of Samadhan, only one incident in her life was sufficient to stir her up at a tender age of fifteen. The incident was, when at the age of fifteen, she witnessed a young girl be the victim of sexual abuse by her father. The girl asked her for help but she wasn't able to save the girl. That feeling of helplessness triggered her goal in life. She understood then the very purpose of her life and since that day she has only focused on the cause of elimination of all kinds of violence against women and children. She was so determined to achieve her goal that after founding Samadhan, she focused on building her own capacities in legal aspects and completed her LLB so as to provide free legal help to the oppressed women and children.

Having lived in India for the last sixty odd years I feel Indians are truly different people. They are complex in some ways, simple in other ways, competent in some ways, and trusting and taken for a ride in many ways. I always think that most Indians are compassionate and good at heart.

Western literature differentiates effective people from efficient people. Efficient people are the ones who do their job well. The job has to be given to them. Effective people are the ones who discover and create jobs for themselves and others. For example, Jeff Haden[1] states the following on nine habits of remarkably effective people after quoting the difference between efficient and effective people following Stephen Covey's differentiation:[2]

There's a huge difference between being *efficient* and being *effective*. *Efficient* people are well organized and competent. They check things off their to-do list. They complete projects. They get stuff done. *Effective* people do all that ... but they check the *right* things off their to-do list. They complete the *right* projects. They get the *right* stuff done. They execute and produce what makes the biggest difference, for their genuine purpose is just effort.

Jeff Haden's conceptualization of remarkably effective people[3] comes closer to the concept of super effective people outlined in this book. The following are taken from Jeff Haden:

1. They always start with goals. Effort without a genuine purpose is just effort. Effective people don't just know what to do—they know why. They have a long-term goal. They have short-term goals that support their long-term goals. In short, they have purpose—and that purpose informs everything they do. That's why remarkable people appear so dedicated and organized and consistently on-task. They're not slaves to a routine; they're simply driven to reach their goals and quick to eliminate roadblocks and put aside distractions that stand in their way. Remarkably effective people set their goals first. So decide what success means to you. You'll find it's easy to stay focused and be effective when you truly care about what you hope to achieve. Even so, once they establish a goal, remarkably effective people don't focus solely on that goal; instead . . .

2. Then they create *systems*. If you're an entrepreneur, your *goal* is to build a successful business. Your *system* consists of your processes for sales, marketing, fulfillment, operations, etc.

For example, Vijay Mahajan started to help the rural poor and then went on to work with NGOs and ended up setting up Pradan to develop, assist and train NGOs in professional management. Remarkably effective people know a goal can provide direction and even push them forward in the short term, but eventually a well-designed system will always win.

'A goal is great for planning and mapping out what success looks like; a system is great for actually making progress toward that goal. Everyone has goals; committing to a system makes all the difference in achieving that goal.'

3. They believe in themselves. They keep trying and they believe that they will eventually succeed. They have enormous faith in themselves and their attempts.

4. They believe they are in control of their lives. Many people feel luck—or outside forces—has a lot to do with success or failure. If they succeed, luck favoured them; if they fail, luck was against them. Luck certainly does play a part, but effective people don't hope for good luck or worry about bad luck. They assume success is totally within their control. If they succeed, they caused it; if they fail, they caused that, too. Remarkably effective people waste zero mental energy worrying about what might happen to them—they put all their effort into making things happen. They know they can never control luck . . . but they can always control themselves.

5. And yet they also embrace 'random'. When your nose is to the grindstone, all you can see is the grindstone. And that means you miss opportunities to spot something new, try something different, or go off on a fruitful tangent. Effective people stay almost totally on-task. Remarkably effective people build in time and opportunity to experience new things, try new methods, and benefit from happy accidents. They're not always trying to reinvent the wheel. But they're more than happy to adopt someone else's perfectly functioning wheel.

6. They find happiness in the success of others. Great teams win because their most talented members are willing to sacrifice to help others succeed. That's why great companies are made up of employees who help each other, know their roles, set aside their personal goals, and value team success over everything else. Where does that attitude come from?

You: Focus only on yourself and ultimately you'll be *by* yourself. To be remarkably effective, find fulfilment in helping other people succeed. In the process you will succeed, too—in more ways than one.

7. They use their goals to make decisions automatic. In a podcast, Tim Ferriss described how Herb Kelleher, the CEO of Southwest Airlines, makes so many decisions every day. Kelleher applies a simple framework to every issue: Will this help Southwest be the low-cost provider? If so, the answer is yes. If not, no. Remarkably effective people apply the same framework to all the decisions they make. 'Will this help me reach my goal? If not, I won't do it.' If you feel like you're constantly struggling to make decisions, take a step back. Think about your goals; your goals will help you make decisions.

That's why remarkably effective people are so decisive. Indecision is born of a lack of purpose: When you know what you truly want, most of your decisions can—and should—be almost automatic.

8. They don't multitask. Plenty of research says multitasking doesn't work. (Some research says multitasking actually makes you stupid.) Remarkably effective people focus on one thing at a time. They do that one thing incredibly well . . . and then they move on to whatever is next. And they do *that* incredibly well.

9. They freely ask for help. Busy people ask for help getting something done. Remarkably effective people ask for help, not just because they need help but also because by asking they show respect for the other person and trust his or her experience, skill or insight. Mutual respect is the foundation of every solid relationship—and the best way to create mutual respect is to first show respect.

Want to be remarkably effective? Surround yourself with people who trust and motivate and inspire you—and in turn are inspired *by* you. Even if you don't achieve all your goals, your life will be infinitely richer.

Have long-term goals

In conclusion, I would like to suggest that it is important for each one of us to be guided by a series of goals. If we need a purposeful life we have to use our talent to the maximum. If we spend our time without purpose, it is like swimming in an ocean without any destination. We will never get anywhere and if we do it is just a matter of chance or luck. We should discover the purpose for which we are meant to be; alternatively, we generate a purpose for each of us. That is where the strengths we could discovered up to a certain point of time will give a purpose. Our compassion and values also may suggest a direction and even purpose. Effective people always live by their goals. In case it is difficult to discover your strengths, at least you can start having goals which are short term.

If you don't have one, develop a set of goals for your life

A person with a high sense of efficacy (a term used in behavioural sciences to mean potential effectiveness) usually exhibits certain characteristics. Pfizer (1969)[4] who developed a manual for scoring an individual's sense of efficacy listed them as follows:

1. Goal orientation or goal making
2. Internal locus of resources or the harnessing of inner resources
3. Problem solving
4. Taking initiative

Now let us examine the contours of the first quality, 'goal orientation', in detail. For other qualities see the source or the book on HRD instruments by Udai Pareek.[5]

The goals are of different kinds: Action goals, essence goals, short-term goals, long-term goals, super-ordinate goals. Different types of goals have different potencies for effectiveness. Super-ordinate goals, explained earlier, have very high potency as they lift the person to very high levels of commitment. Action goals are the next in order. Essence goals are the third in terms of their potency to make one effective.

1. Action goals
People who are driven by goals are often very active. This is because having a goal makes us focused. It allows us to use our competencies and talents in more directed ways, reduces

wastage of time and gives meaning to life. Goals may be of any kind. They could be organization-related, team-related, friends-and-family-related, societal, competency building, service goals, etc. Goals are either long or short term. Long-term goals may include becoming a CEO of a company, changing the values and culture of an organization, reforming society, getting rich, serving the nation, etc., while short-term goals refer more to the immediate circumstances of a person—passing an examination or doing better than the previous year, overtaking someone else, getting a decent job.

Here's a quote from Shantanu Prakash (IIMA, 1988),[6] the creator of Educomp, a multi-crore organization influencing and providing quality education to millions of children across the country:

'I remember, my first office didn't even have a fan. But I didn't seem to mind at all at that point of time. I was so completely obsessed with what I was doing and what I was building. So when I look back, I think that was the coolest year of my life. That I was planning to do the most significant things that I could ever hope to do.'

Vijay Mahajan (PGP, IIMA, 1980)[7] is another example of a long-term action goal-driven individual. Ten years before C.K. Prahalad came up with his notion of 'Bottom of the Pyramid', Vijay Mahajan had established an organization doing just that. He created Basix, a microfinance institution that serves the poor and empowers them to enhance their earnings. Vijay had his encounters with poverty while he was in school at St. Xavier's, Jaipur. While at IIT he sought to solve the problems of the poor through technology. Immediately after his IIM education he set out to address the issues of inequality and injustice. First he formed an organization called Pradan (Professional Assistance for Development Action) which continues to work with NGOs even today and has given birth to many such institutions.

1.1 Action goals may be short term or long term Short-term and long-term goals may co-exist in a person. For example, a student may have a long-term goal of becoming rich through a good posting and a career in one of the MNCs and a short-term goal of doing well in their exam. Many people may have multiple goals: getting a big salary, a foreign posting, a job in a prestigious company, etc. If the short-term and long-term goals are linked, they become an even stronger force for motivation for the person. For example, doing well in one's exams (short term) will most likely lead to getting a job in a good company (long term). Conversely, if one's multiple goals are contradictory, one's sense of efficacy is hampered. For example, becoming rich and serving the poor by starting an NGO could be contradictory goals and it will require a lot of high-level competencies to achieve both simultaneously. At some point, one of the goals will inevitably become stronger than the other. The individual will fluctuate between the two and may feel guilt when he places one over the other. In such cases a person's energy and drive will diminish and his sense of efficacy will become less. Thus it is always better to pursue mutually compatible goals, to be clear-sighted about them and plan them for particular durations. For example, a person may decide that he should focus on getting rich for the next ten years. He may say to himself, 'Once I get rich without sacrificing my values I will start an NGO. It may take place when I am fifty or when I am forty-five but not when I am thirty.'

2. Super-ordinate goals

Super-ordinate goals are not ordinary goals. They are meant to serve a larger principle. In creating and working towards these goals, a person derives satisfaction from the feeling that they are existing for a cause. Perhaps they were born for that. As one starts doing good work, others begin to appreciate them. With every good deed the person gets more power, appreciation and recognition and this has a tremendous force. Take the example of Sarath Babu, the IIMA graduate who decided to set up his own 'idli factory' immediately after his studies at IIMA instead of taking up a high paying, secure job. He has become a success story and a role model for many management graduates to emulate. Recently, he narrated an incident about a troubled young girl who was about to end her life. She came across Sarath Babu's story and was so inspired by his achievements that she decided to live and make something of herself. It is incidents of this kind that help build one's determination to work for super-ordinate goals even though they may be weak at first.

Super-ordinate goals give individuals a high sense of efficacy. People like N. Vittal, Kiran Bedi, Abdul Kalam, Deepak Parikh, Narayana Murthy, Jamshedji Tata, etc. seem to be driven by super-ordinate goals.

3. Essence goals

Essence goals deal with a state of 'being'. The person with essence goals enjoys the status associated with accomplishments like designation, power, etc. When someone says that they would like to be the managing director or CEO of an organization, they desire the state of an MD or CEO but not necessarily focus on what they plan to do. Whereas someone else who expresses it by saying that he/she would like to head the company to change the state of affairs is focussing on action. Having an essence goal is better than having no goal.

Action goals are also powerful goals, although they fall below the super-ordinate category. They refer to those goals where the person sees himself *doing* things once he achieves the goal. Action goals in short represent a state of doing rather than being. Or as the example given above, someone may want to become the CEO of the company so that they can bring a change in some of its policies or practices, or change its direction. Conversely, someone may want to merely be the CEO of a company because they enjoy the position of being the head; once he achieves this, his goal will be to protect 'being called CEO' rather than actually doing something in the position. Doing makes one restless. Being makes one enjoy that achievement and protect the state. Doing goals make one efficacious. Always change your being goal into a doing goal.

It is interesting to note some of the goals of individuals in different categories that have changed the world around them. For example, Mahatma Gandhi worked for independent India and throughout his life with non-violence as the principle. His penchant and drive for independent India is the driving force that enabled him to make several sacrifices. It was this ability to make sacrifices, to achieve continuous action leading a simple life, and not seeking power that made him the greatest leader on earth. In recent years the people who had long-term action-oriented super-ordinate goals include Dr V. Kurien who has single-mindedly worked for making India self-sufficient in milk production and making the farmer get what he deserves. Under his leadership India became a self-sufficient producer of milk. Dr Kurien's goal was to make a success of the cooperative movement and to spread the message of cooperation. After succeeding in this Dr Kurien went on to start an institute of rural development that produced students who could spread his message. Deepak Parikh worked for most part of his life to make low-cost housing available for a large number of Indians in the middle class. Mr Narayana Murthy of Infosys started with a long-term goal of liberating information technology and generating wealth to be distributed among a large number of those who work for Infosys. Kiran Mazumdar-Shaw saw the scope for the application of biotechnology almost two decades ago and pursued it relentlessly to develop this science. She says, 'I may be worth millions on a piece of paper. That doesn't mean anything to me. I'm so happy that I have created this organization with such good people. That is the pleasure I get. It's not the money I get.' (Chary, 2002)[8] Azim Premji, after creating the great company Wipro, started devoting his time to nation building where he has been promoting the education of backward people in rural India. These are all excellent examples of action-driven goal-oriented individuals. It is the goals and their passion for these goals that enabled them to make many sacrifices and overcome many difficulties.

Kiran Mazumdar-Shaw is the chairperson of Asia's largest biotechnology firm and the world's seventh largest biotechnology employer with global sales of $712 billion and a presence in seventy-five countries. She formed her company in a garage after her preferred career as a master brewer hit the glass ceiling due to her gender. She had set up her firm at a time when very few knew what biotechnology was. She has a global vision and would like to see Biocon products in all major countries of the world in the next ten years. 'It has always been my dream to make a global impact with a "Made in India" label. I think a lot of my generation comes from that frame of reference. We have always had to apologize for India. Now is the time we don't want to apologize for our country. We want to be proud of it.' (p. 107, Pota, 2010)[9]

What makes a person a good manager is a high sense of personal efficacy and this arises from the way their goals are orientated —super-ordinate, action and essence. People who approach life without any goals waste their time and talent. Effective managers are goal driven. Where there are no goals they discover some and make them a part of their life.

Once you have identified your goal with confidence you may then convert it into a mission. This leads you to work with a purpose. Then you can accomplish a lot.

Exercise: How to Cultivate Goal Setting and Purposeful Living

In most of the training programmes we give to develop and manage one's own motivation we give an exercise called Life Goals. This exercise makes the individual think, write and share their thoughts, aspirations and plans with others in the team. This is a simple exercise and I am giving below some items that can help anyone to undertake this exercise and plan their purpose in life. This is based on the achievement motivation training module we have been conducting as a part of the entrepreneurship development and motivation management exercises.

Setting: This exercise can be ideally done in a group with the help of a facilitator trained in behavioural sciences. Alternatively, you can try it out in a quiet place with a set of papers and a writing instrument.

1. Draw a picture of your life as you like it to be on a sheet of paper. You can choose an animal and draw or draw any form of picture that represents your life. Write a few lines after you draw it trying to interpret it for yourself.
2. Figure out what is the main motivator or the main motivators in your life. What are you happy with? When you achieve something that is difficult to do for others? Or something that is out of the box? Or something innovative? Or something new and different? If you are normally happy to do something new, or different, or challenging, or better than before, or better than someone else, or when you establish a new standard or accomplish something no one else has accomplished, etc. you may be driven by achievement motivation.

3. If you are achievement driven you need to figure out the core
    competencies which will help lead you to that state. What are
    you good at: Knowledge, attitudes, skills, values, etc.? What
    are your core competencies? For example, Chetan Bhagat
    may say his core competency at one time is to draw from his
    own personal experiences, imagine, make a story and write
    it to communicate to others. Most writers will say that their
    core competency is writing or imagining or communicating
    or influencing or being in touch with reality and being able
    to articulate in a dramatic way and communicate to others
    what is right and what is not right. Your core competency
    may be your values or attitudes or your material possessions
    and your detachment from them, etc. You decide your core
    competencies that you like to put to use to get the best out of
    yourself or multiply them or use them for achieving or doing
    something that makes you feel happy.

4. If you are not achievement driven then you may be one
    of the following: You are driven by the need to impact
    others or change others' way of thinking or change the
    world or the organization. Anything to do with changing
    others including individuals, teams, organizations, culture,
    values, etc. of larger groups of people indicates influence
    motivation. You need to distinguish between the two types
    of such motives. One, changing others for the pleasure
    of changing, or for feeling powerful by changing others
    or impacting others. This is called personal power or self-
    aggrandizement motivation. Most politicians have it. No
    harm. Recognize the same. If influencing others is for the
    sake of group goals or organizational goals or large goals,
    it is social power motivation. It is good to have power
    motivation. It is essential for good managers and successful
    leaders. If you are driven by power motivation you need
    to be aware of it.

5. If you are driven by power motivation you need to develop activities or purposes in life that suit the same. Teaching is a good profession. Choose activities, goals and occupations that will help you to feel happy by lecturing others, controlling others, dictating to others, or persuading others or advocating to others for a good cause. Choose the type of activities that will help you feel happy by influencing others.

6. If you are more happy with relationships, you like to be with loved ones, you want to look after your family, friends and relatives, and you enjoy affection and being with friends, and you value relationships, then you are affiliation motivated. Choose tasks and activities that will help you to be closer to loved ones, that will get you more affection and love, and that will save you time by avoiding conflicts and relationship struggles.

7. It is also possible that you get a thrill out of helping others, or working for a larger cause that benefits the poor, the less privileged, or the larger community, society, etc. Any such desire to make yourself available to help others or to be of service to others is called extension motivation. Decide if you are extension driven and you derive a thrill out of helping others or working for a larger cause. If you have such desires your goals should be extension related.

8. If you don't belong to any of the above you need to reflect and find out what is the dominant motivation that characterizes you. If your goals are aligned with your motives you are likely to work with commitment and passion. If they are not you may be wasting your talent. It does not matter; you can keep trying as some people discover what they want to do late in life and after experiencing many struggles. Do not worry. Decide what interests you at this point of time.

9. Share these thoughts with a friend or a mentor. It helps to clarify the matter sometimes. You may take a few days. It does not matter.

10. On the basis of these thoughts prepare a long-term plan. You can prepare plans for as long as your life lasts. The best way to do it is to write your own obituary the way you want it to be written when you die. Assume that you will live long enough. People lead active lives for as long as eighty to ninety years. You can easily give yourself seventy-five years of life. If you are thirty now you have to plan for forty years. You can't obviously plan for forty years. You can aspire to achieve what is possible in forty years and write an obituary for yourself. Let the obituary be as elaborate as possible. This will reflect what you want to become. It will also bring out your dominant motives.

11. If you want to achieve what you want in your life from your obituary derive a few life goals. Maybe state one to five goals. Two or three will be more focused. State your life goals and everything that you would like to achieve in your lifetime in priority: 1, 2, 3 and so on.

12. State what you would like to achieve in the next five years to move in that direction.

13. State what you would like to achieve realistically in the next three years.

14. State what activities you would like to undertake to reach your three-to five-year goals. These activities are the ones you will do to get there.

15. Anticipate the hurdles you are likely to face in achieving your three-year to five-year goals and state the same.

16. Think and plan the way you will overcome the hurdles you are likely to face in moving towards your goals. The hurdles may be environmental, like finances not being available, government policies, societal sanctions, family support or many more which are outside your control. What help would you like to take to overcome these hurdles? Think and discuss and state them.

17. The hurdles may also be within you, like lack of knowledge, commitment, motivations, qualities, skills, etc. What would you like to do to manage your internal hurdles? Train yourself, learn, take mentors, etc. Plan to overcome the hurdles.

18. Prepare a step-by-step action plan. Assume that you have achieved everything you wanted in the next three to five years. Document the feelings you will have on achievement and as well as the feelings you will have if you fail.

19. Make an assessment of the probability of your success.

20. Write a story of your success in the form of an anticipated autobiography. Complete the story thinking positively. This story will include all the components you have identified and thought of or written so far.

While doing this exercise you may read stories, biographies and autobiographies of people who worked for similar goals or had similar motivations. There are many books available, some of which are given at the end of this book for you to read.

Also watch movies that suit the goals you are working for.

Visit the organizations started by people with inspiring stories.

Document and write your own blogs expressing your desires and aspirations.

14 Reach Out to Many

Reaching out to many is the only way to multiply the use of your talent. Your talent is not yours any more. It gets to be owned by those who learn and internalize; in multiplying your talent you have multiplied your service with the help of others and the methods mentioned in the previous chapters. That is what makes effective people more effective.

From among the people who moved from small beginnings to reach many, include Ela Bhatt, Aruna Roy, Devi Shetty, M.C. Modi, Manjula Shroff, Shantha Sinha, Prathap Reddy, Anil Bordia, D.R. Mehta, Kiran Seth, Anil Gupta, K.K. Nair, Sridhar Rajagopalan, Sharat Chandra, Amitabh Shah, Ashok Agarwal, Rajani Paranjpe, Anil Khandelwal, Abdul Kalam, and Dr Kurien. Others also reached out to many but these are some who stand out.

In sum, the main lesson for moving from an effective to a very effective person is to have a mission and goal in terms of the service you like to offer or the talent you want to make available to others, and your attempt to reach out to many. For this, one needs to do the following:

1. Connect with people
2. Write, disseminate and offer services
3. Use social media

4. Perseverance helps; you don't give up
5. Have a positive attitude

1. Connect with people

Connecting with people is a skill that is required by individuals to be successful in any work. Especially when the work you do is about making people understand the long-term benefits of your work. Communicating your thoughts and your ideas to people, and articulating them in the right way is quintessential to one's journey. An effective person is one with good people connection. They inspire the people to work together for a cause, at times persuading them and their kin to go the extra mile, even during times of difficulties. It is the characteristic of an effective person to push people, colleagues and others to keep on working, even when faced with failure. A communicator is one who sensitizes people about the ills of society by raising awareness on such issues. They need to be persuasive and determined to voice their opinions against social taboos. Changing the mindset of the people requires positive influencing. It is through proper dialogue that one informs individuals about their rights. Often, for societal work, one needs to get financial grants or administrative help. A person who is a good communicator and networker is able to establish a rapport with the persons concerned and ensures that the main objective is fulfilled. An effective person ensures that the process initiated by them spreads, branches, and through mentoring and institution building, they ensure that the lineage of their work is carried forward. It is through these threads of connections that the work remains sustainable and continuous. As a human being cannot be omnipresent, it is important to share and delegate responsibilities for comprehensive growth. In this way a person creates involvement of the people in the cause.

If one wants to change the lives of others, one should be able to connect with people, to understand their problem and to make them understand their advice. Aruna Roy has this ability to adapt to the surroundings she is working in. She is a Tamilian, so it didn't take her much time to adapt while working in Tamil Nadu as an IAS officer. But when she went to Tilonia, Rajasthan, to work with her husband with SWRC, she understood that she had to adapt according to the local traditions and learn Rajasthani to understand the problems of the locals effectively. Aruna had to deal with hostility from the prosperous sectors of the village, but this helped her to gain a better understanding of the caste system prevailing in Rajasthan. She believes in the equality in relationships and became fascinated with the kind of relation her husband had with the villagers without any unwanted formality. She has also worked with the craftsmen of the Dalit community and always took part in their meetings to listen to their problems. She formed a strong bond with a local woman, Naurti. Along with Naurti, she was able to get minimum wages for the workers in the region from the Rajasthan government. Her modest nature has made it easy for her to connect with local villagers and gain their trust.

Dilip Banerjee is working on environmental conservation and disaster relief management in rural areas. He has been proactive in fighting disasters by ensuring that communities become self-reliant. He has achieved this largely due to his mobilizing and influencing nature. He works with village-level government institutions, communicating to them about their roles and responsibilities; he creates a team of villagers and involves them to solve their problems. His work has enabled them to identify their goals based on priority and to devise solutions for long-term sustainability. After creating groups to look after themselves, he delegates the entire responsibility to them. He sensitizes the people about the various government initiatives and how to use them properly. His seamless connection with the rural folk helps him to connect with them. He also conducts workshops to involve and make people aware of their roles in collaborative development.

As mentioned earlier, changing the mindset of people requires positive influencing. Uttam Teron, working in a tribal-dominated village of Assam, started a school for the tribal children. Faced with the ignorance of the parents for whom education had no significance, he started with just four students in his school. He has been vocal about children assisting their parents in stone quarries and farming. Through repeatedly persuading the parents and his good work, he has been able to increase student enrolment. He has been successful in articulating his vision to the parents and his students, for whom learning has now become interesting. His motto has been to educate all in his village but he has also branched out his activities to vocational courses, whereby students can learn and earn. It is through his networking skills that he has been able to connect with people even outside India, people, who help financially to his cause. Even volunteers across the globe come to help. It is through his networking that people from as far as Australia are aware about his institution and help him in improving the methodologies of teaching.

For a person who spent most of his young life in the USA, communicating seems easy! Influencing other young people to visit old age homes is a little more challenging. Amitabh Shah has mobilized and inspired the youth to be a part of societal development. You meet him and see the positivity which he transfers to the other persons almost inductively! Seeing his positivity in life, a person gets motivated. His work philosophy of any person dedicating two hours a week brings a sense of inclusivity to the society. One comes across open events of YUVA Unstoppable where people attend for the music and also to listen to Amitabh Shah speaking on the need for a collaborative development with the government. It is his excellent networking skills with the corporates that ensure that someone like Sudhir Mehta of Torrent Group adopt 100 municipal schools in Gujarat. His team is self-motivated, largely due to the inclusive, delegating nature of Amitabh Shah. His work has inspired many youths and has led to forty branches of YUVA across the country.

Communication is an important trait of effective persons, as emphasized by Renu Singh. According to her, an effective person is one who is a positive communicator by default. The kind of work that she is doing, i.e. empowering rape survivors, brings her a lot of flak from the society. Society, especially in rural areas, is still very primitive when it comes across the evil of rape crime. They generally isolate and look down upon the victims. Renu Singh tries to change this mindset and counsel the rape survivors by conducting 120 regular legal awareness camps every year. She is also a regular speaker on well-known FM radio channels on women's empowerment and legal awareness programmes. Clearly communicating the problems faced by these oppressed people and the benefits of the work done by her to the people is an important task for her.

2. Write, publish and disseminate

Starting in a small way it is the efforts of K.K. Nair—Ahmedabad Management Association—that reach out to several thousands of individuals in the country. Its coverage of 12,000 professionals with 622 management development programmes a year is just about six times its neighbouring IIMA. Though the clientele is different, it is AMA that truly works for professionalizing management in all sectors of the society just as IIMA aims to. What IIMA aims at, AMA implements, both being the brainchildren of Dr Vikram Sarabhai. K.K. Nair, the executive director of AMA, made a difference. He connects with people, welcomes any innovations and always has a positive attitude. AMA publishes a monthly calendar and sends it to all current and potential members. Every month it brings out different newsletters, including one for schools, one general and another for exports. Every alternate day there are open lectures attended by around 100 to 300 people. In 2014–15 AMA conducted 135 open lectures, and 132 international trade programmes. The brain behind all this is K.K. Nair. He connects with others, involves them and assigns tasks and gets teamwork done. He gives them all due credit. Hence AMA has been the most successful and award-winning management association consistently for the last two decades.

Dr Kalam's books are evidence of the need to reach out to people through books. *Wings of Fire, India 2020: A Vision for the New Millennium, My Journey* and *Ignited Minds: Unleashing the Power within India* have become household names in India and among the Indian nationals abroad. Professors like Vijay Govindarajan and C.K. Prahalad are known by their writings. There are many professors in Indian institutes who are great brains but they don't write and limit themselves to their classrooms and as a result their talent remains in limited circulation.

Among bankers, besides doing great work of turnaround, it was through writing about it in his best-selling book *Dare to Lead* that Dr Khandelwal could catch the attention of many in disseminating the idea that the public sector needs daring leaders.

The HRD movement gathered momentum due to the numerous publications by Udai Pareek and me, which are acknowledged internationally. Books like *The HRD Missionary, Recent Experiences in HRD, HRD Audit, HRD Score Card 2500, Hurconomics, Power of 360 Degree Feedback* and *Future of HRD,* etc. have disseminated the concepts and have established a new meaning for the HRD field.

Sometimes biographies and autobiographies help disseminate your philosophy and values and also help you clarify rumours and miscommunications that may have occurred in the past. Doctors will do well in publishing their wisdom in ways that will help all citizens. Deepak Chopra is a good example of such dissemination reaching millions. Professors like Khandwalla and Ramachandran are known for their publications. A number of people talk about the ten principles for running family business outlined by Kavil Ramachandran. Books by Anupam Kher and books on actors like Rajinikant reveal a lot about their childhood and acting experiences. Several people find them inspirational.

3. Use social media
Social workers, civil servants, educationists and others have made great use of social media. Actors like Amitabh Bachchan, Aamir Khan, Shah Rukh Khan, Deepika Padukone and many others use Facebook and Twitter very effectively. Twitter and Facebook help you to keep all others informed about your thoughts, work, events and ideas. They connect you with people and also gets you direct feedback about your moves and activities. They also create potential for self-correction while helping you disseminate your ideas.

Anil Gupta is very active in social forums and reaches out to many people.

4. Don't give up when faced with challenges: Persist
A task which is difficult to deal with brings with it some adversities. Problems are part of life and help in the growth of individuals. The act of never giving up is called perseverance. An effective person with the trait of perseverance aims at the end result and stays ready to confront the pitfalls. For them the journey towards success remains equally occupied with failures and struggles. Their perseverance keeps them calm and

determined. It enhances their strengths and helps them have a clear focus on their goals.

Their dedication makes them believe in themselves and hence they become effective persons. These people never think of giving up before the race finishes. Their approach remains very clear and they have the realization of the dos and don'ts right from the beginning. Their confidence makes them unstoppable and distinct. They believe the end is not attained till the time they accomplish what they desire. This helps them grow in their life.

Jadev Payeng becomes an example of one who has faced many challenges in his journey but has overcome them with his persistent efforts. When he first planted saplings and they used to die in the hot river sandbar, he was unaware of the reason. He took guidance from elders and implemented their suggestions. He was very determined in his efforts despite all difficulties. Every plant's survival was a challenge for him and he looked after them till they became self-sustainable. Elephants were another problem for him. They used to destroy crops in the village and the villagers were furious with them. He thought of producing more bananas to stop those elephants entering the village, and so he started a large banana plantation. He was always clear and confident about his goals and his perseverance led him to achieve what he wanted to.

A person who has embarked on a journey, and has never stopped since is Ayyappa Masagi. Probably it is easier to face criticism from the outside world; but when one is faced with criticism from one's own kin, it is difficult. His own wife termed him to be useless because of his decision to quit his job and start farming! He faced nature's vagaries in consecutive years, once floods, and the next year drought. He was hell-bent on proving that in dry areas of northern Karnataka, one can produce good crops in spite of the scanty rainfall. He has innovated a borewell recharging technique, combining the knowledge gained from his father, and experts like Rajendra Singh, to ensure that dead borewells were yielding potable water. He was faced with a situation where he had to choose between his job and his dream of contributing to farming through scientific innovation. He chose the latter! It is his grit and determination to succeed and make the country water efficient that has led to many farmers' happiness. It is his hard work and dedication which has ensured that areas which were contaminated by chemical effluent from industries are getting clean drinking water for the populace. This effort was a surprise to many experts in the field too.

Narayanan Krishnan had a similar experience. Seeing a man eating his own waste moved him so much that he left his lucrative job and started serving the needy. His parents didn't support his idea and he was asked by his own relatives to visit a psychiatrist or priest, but he was confident about his initiative. When his mother saw what he was doing, she was touched. He was so committed towards these poor people that he not only gave them food but bathed them, shaved them and cut their hair himself. Today, his trust takes care of around 450 people and it's not easy for him to handle them but his patience helps him. His commitment and dedication has led the Madurai district to be free from mentally ill and old people on the roads.

Similarly, when T. Raja started the New Ark mission he faced financial difficulties but he didn't stop and kept propagating his initiative. He encountered numerous problems in handling mentally challenged persons and he learnt that they can only be controlled with love and care. His patience and dedication kept him engaged in his project. He believes that one should work hard and sacrifice to do any charity. He himself has worked for twenty-four hours continuously. He doesn't consider any job as small or big, and he himself takes care of the things that crop up in between.

K.K. Nair is of the firm belief that peer pressure and such things would never affect you if you are loyal to your work. He learnt from his professor that to achieve something there has to be a 'willingness' to do the work, and the general attitude one has towards it matters. He believes he achieved his goal through honesty, innovativeness and willingness to go the extra mile. His plan is to open a facility for research and development in order to help students who are interested in research work. This shows his integrative mindset and innovativeness to be at par with competitors despite being a not-for-profit organization. He thinks that passion is very important to achieve anything in life; if you have passion, you will automatically have something to do. All that is required is the willingness to do things without expecting anything in return. Work is how one proves oneself. If and when you get an opportunity, grab it, do it perfectly and prove yourself. Have small goals, and work towards them with integrity and passion. Large goals do not always work. He believes that once people see the sincerity with which someone is doing their work without any expectations they respect them and come forward to help.

5. Have a positive attitude

Positive thinking energizes and motivates a person and their surroundings. It helps one handle the day-to-day affairs more smoothly. To have a lasting impact on someone else, a positive attitude is binding. Positive behaviour gets followed by optimism. Life gets revamped with constructive and bright ideas. One can then become close to success. The confidence level goes up and the person start enjoying the work they do. The focus always revolves around the belief that things will happen at some point of time. This self-belief automatically enhances one's capabilities. The solution side is targeted rather than struggling with the depression arising out of the problem.

The people around such persons start getting inspired. With so many privileges of viewing a better side of life, the person becomes more appreciated, not only by themselves, but by those in contact with them. So a positive mindset is worth nurturing. It is actually a matter of choice which encourages one to achieve things which otherwise might not be possible.

When Jadav Payeng started planting the saplings, he didn't know that one day he would be able to build a forest of 1360 acres. He was disappointed by the deaths of birds and snakes. When he came to know that planting trees is the only solution, he asked the forest department officials to help, but they insisted he do it himself. Without giving it a second thought, he started planting bamboo saplings on an island on the banks of the Brahmaputra. With all his effort he soon converted it into a bamboo thicket. This gave him hope and he then planted other varieties of saplings. He has faced many challenges but his commitment always led him to overcome them. He is focused towards his goal. His attitude towards any natural disaster is very positive. He thinks nature is doing its job and he should do his.

For any person, losing a job is hard; especially when you are an MBA and have had a good start to your professional life. It is extremely rare to find people who turn around such an adverse phase in their life into an opportunity. Parikshit Borkotoky did exactly that. Faced with such difficult times ahead, he started his own social enterprise. Coming from Assam, he was aware of the abundance of natural resources there; if they were properly utilized, they could do marvels for the place. This led to the birth of Kaftinn, an organization which focuses on selling bamboo and water hyacinth products across India. His business employs local artisans, who get a platform to project their work on a national scale. Faced with difficulties in business, he constantly reads and learns from others. It is his positivity of doing things better through learning which has helped improve business and maintain good-quality products for the customers.

Nothing is impossible for a person who has self-belief and a positive attitude. They always look out for other options if one option is closed but never lose sight of their goals. In the case of Rajesh Kumar, unfavourable circumstances, tough challenges and no or meagre support couldn't deter him from achieving his goals. He wanted to teach the children of construction workers, labourers, roadside vendors, etc. who are not able to attend government schools and he is doing it without anyone's help. He started a school under a metro bridge and started devoting time to them. His financial condition is not good either but that didn't succeed to lower his determination. Instead of getting bogged down by the challenges—financial, lack of resources and many more—he is still imparting education to over sixty students by investing his time and money. A positive attitude causes a chain reaction of positive thoughts, events and outcomes. Among several other people, IIT students have come to assist him in his noble cause.

M.C. Modi's forte lay in his incredible swiftness. He was known for his dexterity as a surgeon and his diagnostic acumen. It was around the mid-70s in the holy town of Tirupati that he performed 833 cataract operations in a day and entered the Guinness Book of World Records. Due to his commitment towards society, he had examined more than 10 million patients and performed a record half million eye operations since 1942. He enjoyed his work and his confidence made his success rate a whopping 99.5 per cent—the odd case of failure was because of the patient's ignorance. Selfless service was all that mattered to him. He was an eloquent speaker and adept at making people take up voluntary work. After forty-five years of service, the doctor was not tired. He never postponed or cancelled his eye camps. He used to say, 'How can I rest when I know that every minute I work I can save a poor villager.'

Mukesh Patel thinks his positive attitude has really helped him in the various challenges that he has come across in his life. Once, when all his colleagues had given up because they weren't being able to acquire land for AMA, he did not give up and continued with his persistent effort. Ultimately he was able to collaborate with ATIRA and make the dream come true. Also, for resources, they needed around Rs 4 crores, which is a pretty high amount. He along with his colleagues was able to come up with various ideas that really turned things around. The 'never say die' attitude has always worked for him. He believes that persistence pays. Once you are focused on your aim you will achieve it no matter what. Many times he has a dream and it happens that when he is just about to give up on that dream, he doesn't realize that success is round the corner. It is always the attitude that made the difference for him. He thinks that 'effectiveness' is not just material progress but a holistic progress which includes your mental, spiritual, physical progress. Only money or material success should not be considered as a parameter of success.

Self-assessment Test on Personal Effectiveness
Answer the following 'Yes' or' No'

☐ 1. Do you have an idea or service which is of benefit to others if shared?

☐ 2. Have you tried it out with a few?

☐ 3. Have most of them or at least a sizeable number of them benefited?

☐ 4. Have you written a paper on it or an approach or short note?

☐ 5. Have you discussed it with a few of your friends or mentors?

☐ 6. Have they appreciated it and encouraged you to pursue it?

☐ 7. Have you tried sharing it on the social media: tweet it, blog it, share on LinkedIn, Facebook or Yahoo groups, etc.

☐ 8. Did you receive good results?

☐ 9. Have you lectured or made presentations to any groups or students or Saturday start-ups and such other groups?

☐ 10. Are you convinced that this needs to be disseminated to benefit a large number of people?

If your answer is yes to all of the above, then you are ready to launch your service or share your talent with many. You are now ready for action and you can use the various strategies suggested in the book and prepare an action plan.

THE STORY OF HRD IN INDIA

India was the first to start a dedicated HRD function with a definite philosophy. This was done by the two of us (Dr Udai Pareek and me) at Larsen & Toubro in 1974–75. We proposed a new concept of the HRD system and a separate department to implement it. HRD as we envisaged it had a definite philosophy. The two main features of the proposed concept of HRD were that HRD dealt with all the human units of the organization (from persons to the total organization), and that it was value-based. The following fourteen principles were shared with the organization as the guiding principles for designing the HR function. The HRD systems should:

1. *Help the company to increase enabling capabilities*
2. *Help individuals to recognize their potential and help them to contribute their best towards the various organizational roles they are expected to perform*
3. *Help maximize individual autonomy through increased responsibility*
4. *Facilitate decentralization through delegation and shared responsibility*
5. *Facilitate participative decision making*
6. *Attempt to balance the current organizational culture with changing culture*
7. *Balance between differentiation and integration*
8. *Balance between specialization of the function with its diffusion into the others*
9. *Ensure responsibility for the function*
10. *Build upon feedback and reinforcement mechanisms*
11. *Maintain a balance between quantification and qualitative decisions*
12. *Balance between external and internal help*
13. *Planned as an evolution of the function*
14. *Promote continuous review and renewal of the function*

In sum the integrated HRD systems approach designed by us had the following elements: (i) A separate and differentiated HRD department with a full-time HRD staff; (ii) Six HRD subsystems including performance appraisal, feedback and coaching, potential identification and development, career development, training and OD; (iii) Interlinkages between the various subsystems; (iv) designed with fourteen principles in mind; and (v) linked to other subsystems of Human Resource Function.

The Factors of Its Success

The implementation of the integrated HRD systems approach in L&T was one of the most successful change management experiences. Several factors contributed to the success of change. Some of these are briefly mentioned here: 1. Committed top management including its chairman, Mr N.M. Desai, and founder Mr Holk Larsen who showed deep interest in redesigning the personnel system; 2. Appointment of a high-level implementation task force; 3. Placement of the system at a high level in the organization—L&T was the first to assign a top level position to HRD in those years; 4. The competent head of the function—S.R. Subramanian, a competent engineer was heading the function; 5. The strong internal resource: Dr Pereira was the first to head the HRD; 6. Involvement of all levels of the organization; 7. Developing internal competence: Over a hundred internal managers were developed to communicate the system all through the company and the term L&T University was used informally by these members.

This was followed by the State Bank of India and its associates starting the HRD with all its philosophy envisaged in L&T. BEML, Crompton Greaves and a few others followed. By 1982 many started HRD, some without understanding the basic philosophy and tenets. Others renamed training as HRD, and a few rechristened the personnel functions HR without changing anything else. By 1982 HRD was beginning to be diluted. Sensing this, I took up the challenge of starting a centre for HRD at XLRI. The XLRI centre could hardly conduct a few programmes in a year, perhaps covering not more than 100 managers. We held a national seminar in Mumbai and created a network to communicate the message of HRD to many others who wanted to implement it. The message had to be spread. We started printing a newsletter called HRD Newsletter. We made it a quarterly with special features. Each issue was sponsored by a company that implemented HRD the way we envisaged it. The newsletter was dispatched to around 2000 managers for free. We registered a not-for-profit society called National HRD Network (NHRDN) with wing no. 15, IIMA, as the registered *address. Between 1985 and 1988, in three years, we must have reached at least a few thousand personnel, HRD, training and other managers, promoting HRD concepts and philosophy. Then we inserted a perforated form to enrol members into NHRDN. We held a national conference on HRD in 1987 and made it a benchmark conference. It had many firsts. Around ten CEOs presented their philosophy on HRD, including prominent persons like Dr Krishnamurthy, K.K. Nohria, M.V. Arunachalam, M.V. Sunbbaih, Suresh Krishna Venu Srinivasan, Deenadayalan and CEOs of SBI, L&T, etc. The* Economic Times *brought out a special edition of the paper on HRD. Government officers were involved. A book was brought out containing conference papers and distributed on the first day of the conference. An AGM was held on the last day and the next conference theme was decided in the AGM at the suggestion of one of the members who was critical of HRD, and it was suggested that the focus be on workmen. It was decided to hold the next conference on HRD for workmen. The next president was also chosen to mobilize funds and the venue was chosen as Delhi to mobilize participation. The conference attendance boosted up to 600 from 200. The new president was elected and a mission vision workshop was held in 1989 to work out the future course of action. NHRDN had come to stay as a professional body to be reckoned with and a body meant to seriously promote HRD philosophy. Prominent professors from various IIMs, ASCI, IITs and other important centres were involved. Today, NHRDN has over forty chapters, thirty books, forty issues of journals, 1400 articles, and over 15,000 members and a president who is determined to make it to a lakh.*

The story of NHRDN has a lot to say on multiplication and use of a few peoples' talents to benefit many. You need a clear-cut philosophy and a reason that gives birth to a mission, a super-ordinate goal to be pursued with missionary spirit. NHRDN had all that. A few individuals like Fr E. Abraham, P.V.R. Murthy, M.R.R. Nair, S. Chandrasekhar, Anil Khandelwal, K.K. Verma, D.M. Pestonjee, P.K. Sarangi, Anil Sachdev, Shashi Khanna, Rakesh Kumar, Keith

D'Souza, T.P. Raman, Kishore Rao, Rupande Padki and R.R. Nair joined the originators of the movement. They were all infected with the philosophy of HRD and the need to disseminate the right concepts and prevent the misuse of the term HRD. There was a mission and there was a vision. There were values like financial integrity, transparency, honesty and commitment. Many of those who joined worked for free and in fact contributed in their individual capacity. There was passion, not compassion.

Thus effective people committed to disseminate their talent, once they had their mission clear, that they should work on the next step of reaching many. These could be potential users or beneficiaries of the talent, or multipliers and disseminators of the talent. One needs to work like a talent machine. From the experience of NHRDN one can draw the following lessons for reaching out to people:

1. Conceptualize the change you want to bring in. It could take the form of a vision, mission, desired state, what is wrong with the present, creation of a new hope for the future, a solution or a philosophy, a tangible or intangible process, etc. In the case of NHRDN it is the HRD philosophy and integrated systems approach and the role of HRD managers as competency, commitment and culture builders.
2. Create a band of supporters or intensely involved promoters. They need to be infected with enthusiasm. In the case of NHRDN it happened on its own; it was not planned to have such promoters of HRD. Being at XLRI and IIMA helped immensely to get a team of supporters. Some of these institutions have a knack of giving you such supporters. This is what Shantha Sinha and Trilochan Sastry both experienced. Pillai had his students to support him after he left SCMLD.

3. With their help, disseminate your ideas through conferences, seminars, etc. The foundation was laid by the first seminar in Mumbai in February 1985 at the end of which I asked if we should wait for XLRI to organize a seminar in order to learn from each other. Why not continue to learn from each other? When the answer was yes, we could continue to learn from each other, I raised another question, should we limit such learning to only when we meet at Mumbai or Delhi? Can we not learn from each other more frequently and from our neighbours in the same city? This gave birth to the first few chapters in Mumbai, Bangalore, Madras (now Chennai), Delhi, Ahmedabad, Baroda, and subsequently other chapters were added.

4. The promoter has to travel, work hard and become a missionary. It involves hard work, sleepless nights, living, eating and breathing the mission at hand. A lot of hard work went into the first five years of the NHRDN. No one knew about it. There was neither Internet nor e-mails. STD and ISD were being conceptualized and not yet introduced. My task was to travel from town to town and disseminate innovative practices reported in one town to another, mobilize participants, enrol members, distribute newsletters, enthuse them with the true concept of HRD. We had to reach out to many with the help of others and through our own hard work. If your mission is clear and you are a value-driven people a lot of help comes on its own.

5. Use newsletters and other mechanisms to network and disseminate. The *HRD Newsletter* became a very handy tool. Fr Abraham was editing it staying in Ahmedabad and St. Xavier's school students were helping him insert them into envelopes and paste mailing addresses . It was being mailed for free to 2000 managers at a time. It disseminated and passed on a lot of information. It became a great networking instrument.

6. Keep conducting national seminars and conferences. Conferences became the most critical instruments for reaching out to many. CEOs were involved. Prominent personalities were roped in and a concept called *member honorius causa* was introduced. Prominent leaders like Dr Kurien, Amrita Patel, M.V. Subbaiah, N. Waghul, Suresh Krishna, K.K. Nohria, etc. became members honorius causa, lent their names and promoted the concept of HRD the way we conceptualized it.

7. Use the media to disseminate the philosophy and practices. Besides the *Economic Times* publishing it, we invited Indira Gandhi Open University to film the proceedings and use the footage in their distance education courses. Even today they are using a few of the videos shot during that period of the late eighties. This has gone a long way to disseminate the concepts of HRD. A team from NHRDN even wrote chapters for the PG degree courses of IGNOU. MS 22 was written by several of us in those days.

8. Publish books and journals wherever you can to disseminate information. They go a long way.

9. Encourage students and teachers to use your knowledge by instituting awards, fellowships, etc.

10. Award people who do great work and recognize and publish them and avoid, as much as possible, to get into controversies. Keep away from politics and protect yourself from politicization to the extent you can by avoiding divisive elements. It is difficult but has to be done tactfully.

15 Take Initiative: Build Institutions

One major characteristic that implies how effective a person can be is via the initiatives they take to tackle an issue. Taking the first step requires courage and risk, and effective people exhibit this. One should be brave enough to put forward an idea. All the initiatives rarely become successful in the beginning; hence one should be ready to embrace all the failures and should learn to rectify them. The failure should not be treated as a hurdle, rather it should be considered as an opportunity to better oneself. The real wisdom lies in being open to failures. Only then can a person be differentiated from the masses. In order to have an impact, one should pick the relevant issues and address them to lead to some specific outcomes. Patience is a virtue, so one should not lose one's calm with the passage of time.

Once an effective person succeeds with original ideas, they then disseminate them to larger numbers by extending the service or benefit through a variety of means explained earlier. Institutionalizing service graduates the person from being effective to very effective and then to super effective. As mentioned earlier, super effective people left a legacy and imprint of their talent through institutions. Even when some of them are no more, the institutions they left go on building further on the original tenet and multiplying the same. The Indian Space Research Organization, IIMA, the Physical

Research Laboratory left behind by Dr Sarabhai, the Indian Institute of Science, National Institute of Design, missile technology, the NDDB, IRMA, the Apollo hospitals, Mother Teresa's series of homes for destitute and the poor, etc. all continue to exist and serve people. Building lasting institutions makes effective people super effective. It is not enough to build institutions, it is equally important to build sustainable institutions.

In this chapter, first we give a brief outline on concepts of institutions and institution building and then we draw lessons for building institutions.

What Is Institution Building?

In his book *Beyond Management*, Dr Pareek[1] postulated, while tracing the history of management and differentiating it from institution building, the following: Administration was replaced by management. Management should be replaced by institution building. Administration has been concerned with the successful maintenance of an organization and its running according to laid down rules and regulations.

Management brought in a change in emphasis and is primarily concerned with efficiency, i.e. accomplishing tasks with minimum resources. In recent years, in addition to concern for efficiency, organizations are striving for two other aspects: continued growth and development (self-renewal), and creating a larger impact on a segment of the society or the entire society. For public systems, the importance of both these aspects is obvious. While management is concerned with getting results, stability, quality, effectiveness, strategy, achievement motivation and competence, institution building focuses on vision, future, trendsetting, networking, culture building, mentoring, extension drive and empowering. Dr Pareek differentiated institutions from organizations. To him, 'Institutions are distinguished by their mission, values and impact on society.'

Institutions should be agents of change in the society and the community. Knowledge utilization is a focal point of an institution's impact on the community. Institutions have self-renewal processes.

One main contribution of an institution is to generate new values in the society or into the field of its operation. The nine criteria suggested by Dr Pareek for institution building are:

1. Attention to process
2. Significance of goal or uniqueness of the field, urgent social needs
3. Innovative nature
4. Autonomy
5. Generating new values
6. Impact
7. Multiplication of know-how
8. Linkages
9. Development of people

Institution builders make a lasting impact by leaving the service they were first doing as individuals to the institutions to perform. Those who are founders of institutions are serving the society many times by extending their and other people's talent for the service of others.

Institution Builders

In my view the physicist and founder of ISRO (Indian Space Research Organisation), Vikram Sarabhai, and Ravi Matthai, the founder of IIMA, are two great institution builders. Sarabhai built a number of institutions in different fields, most importantly in space and management. Ravi Matthai promoted his belief of professionalizing management and actively demonstrated in his own life how management should enter all sectors.

Take IIMA. The symbols that differentiate people and communicate that you work for a team or group are minimal here. Every faculty member gets the same-sized room and each one, irrespective of their designation, shares the same secretary and privileges. You charge the same consulting fee irrespective of the designation. You are addressed as professor, irrespective of whether you are a professor or assistant professor. There are no departments and there are only areas. The term 'area' signifies a broad categorization. You may be a member of more than one area, group or centre. You may also change areas. All these are organizational mechanisms to create a larger identity and bring down the overheads or transaction costs associated with management of the system. IIMA follows most of the principles Udai enumerated.

(Reproduced from T.V. Rao, *Managers Who Make a Difference*, IIMA Books, Random House, 2010.)

Kavil Ramachandran[2] maintains that institution building is like a relay race. 'The founding leaders who realize this and set norms for the successors to follow do well for the creation of institutions out of organizations.' Professor Ravi Matthai took over as the director of IIMA without any specific end to his tenure. He could have continued indefinitely, but chose to step down after six years because he believed that the institution required fresh thinking on a regular basis. After stepping down, he set a new norm by becoming a regular faculty member like all his colleagues and worked from a faculty office like anybody else. For him, the continued success of the institution was more important than anything else. 'He was not at all concerned about symbols like having a large director's office or house or its location. Succeeding generations get inspired by the examples set by leaders like Professor Matthai.' Institutions that believe in the relay race principle have a clear succession plan as well.

Ramachandran points out a few more tenets of institution building using similar concepts to those of Udai Pareek and Ravi Matthai. 'Another key observation is that people trust each other a lot in such institutions. There is always an element of informality, and colleagues can get a lot of things done over the phone or across the table, all based on mutual trust. You can always follow up many things through an email confirmation but action is not delayed for want of an email or formal communication. Trust will grow only if it is practised as a value, top down. Team members, particularly division heads and faculty members in academic institutions need a lot of freedom to operate. While accountability is a critical must, individual team members should have adequate freedom to do things, all for the benefit of the organization. In essence, empowerment should happen regularly and routinely.'

One of the key qualities of a good institution builder is his or her ability to listen to others, encouraging criticism and disagreements. Such leaders know that there are smarter and more capable people around and there are many ways of addressing organizational challenges. All great academic institutions have completely open faculty meetings where leaders encourage dissenting views.

Some individuals may not develop an institution but leave behind a legacy by virtue of the work they have done. This legacy, their style, approach and the documentation they do, leaves a lasting resource for others. They transform existing institutions and leave their stamp. For example, N. Vittal always fought for transparency in the system. His risk-taking behaviour coupled with an 'open to failure' attitude has helped him overcome the hurdles in his way. He has remained consistent in implementing his initiatives, and has displayed a positive attitude throughout his life, which has established him as a leader and initiator of change. He is cited as an institution by himself, a civil servant and a role model for others.

Education is a vital aspect in a child's life. Kiran Bir Sethi has always believed that children should be given responsibilities and community work to gain confidence in their city. Today there is hardly any institution that allows kids to explore on their own. She started Riverside School in 2011 and taught the students to be optimistic. She thinks shamelessness is a characteristic that everyone should have, if they want to do something. She is never worried about rejection in her attempt to bring about a change.

People of action do, when others only think! The miles of distance between his country and the USA couldn't stop Balaji Sampath from helping his motherland. Being a part of AID India, in far USA, he mobilized people to support his fellow countrymen in development. Even before this he was instrumental in teaching rural, poor children during his stay at IIT, Madras. Probably the biggest reason for his success is his desire to learn from the students himself. He constantly asks for feedback from the students and trusts their ability to make the courses and methodologies better. His focus is to widen the scope of innovative teaching across India, to make learning enjoyable.

All Super Effective Persons Have Built Institutions

They took initiative and designed entities to promote or disseminate their talent in service of others.

Step 1: The first step to institution building is initiative and planning. The plan need not be a grand one. All institutions are built with small beginnings and in small steps. So are organizations. Sometimes the institution builder has to keep slogging for a long time until the right break comes. Our modern business leaders like Narayana Murthy, Kiran Mazumdar-Shah, Anu Aga, Azim Premji and Kurien, are all good examples of the time it can take for individuals to build institutions. Some of them took as long as two to three decades or more to start the acceleration process and luck or chance facilitates the speed sometimes.

The second step is like the earlier one, extending your vision to a larger number of people, with perseverance and a never-give-up attitude. Civil servants like Anil Bordia persisted with their interest in education and promoted many institutions they are associated with. Jagdish Pandian was able to facilitate the development of PDPU in Gujarat and was fortunate to stay in the same ministry for long years.

Step 3 requires defining what you and your institution stand for, its values and the culture you would like to build, and pursue the same relentlessly. Without a clear purpose, culture and values, foundations for sustainability cannot be laid.

Step 4 is to develop talent and succession to manage the show or the institution. For this it is important to finding the right kind of people to lead, manage and propagate your philosophy, mission, vision and values. This is a very critical step as if one errs in this the institution may become a hotbed of politics. People may be considered your shadows but it is necessary to identify those who subscribe to your mission, vision, values and culture.

Step 5 is to delegate and release your time to spend on expansion or change to another sphere of activity. Dr Sarabhai has done that. From space to management to physics to culture and environment, etc. Ravi tried to do that from IIMA to Jawaja to education systems and rural entrepreneurship. Samuel Paul has delegated totally and shifted to other areas like anti-corruption, North–South development differences and Christian Medical College Vellore and its development.

Step 6 is, if necessary, to get out so that others can grow and develop. There is a risk involved. There is no guarantee that vested interests will not be developed. For example, in NHRDN, once Udai and I started withdrawing, the new leadership took it in the direction they wished. The direction by itself was not wrong, but slowly the new direction consumed so much time the old mission and vision got neglected. It may be good, but once a path changes and takes a new direction the great dream of the founders may not be realized. The dream of NHRDN was to serve other sectors, while many presidents in recent years have felt that the path should be to have successful conferences attended by large numbers of people and generate revenue. The founders can get into very tricky issues. If they suggest and point out that the direction is not right, they are interfering. If they don't, there is no guarantee that their vision will be carried out in the true sense.

Step 7 is to expand and influence globally or in other regions. Almost all the super effective persons described in the earlier chapters have expanded their institutions in different ways and continue to impact the people they intended to serve. Many of them have given models to the world. Ela Bhatt, Samuel Paul, Prathap Reddy, Devi Shetty and Shantha Sinha have all impacted the thinking in other countries and set up institutions or are helping others to carry out similar work.

When institutions grow and the founders get awards and admiration, then other kinds of issues start coming up. It is here self-awareness and self-management skills come into play. A super effective person will remain humble and not get inflated by the awards and recognition and will be periodically examining and renewing themselves and the institutions. Of course there always comes a time to withdraw for the sake of the institution you have built. They can continue the association by donating the award money to the institutions they have set up. Nobel laureates like Mother Teresa, several Magsaysay award winners like Ela Bhatt, Shantha Sinha, etc. have done the same. This adds to their commitment as institution builders.

Institution building involves a lot of delegation and empowerment as observed earlier by Ramachandran and Pareek. Empowering means to make someone stronger, independent and confident about controlling their life. A person who through their work ensures that others are becoming self-reliant—economically, intellectually, socially—can be termed as an empowering individual. In a social context, empowerment means to spread awareness about the rights of individuals, and the duties and obligations that people have to the society. In an intellectual context, empowerment means to ensure that true learning takes place which elevates the state of mind to think, behave and live responsibly and with pride. In an economic context, empowerment means to be financially strong enough to lead a life with dignity. Empowerment helps individuals to think for themselves, to decide for themselves and to judge between right and wrong. This self-actualization is what empowering people imbibe in individuals. There are many people who need a platform to contribute; effective people are those who mobilize people and channel their energies to do something positive. They create institutions which bring many people together for a cause—sometimes the cause may be for economic well-being, sometimes for educational pursuits. Empowerment goes with the philosophy of inclusiveness, that is to involve everyone in their pursuit for a better life. Empowering individuals create a team, and feed off the energy, complementary skills and ideas of others to be more effective.

They inspire people by trusting in their abilities and their hard work to create a better society.

Effective people work for empowering others in various ways. Anil Gupta is working for empowering the rural people by providing them with the platform to express their ideas to solve a particular problem and providing proper recognition to them. He saw innovations and talent in rural India that were not being supported. In response, he started the Honey Bee Network and began searching the country with colleagues, often on foot, finding myriad inventions developed out of necessity. These discoveries are documented and often shared with the global community. The Network has made it a norm to acknowledge the knowledge provider with name and reference, if not otherwise desired by the knowledge provider. This particular practice has come handy in protecting the IPR of the knowledge provider. He has also worked with the Government of India to establish the National Innovation Foundation, which holds national competitions to encourage new inventors and helps sustain them through the National Micro Venture Innovation Fund. He believes that in rural areas, people solve their problems through innovative mediums. Through the National Innovation Foundation, he has uncovered many useful devices such as a pedal-operated washing machine, a micro-windmill battery charger, a hoe powered by a bicycle, and many more.

The waterman of India, Rajendra Singh, has totally changed the landscape of Rajasthan. Rivers which were drying up, land which had become arid and people who were flocking to the cities have all regained their lost glory. All of these things have been made possible by the hard work of Rajendra Singh. His dedication has made the rivers in north-eastern Rajasthan perennial, impacting the lives of many. His methods of collecting the rainwater in man-made *johad*s, have helped the farmers in their daily practices of farming. His awareness campaign for Gram Swawlamban which coincides with traditional village rituals on soil conversation, improved seeds, and collection of herbal medicines has helped these poor farmers to get a better life and also protect the society. He has played a major role in rural development and employment generation in 1985 at Gopalpura village through water conservation. His actions led to the Supreme Court's ruling in stopping illegal mining and protecting the rivers used by the village farmers. His actions have stopped poor villagers from relocating and helped them carry out their farming with better means.

IMPORTANT INSTITUTIONS

The Indian Institute of Management Ahmedabad (IIMA) has emerged as a top-ranking institution in India and has also established itself globally. Every year it graduates around 500 postgraduates and another 100 practising managers, as well as 10 doctoral scholars, and educates over 3000 executives through various programmes held on the campus. Those who graduated from this institute teach in other B-schools, including those in the USA. IIMA has over the years contributed to over 10,000 postgraduates, around 300 doctorates and several thousand executives. At a conservative estimate of annual value addition of a million rupees by every graduating student, the IIMA graduates together add Rs 10,000 million or Rs 10 billion annually to the GDP, and every graduate and its doctoral students add another Rs 3 billion at a conservative estimate by training other MBAs who add value of Rs 1 lakh per student, with each doctoral candidate contributing Rs 1 lakh per student trained by them every year. The IIMA faculty publishes over 100 cases and over 100 articles every year. Cumulatively, the IIMA faculty, between 1967 and March 2010, had produced 541 books, 445 monographs, 3762 scholarly articles and chapters in books, 4696 registered cases and notes, and 2201 working papers. Today, IIMA stands out as a globally acknowledged institution of excellence. The institute was set up by Dr Vikram Sarabhai, and Ravi Matthai provided it the soul and made it what it is today. Both of them were super effective persons.[3]

The Ahmedabad Management Association[4] today emerges as an organization that caters to the educational, training and development needs of every section of society. In 2014–15 alone AMA conducted 622 management development programmes, with participation from over 12,000 professionals. They conducted forty-two in-company programmes, 132 international trade programmes, 6 diploma programmes, 135 open lectures and 8 industrial visits. The benefits of AMA to the citizens in and around Ahmedabad are enormous. The diploma holders from AMA are known to get employment once they step out. The credit for this largely goes to K.K. Nair and to Dr Vikram Sarabhai, who founded the institution in the late fifties. Effective people like Mukesh Patel, who is featured elsewhere, were its presidents.

The Indian Institute of Health Management and Research (IIHMR), established about thirty years ago, has four campuses in Jaipur, Delhi, Bangalore and Kolkata. It conducts six different types of PG programmes in health management, and its graduates take care of the health management needs of the country. It has also conducted over 500 research projects and a large number of management development programmes for practising health managers. The institution has grown to be a university and has been self-financing since 1995. Dr Ashok Agarwal established it and is considered a very effective person.

Narayana Health, headquartered in Bangalore has come to be one of India's largest and world's most economical healthcare service provider. Since its inception in 2000 by leading cardiac surgeon Dr Devi Prasad Shetty, as a 225-bed cardiac hospital, Narayana Hrudayalaya, the NH Group of Hospitals has grown in to a healthcare conglomerate with a network of thirty-two multispecialty and super specialty hospitals spread across twenty locations with 6498 beds. The group was rebranded as 'Narayana Health' in 2013 to convey organizational vision, values and objectives beyond just cardiac care. The NH group offers services in all areas of medicine with a special thrust in the areas of cardiology and cardiac surgery, cancer care, neurology and neurosurgery, orthopaedics, nephrology and urology, gastroenterology, general surgery, solid organ transplant and critical care, and it is focused on awareness, disease prevention, screening and early intervention.

Over the last decade and a half, NH has set up clusters in the south, east and west of the country and plans to create similar clusters in northern and central India and globally. 'We have set our global footprint with the establishment of Health City, Cayman Islands, North America that replicates the NH model of healthcare delivery. NH plans to reach out to people in Tier II and Tier III cities of India systematically, ensuring and providing them with quality care. Recognised world over for its social enterprise model, NH is committed to the principles of Compassion, Quality and Affordability in healthcare and leverages technology to achieve this . . . NH has also been striving to build a self-sustaining healthcare ecosystem through various initiatives like building Health Cities to bring down the overall cost, leveraging economies of scale, CSR initiatives/donations from corporates/charitable trusts, offering academic programs, vendor management, thus addressing healthcare dynamics in a systematic manner. For its ability to reconcile quality, affordability, scale, transparency, credibility and profitability NH has emerged as a global industry model.'[5]

ACTOR PREPARES is among India's finest acting schools for talented individuals who wish to pursue careers as actor-performers in the entertainment industry. Established in 2005 by Anupam Kher, it is the only school for actors in the world to be founded by an actor who is professionally active. The intensive professional-level course provides specialized training in acting. The classes at ACTOR PREPARES are conducted by competent in-house faculty members who passionately teach the craft through practical and theory classes, games, exercises and extensively filmed practicals. In addition, there is a roster of Bollywood celebrities, which comprises the school's visiting faculty, who share with students their invaluable on-the-job experiences and tips to success. Above all, each student receives individual guidance and counselling from the country's most successful trained teacher-actor, Anupam Kher, throughout the programme. Its alumni include Preity Zinta, Deepika Padukone, Richa Gangopadhyay and Varun Dhawan.[6]

The Mamidipudi Venkatarangaiya Foundation (MVF) graduated from doing actual education for schoolchildren by bridge courses to be a resource centre and is guiding villages and governments in other states and countries. It is building the capacities of community in rural and urban areas for the abolition of child labour by universalizing social education. It uses an 'area-based' approach instead of a target-based approach. The area-based approach concentrates on protecting the rights of every child and ensuring that all of them attend full-time formal education. It draws plans for children to withdraw from work and prepares them to be integrated into schools. Schemes were also designed to ensure that children are retained in school and will continue to attend without any disruption. Over the years, over 1,000,000 children have been freed from child labour, enrolled and retained in school, more than 4000 bonded labourers have been released and 168 villages in Andhra Pradesh are now child labour free. The core strategy of the MV Foundation to achieve its objective of transforming child labourers to students is through the residential bridge camps. It has been implemented in more than 6000 villages and an estimated 45,000 child labourers have benefited from these bridge camps. Through the Stop Child Labour Campaigns and Child Rights Protection Forum (CPRF), they have successfully mobilized communities to establish a social norm against child labour and have helped people to understand that school is the fundamental right of a child.[7] 1500 villages are child labour free and all the children are in schools.[8] As the government takes over the responsibility of getting all children into school, the reach has expanded all over India, to children outside the areas where the the MVF works. The scope is broadening with the help of the government which is causing the MVF to implement less. MVF has gone from being an implementing organization to becoming a resource organization, and its role will continue to change as child labour is eradicated in India.[9]

By 2013–14 the Public Affairs Centre (PAC) completed twenty years. Mission PAC is dedicated to improving governance in India by strengthening civil society institutions in their interaction with the state. The centre's mission is to identify and promote initiatives that facilitate a proactive role by citizens to enhance the level of public accountability and performance. Values practised include: integrity in terms of committing themselves to their vision; credibility through consistent practice of transparency and accountability; non-partisanship to maintain an independent stand on governance issues; constructive engagement to reduce conflict and ensure constant dialogue for coalition building; knowledge-driven action support to encourage/promote informed advocacy. For over twenty years now, PAC has been a pioneer in creating and promoting the use of citizen-centric tools for the consolidation of grass-roots experience that is critical to the understanding of how government programmes stumble, fail or sometimes even succeed. In this time, PAC teams have researched almost every sphere of governance, worked in many sectors, and established friends and well-wisher groups in many countries. Internally,

PAC's reconstitution as a team with a common mission of knowledge creation, often outside the boundaries of their discipline and skill sets, allowed for a more holistic expression of their research results. There are four research groups: Public Policy Research Group; Participatory Governance Research Group; Citizen Action Support Group and Environmental Governance Group.

The annual report says, 'The Public Affairs Centre is twenty years old. Through its chequered life, the Centre has striven to give voice to citizen experience and aspiration through the medium of Citizen Report Cards and other social accountability tools. These efforts have been instrumental in engaging governments and policy makers with thought leaders, communities of action, and researchers to improve the fabric of governance in India and elsewhere. Social accountability of governance processes is now an established idiom in several branches of government and it has proved to enrich and vitalise policy design, and improve programme expression.'[10]

Bhagwan Mahaveer Viklang Sahayata Samiti (BMVSS) is the world's largest non-profit organization serving the disabled. BMVSS's services have benefited over 1.3 million people with physical disabilities.

Founded in Jaipur in 1975, BMVSS has twenty-two branches across India. From just fifty-nine artificial limbs fitted in 1975, the organization has scaled up its operations to distribute about 60,000 aids and appliances to handicapped people annually.

BMVSS holds field camps at various locations within the country to help patients who have financial and physical difficulties in travelling to the main centres. Doctors and technicians travel with equipment and materials to the various locations. On-the-spot fabrication and fitment of prosthetic limbs and other aids and appliances are provided by the organization at these camps.

In a year, over fifty such camps are held. BMVSS workers and volunteers also use mobile vans to access remote areas. As a humanitarian organization, BMVSS knows no frontiers. The disabled all over the world are its concern. To date, it has held more than fifty on-the-spot artificial limb and caliper fitment camps in twenty-six countries in Asia, Africa and Latin America. As done within the country, BMVSS doctors and technicians travel with equipment to the camps held abroad. The fitment camps are supported and organized by local donors, local governments and others to provide on-the-spot limb fitment facilities. Patients do not have to come twice as they would in the general healthcare system. BMVSS has established associate centres in Pakistan and the Philippines and has set up a joint venture in Colombia, the Mahaveer K. Mina Foundation. It has also helped set up independent prosthetic fitment centres in Asia, Africa and Latin America.[11]

The T.T.K. Hospital managed by Shanthi Ranganathan has 100 beds, and admits substance dependent patients and treats each of them over a month. Thus every year about 1200 substance dependent people are rehabilitated. Additionally, the centre works as a Regional Training Centre and supervises the activities of another over hundred NGOs in south India. It also serves as an internship centre for interested students.

These are just a few illustrations of the processes underway in the institutions built by effective people. They have certainly graduated from being effective people to institution builders. Their contributions are of a far higher degree as compared to those who stop at making available their talent to the society. Hence the message for all is, 'Don't stay merely effective, graduate to be very effective by reaching many and graduate from very effective to become super effective by building institutions. Institutions are lasting contributions you can make and leave behind. Build institutions.'

Two Models of Institution Building

I call the first model the Ravi Matthai model and the second model as Dr Kurien's. I have talked about these models in several forums a few years ago. I worked closely with Ravi Matthai, the first full-time director of IIMA who took over from the then honorary director, Dr Vikram Sarabhai. I observed Dr Kurien from a distance. I had only a few interactions with Dr Kurien as HRD consultant to NDDB. Everyone fondly addressed Ravi Matthai as Ravi, and perhaps there is something about your philosophy that gets reflected in the way you are addressed. The legacy to address Dr Kurien formally as Dr Kurien perhaps has come from the need to build a different type of organization like the National Dairy Development Board where a certain degree of formality is required. Ravi stepped aside as director seven years after he became the first full-time director. I joined IIMA just after Ravi stepped aside (whenever we talked about his stepping down as director, Ravi used to correct us by saying that he stepped aside rather than stepped down, and he used to say that the director was never above the faculty to step down). The way in which he stepped aside is also interesting. He got an 'IIMA Review Committee' appointed to review IIMA and give it a new direction. As the committee was completing its deliberations and giving its final touches, he stepped aside and said that the new director should take the institution forward using the direction set by the review committee (and not the previous director!). The tradition continued thereafter and such review committees get appointed every time the director's tenure is coming to an end, and this provides new opportunities for the faculty and the new director to give a new direction to IIMA. I had the privilege of serving in one such committee chaired by Dr C. Rangarajan during Samuel Paul's time. Ravi not only stepped aside but continued as a professor in the institute. The most interesting thing to note is what the person does if he continues to be in the same institute. Ravi wanted to facilitate management in various sectors. He chose the education sector and worked until he died in 1984 on linking education with development through professional management. He never interfered in the running of IIMA once he stepped aside as director. There was a gradual withdrawal of guidance to the new director also. For a few years he was on the board and the faculty evaluation committee. I still remember how the faculty discussions used to take a new turn if he attended a meeting and gave his views. He used to feel uncomfortable that the faculty should be swayed by his comments, and gradually he spoke less and also withdrew from the board. In my view, this is what has built the IIMA culture and has thrown up several leaders. There was a great degree of faculty autonomy, and sometimes we felt that this autonomy was even to a dysfunctional extent. I think if IIMA is what it is today it has great foundations laid in terms of its culture by Ravi Matthai and Dr Sarabhai, from whom apparently Ravi learnt a lot.

I have used the Ravi Matthai model very successfully with the National HRD Network which is now an internationally recognized body—this institution was born in Ahmedabad at IIMA.

Perhaps NDDB needed long-term leadership given the nature of the organization, and Dr Kurien was justified in his long tenure with NDDB. It was this long-term tenure which got the white revolution going and changed the cooperative movement, besides benefiting millions of farmers. However, the issue is different when it comes to an educational institution like IRMA. It is to the credit of Dr Kurien to build IRMA and supply a huge manpower of trained professionals to be available to the rural development sector where no one dared to go. It is not a small contribution he has made. Understandably it became difficult for him to believe that the institution can be on its own.

During Ravi's time and to a large extent thereafter, IIMA always welcomed back its professors even when they left. Even when professors left to work abroad, IIMA maintained their names on the faculty list and welcomed them back. Ravi maintained that the faculty is the intellectual capital of the institution and they should be attracted back even if they leave for short or long periods of time. I understand that IRMA has a policy of not welcoming back its faculty once they resign or leave—a policy largely promoted in Dr Kurien's model, perhaps as a legacy from NDDB. The basis behind this is perhaps the need for long-term commitment to an institution which Dr Kurien strongly believed in, and therefore he would not forgive any faculty who left to join another place which was not in tune with IRMA.

I do agree that managing NDDB is not the same as managing IRMA. Dr Kurien should be credited for demonstrating the importance of having non-negotiable value of service to the rural poor as a basis in both the institutions. None else could have done this apart from Dr Kurien as value establishment requires long-term involvement. As an educational institution, the backbone of IRMA is the faculty and students. Educational institutions need complete autonomy as the main resource they have is their intellectual resource and it needs to be constantly generated. Faculty and students need to be protected from outside interferences so that they can devote their time to learn and generate knowledge. If the leaders fight, it could be very demoralizing to the institution. We experienced it at IIMA once when there was a great delay in appointing the director by the HRD ministry.

Whatever may be the case, too long a tenure of a chairperson of an educational institution is not perhaps in the best interests of the institution.

In the case of another institution, the Academy of HRD, where we tried to follow the Ravi Matthai model, it did not progress when the founders withdrew. They withdrew within a short time and handed it over to a director who was associated with both IIMA and IRMA. It did not grow the way it had grown in the initial years and it was perhaps a big mistake of the founders to withdraw from it too soon. From this perspective, Dr Kurien should be credited for not following Ravi's model. Dr Kurien was also needed to ensure that the institution became stable. He hired many luminaries as directors in the initial years (Dr Kamala Chowdhury, Dr K.R.S. Murthy, Dr Haldipur, etc.) and remained until it was stable. Sometimes it is difficult to judge exactly when to say goodbye and how long to treat the institution and its caretakers as children.

In the initial stages, when the director of another IIM tried to get himself a long tenure, the institution did not grow until he left and made space for a new director to come and provide new leadership. Once he left this IIM grew at a high speed and has become one of the best. There is every danger of personal interests getting mixed with institutional interests and public institutions getting privatized. It often becomes difficult to differentiate personal interests from institutional interests. Especially when one holds strong values and believes that institutions should be run following those values only. The Kurien model of long-term tenure may be fine with NDDB (up to a point of time) but educational institutions like IRMA deserve a better model with properly timed withdrawal of the founders and directors. Institutions are larger than individuals and no one individual can be bigger than the institution. If anyone tries to be bigger, they are limiting the growth of the institution and are assuming too much about themselves.

We all admit that AMA is a great success story. It has surpassed the All India Management Association. It has a new president every two years. However, there is one person who has not changed for the last thirty years and is one main factor behind its success. We all know how much difference this person, as executive secretary or executive director, made. Perhaps it is wrong to conclude that one model is better than the other, but the timing is very important and one should exit before one becomes a source of politicization, which in turn affects the institution.

In the case of highly skill dependent professions like cardiac surgery and the medical profession, it becomes very difficult for the founder to exit and follow the Matthai model. It may become necessary to follow the Kurien model and continue for a lifetime. However, self-dispensing leaders build many institutions while self-dependent ones may build only one and spread it to many places. Dr Devi Shetty and Prathap Reddy are good examples of spreading institutions to serve a larger number of people and one can be reasonably certain that the institutions will continue to exist for long periods to come, like the one built by Mother Teresa.

Institution Building Insights

Institution building is a long-term job. As recommended by Dr Pareek, institution builders and heads of institutions should be assessed and trained in the following roles and the extent to which they are discharging their roles:

1. Identity creation role or the extent to which they promote unique identity for their organization and at the same time ensure societal contributions of the institution;
2. Enabling role in which they develop a variety of resources in the institution including human resources;
3. Synergizing role in which they ensure collective contributions and collaborative culture, make the organization integrate

various resources systems and achieve more than the sum of its parts;

4. Balancing role where they balance conformity with creativity and short-term with long-term goals and activities;

5. Linkage building role where the CEOs create the linkages required with external agencies and subsystems;

6. Futuristic role where they develop the capability to anticipate the future and future changes, and prepare the institution to meet these needs or creates its own future;

7. Impact making role where the institution makes both internal impact through its achievements and the climate it creates, as well as external impact in terms of influencing the policies in the field in which it operates;

8. Super-ordination creating role where the top executive gives a sense of fulfilment to its members by deeply connecting what they do to the larger good of the society.

Institution building needs a lot of thought before action; once the thoughts are clear, then the plan of action follows. The thoughts should focus on the vision, mission, values and objectives of the institution you plan.

Role of the Founders

When SEPs build institutions, they run the risk of becoming possessive. Dr Kurien was the brain behind IRMA, and after he retired from NDDB he found it difficult to dispossess IRMA which provided him the scope to lead it as chairman. However, it has resulted in restricted freedom for others who were good at managing IRMA. Dr Kurien had different views and this led to confrontation and avoidable bad publicity. On the other hand, Matthai stepped aside and kept himself off totally. Using the Ravi Matthai model, I left the Academy of HRD, started in

1990, to be managed on its own. However, many well-wishers of the AHRD feel that it was a mistake I made as it did not grow the way it was envisaged. The vision when it was started was to make it an internationally known centre for research and higher education in HRD with its own campus, residential facilities, library and research centres. It has contributed in terms of research and doctoral studies. About thirty students completed their doctoral-level fellow programmes and seventy are in different stages. A number of books have been written by the faculty but other things remained unfulfilled and it still has a long way to go. Sometimes, on reflection I feel that I made a mistake by following the Matthai model instead of the Kurien one. In the case of NHRDN I withdrew but chipped in whenever there was a crisis. At one time when the fourth president left for abroad within six months of his taking up office, I took up the position of interim president. The second time when it reached a new low in terms of its activities, I volunteered to chair a rejuvenation committee and rejuvenated it with the help of a team. My withdrawing subsequently has worked well. While no one can predict what would have been a better model in retrospect, the dilemmas remain.

Some Questions for Prospective Institution Builders

The following questions need to be answered to begin to build an institution:

1. What exactly is the skill or talent you have which you would like to make available?
2. Who are your target group of beneficiaries?
3. How will the institution help them?
4. Who are going to be the service providers?
5. What skills do they require?

6. Where do you get them? What price (salaries, perks, housing, etc.)?
7. What time is required to build them up?
8. What is the physical infrastructure required?
9. Service area, classrooms, hospital beds, operation theatres, office space or residential space, etc. All infrastructure requirements.
10. What is the equipment required?
11. What are the other social requirements for the kind of services you want to offer?
12. Where to get them?
13. What is the financial base required?
14. How many do you want to serve in the first, second, third year and so on?
15. Affordability of service for those whom you want to serve.
16. What is the source of revenue? What is the level of capital investments required?
17. How and who will mobilize funds?
18. What is the basic philosophy you stand for?
19. What is the training you need to give to all the staff?
20. What are the processes and systems you want to follow from the beginning? Who takes care of the administration? Supervision?
21. What amount of technical people's time is involved?
22. Which services can be outsourced?
23. How do you disseminate information to get beneficiaries to use facilities?
24. What is the long-term plan and vision for the future?
25. How will the institution look like after 5, 10, 15, 20, 25 and 50 years?
26. What milestones do you expect to keep for building the institution?
27. Who are the collaborators?
28. Investors? What returns will they get and across what period?

16 Be Integrative Not Divisive[1]

This chapter may be an unusual chapter. Unlike the earlier chapters where I have described the qualities that characterize effective people, in this chapter I have attempted to go deeply into the thought processes behind effective people. Part of this chapter is based on my personal observations and experiences in life.

When I was young, in my village there was a strong caste system. I was born to parents from different castes. My father was from a higher caste and my mother from a lower caste. I lived largely with my grandfather and mother as my father left my mother to marry and live with his second wife from his caste. I used to watch and experience the distinction of the caste system. All my friends in my class were from different castes or what are now called as community groups, and a few were from what is now called as Scheduled Caste. Among my friends I had friends from different caste groups and religions. In school we never felt any difference. We celebrated all feasts together—Deepavali, Dussera, Vinayakchavathi, Sankranthi, etc. and we also used to enjoy the Muslim and Christian festivals. We had a lot of nationalism. There was a caste system but there was a lot of integration and respect for each other. Some of my best friends were Rambabu (Brahmin), Gandhi (Kamma), Abdul Gaffar (Muslim), Munnangi Venkateswara Reddy (Reddy), David (SC) and Nattah Kripa Rao (SC). I would go to sell some of the handmade products made by my mother in the nearby villages and when it was lunchtime I would

371

eat in the house of one of my friends who lived outside a nearby village because he was supposed to be a Mala (untouchable). Though the concept of caste was there, it never bothered us. We would mix freely. Today in urban India there are no caste differences. We mix freely irrespective of caste and community, religion, state, language and so on. India has come a long way from the old days. This is one India and we are a highly integrated nation. There are many movies that indicate that there is no difference among human beings and they are all from the same God and they have a lot more similarities irrespective of caste, community, religion, language and so on.

I wish this were true always and everywhere. When people compete with each other, caste, community and religious differences come to the forefront and they get an exaggerated importance. When it comes to discrimination at the time of admissions by caste, community, socio-economic status, etc. the differences come to the forefront. Promotions and reservations create some mischievous divisions among people and pit them against each other. This is also fine. However, sometimes some people tend to exploit the various identities we have for selfish reasons to get ahead of others. The Indian caste system was originally invented to be an occupational classification. All are supposed to be equal as long as they carry out their 'dharma' and that is what they are skilled at. Everyone is respected. Lord Rama cared for a dhobi's words and asked Sita to be left in the forest; he did not say he is, after all, a dhobi. All good kings made sure that the poor were cared for. However, in a competitive world, in order to gain importance and have significance some people created different types of caste systems everywhere. Organizations are classified as micro, small, medium, large, private, public, MNCs, etc., and we ascribe a different status to each of them. Similarly, we classify institutions and ascribe a status to them. If you are from IIT, you're high status, and if you are from a lesser-known MBA college from a small town you are an unknown entity. You may be a great doctor with a high service mind and highly skilled from a small medical college no one knows. But a less skilled person from an AIIMS or any other well-known medical college gets a lot more respect and if you are 'foreign-returned' you are even greater. Even today professors with American degrees are paid more and are more respected than those who are locally bred, irrespective of their competencies. In organizations we classify people from various departments with varied statuses. Finance departments are supposed to be more powerful than any other, or marketing departments are the highly incentivized departments.

Government service has a classification of IAS, IPS, IRS, IFS, IAAS and so on. There is a classification among them and state services are considered lower ranks. Even among the central services there is further classification with IAS at the top. It is in our minds, and these divisions have been created by some self-serving people who want to be powerful. Unfortunately this caste system in services, organizations and everywhere is creating conflicts and preventing talented people from moving forward. It is not in the interest of the country and not in the interests of humanity. I call this way of thinking a divisive mindset and it has continued from ages and is spreading like wildfire. When decisions are made and privileges are given on the basis of ascribed statuses and associated competency perceptions are not based on reality society does not progress. Those who promote this and strive for this are called divisive minds. They are not effective people. This chapter examines these 'divisive personalities' and promotes 'integrative personalities'. All effective people in my view are integrative people.

Those who work for widows to be treated better, or the destitute to be taken care of, or provide alternative forms of education for those who need it, and those who serve the health needs of the poor, and almost all the effective people I have covered so far are integrate people. People who integrate the less fortunate into the larger human kind, and lift them up from their current status and provide a better status are all integrative minds. Compassion comes from such integrative minds. It is this that made Mahatma Gandhi strive to make India independent. All his life he fought for integration and we are experiencing even today the negative consequences of divisive mindsets.

This chapter is devoted to highlighting such integrative mindsets and draws heavily from my personal experiences.

Divisive Minds

To divide means to separate into parts. It also means to make people disagree, or the existence of disagreement or difference between two or more groups. Division is the act of dividing people into groups.

'Divisive mind' is a tendency or mindset a person has to assign to self or other people, quickly, a group identity (for e.g., caste, community, linguistic, professional, occupational, cultural, social, batch, national, etc.) and anchor subsequent behaviours and decisions on the basis of that identity.

Individuals with a divisive mindset may be called divisive people just like people with an internal locus of control are called internals. Divisive individuals often differentiate and attribute group characteristics to divide people into groups that cause disagreement and competition against one another. By nature division has the potential to create competition and conflict rather than collaboration. Collaboration does not require divisiveness. It is a mindset. All of us perhaps have this mindset. I have it, you have it. It is perhaps our nature. However some live on it and promote it, while others are either beneficiaries of it or victims of it. The sum of results arising out of divisiveness is likely to be less than those that could be obtained without it or with integrative mindsets. While divisiveness in the short term benefits some people, in the long run it hinders overall growth, consumes a lot of resources and increases overheads or transaction costs or process costs.

Integrative Personality

To integrate means to combine parts into a whole. It also means to make some one accepted within a group.

'Integrative personality' is intended to depict a constellation of behaviours that strive towards inclusion, integration, cooperation, emphasis on the whole, and benefits to larger groups of people or entities including humanity at large. A divisive mind gives importance to parts or small groups while an integrative mind focuses on the whole and strives to build the whole and use the strengths of the whole.

The term 'integrative personality' is preferred here to 'integrative mind' to communicate the desirability of developing constellations of qualities that promote integration in the society. Divisive mind is a mindset that can be changed, while integrative personality is a personality trait that can be developed with consciousness and training.

In my view Dr Vikram Sarabhai and Ravi Matthai are two great integrative personalities. Dr Sarabhai built a number of institutions in different fields including space and management. Ravi Matthai promoted the mission of professionalizing management in all sectors of life and actively demonstrated by his own life and example how management should flow through all sectors. Their design of the institutions they were associated with speaks for their integrative mind. Mahatma Gandhi of course is an embodiment of integration. His passion for one India is unparalleled. All corporates working to uplift the local communities where they are located without being asked to do so are also indicating a high degree of integrative tendencies. Any inclusive mind leads to the development of integrative personality.

A divisive mind is a mind that shows tendencies to constantly divide people into smaller groups and use the groups for decision making and various other purposes. Integrative personality is a personality that always gives importance to the whole rather than the parts. The integrative personality thinks of larger goals and larger society while a divisive mind looks after the short-term interests of self or the small group with which it is associated.

A group within the faculty of a university, or an institution opposing the allocation of resources or blocking the growth of another department because it is growing out of proportion, is an outcome of a divisive mindset. The divisive mind always sees the benefits to a part and often ignores the benefits to a larger community. In this case the clients served, the number of people benefited due to services rendered by the fast-growing department, etc. are ignored, and only the benefits availed by the fast-growing department are highlighted, and issues of equity and fairness are brought in. This largely rises out of a divisive mindset. A group of faculty of one institution blocking the collaboration between two institutions as it may bring the second institution fame though together they may be doing a great service to the country is also an example of divisiveness. Divisiveness involves differentiation in terms of 'I' and 'you' and 'ours' and 'theirs'. The term 'we' is interpreted narrowly and boundaries are put and maintained strictly. Jealousy, mistrust, insecurity, intolerance, narrow-mindedness, etc. are perhaps the root causes of divisive mindsets. Sacrifice, trust, strong spiritualistic orientation, self-confidence, respect for each other, empathy, vision and long-term thinking are perhaps associated with integrative personality.

There are a number of stories including Panchatantra stories that tell us a lot about the consequences of divisiveness and the utility of staying together or united. The story of five bulls fighting a lion when they stand united or the story of how a group of birds flew away along with the net and escaped from the bird hunter are all stories that aim at promoting integration.

What Causes Divisiveness?

We are taught from childhood to be divisive. It happens culturally. In some of the Asian cultures divisiveness is high. All Asian cultures have enough reasons or parameters to be divisive. Some of them are more divisive and others less so.

A few years ago I was working in Indonesia as a USAID consultant to the ministry of health. As part of my work I had to take a group of doctors on field trips to teach them task analysis, a technique we introduced to bring more professionalism in the management of health services in Indonesia. Whenever I asked the team to choose a health centre for fieldwork, they would talk among themselves and in five minutes' time come up with their proposal and it was always unanimous. I was amazed at the teamwork and remarked about the same with appreciation to the participants who were doctors. One of the lady doctors narrated to me the following in response to my compliments. I reconstruct this from my memory:

'Professor Rao, I agree that we in Indonesia work like a team. We care for each other and respect each other. There is a lot of sharing that takes place. I also agree that it should strike you as an important part of our culture as I believe that your country which taught us a lot at one time has this one aspect very much lacking in them. I am sorry to say this as I had only one experience which I would like to narrate.'

She continued, 'Professor, a few months ago I was attending a meeting of UNFPA in Bangkok and it was attended by participants from various countries. Each country had two or more delegates. We had delegates from Sri Lanka, Pakistan, Malaysia, Singapore, Bangladesh, the Philippines, Japan and India, etc. One thing I noticed was, whenever a Pakistani spoke about his country his colleague supported it. Whenever a Bangladeshi spoke about his country his colleague from another department supported it. Whether it was a Sri Lankan, or Pakistani or Bangladeshi or Malaysian or a Singaporean, they supported each other in their presentations. However, whenever an Indian spoke the second or third Indian contradicted him and said, "What my colleague said is true in his state, as he comes from Tamil Nadu but the situation is different in my state, as I come from UP," and the third person gave a third story. The convention was filled with contradictions by Indians. Surprisingly the contradictions extended even to fights. We found that by the fourth day the Indian delegates were even staying at different places and coming at different times to the conference. So I understand that in your country teamwork is difficult as every Indian seems to differentiate themselves a lot more than integrate, unlike other countries. We are an integrating nation and we help each other.'

This episode left strong impressions in my mind about how divided we are as a nation. I am deeply pained to see that we have not learnt lessons from our own past and from others and are pursuing policies that divide the nation more than integrate the same.

Integration and Diversity

Having made the above observations, I would like to say that there is perhaps a lot in ancient India that promoted integration and tolerance. We need to discover the same. On the positive side it is amazing that a country as divided as ours still runs well as a democracy. Perhaps we are not using this diversity adequately and divisive policies are taking over and having an overwhelming impact on integrative personalities. Divisiveness is normally intensive and has a larger emotional appeal than integration. Integration becomes a philosophy while divisiveness becomes a reality. Divisiveness serves the short-term interests of certain vocal sections of people and therefore is paid attention. Long-term interests are postponed and integrative personalities get frustrated.

Asian cultures and particularly the Indian cultures seem to be either role-bound or rule-bound. They exhibit 'it is not my job' syndrome. For them the first level of importance is the 'self'. There are of course those who go beyond the self and go for selfless service.

The most enjoyable time I had, where I found work to be smooth and individual dignity maintained from day one, was at IIMA. The symbols that differentiate people and communicate that you work for a team or group have been minimized. Every faculty member gets the same-sized room and every faculty member, irrespective of designation, shares the same secretary and privileges. You charge the same consulting fee irrespective of your designation as per the norms of the institute. Irrespective of whether you are a professor or an assistant professor you are addressed as 'professor'. There are no departments, there are only areas. The term 'area' signifies a broad categorization. You may be a member of more than one area, group or centre. You may also shift your area. All these are organizational mechanisms to create a larger identity and bring down the overheads or transaction costs associated with management, the system they contribute to, and the growth of the organization.

However, there could be other forms of divisiveness even in the best of organizations. For example, teaching staff versus programme staff. The norms for teaching staff were different from those of the administrative staff. It has always been a sore point. However, the administrative staff always took pride in the fact that they belonged to the IIM. The internal processes were designed so that they receive respect for the roles they are performing. For example, the activity head depends a lot on the programme manager as the latter is an embodiment of experience and information. The activity head keeps changing but the programme head is a lot more permanent.

The IIMA experience indicates that it is possible to institute structural mechanisms to promote integrative tendencies. Integrative personality can be developed. Conscious effort and emphasis on super-ordinate goals helps in developing the same.

Win as Much as You Can

The behaviour of most participants in the game of Win as Much as You Can is a good example of the divisive mindset. In this game most often (almost 90 per cent of the time) I found it very easy to develop mistrust. The moment a team is given a label like (A or Red or any other) they saw the other team as an adversary and worked for narrow interests. It is extremely rare to find a team that interprets 'we' as the totality of all four teams. I have used this game hundreds of times in my career but only on one occasion I came across a situation when the groups interpreted 'we' as the total team and started playing win-win. Even in this group it only required four attempts for one of them to try some mischief and once the trust was breached by any one party it never returned. I still remember an occasion when an army officer was trying his best to convince his team to play a win-win game and failing, and then he started crying. This is an integrative personality. The overall score of the group went up but he was very upset that the groups behaved in a divided way. He saw this happening in his country.

What Do I Conclude from All These Experiences?

Divisiveness is the order of the day. It is the easiest thing to divide people. The divisive personality operates perhaps in all of us. We are perhaps socialized in a country like India to be divisive from childhood. Caste identities, community identities, linguistic identities, social identities and groups make us develop an affinity to select groups and deny a larger identity as Indians, perhaps as people. While grouping or dividing people into groups and labelling serves some purpose sometimes, it has an inherent danger of increasing conflicts, decreasing trust, and affecting individual, team and organizational as well as national and global productivity and improvements in quality of life. Divisiveness or labelling needs to be done extremely cautiously. Indian society is filled with such divisive tendencies.

The good news is that post-liberalization it is changing as organizations are becoming less hierarchical, more flexible and competency based rather than group based. Group-based interventions, though well intended, will promote the growth of some groups but inherently at the cost of some other groups and the whole (nation or organization). The development-oriented division needs to be very carefully orchestrated. A lot of education is needed to take care of the negative side-effects of divisiveness. Integrative personalities are needed at the helm of affairs, whether it is in an organization, an institution or in a country.

Developing Integrative Personalities

An integrative personality can be developed and identified. We need to develop more and more integrative personalities.

Cultivating an integrative personality should be a way of life. An integrative personality always thinks long term, sacrifices and enables people to sacrifice short-term interests and small-group interests in favour of long-term interests and larger-group interests. Such long-term and larger-group interests also benefit all those who make sacrifices or postpone immediate gratification for the sake of long-term gratification. Nation building and organization building today requires such integrative personalities more than before as there are more opportunities for growth and avenues for growth.

Some of the methods of developing integrative personalities may include:

1. Continuous education
2. Introspection
3. Self-renewal exercises
4. Collaboration exercises
5. Job rotation
6. Field visits to places of high integration
7. Vision dissemination and training in super-ordinate goals

People need to be educated on the crippling outcomes of divisiveness and the advantages of integrated living. Continuous education should start from schools and extend to training programmes. A large part of team-building exercises taught in high-class B-schools are nothing but attempts to bring and develop an integrative mindset. This education should go on.

People should be encouraged to fight their own divisive tendencies. Many courses on meditation including vipassana, sensitivity training and many other forms preach an integrated approach to life. All religions emphasize the fact that all of us are created by God and we should do our duty rather than spending our life pulling each other down. We should instead try to pull each other up. Introspection should be encouraged.

Organizations and teams should undertake self-renewal exercises. In the corporate sector, in government and in other NGOs there could be self-renewal exercises to examine the extent to which they are working as a team. Self-analysis and self-criticism could be action plans to become more integrating. Self-renewal exercises focus on self-diagnosis of problems and issues and plan mechanisms to improve the current situation. Such renewal exercises throw open a lot of teamwork-related issues and reveal how divisive mindsets work. Through the exercises, they can be brought out into the open and strategies made to strengthen teamwork and collaboration.

It is quite common for organizations to undertake role reversal and image sharing exercises. Such exercises facilitate the working together of people. For example, such exercises were conducted by the author to bring more collaboration in residential schools between the headmaster, housemasters, heads of departments, support staff and students. The recent innovations on whole system transformation are useful tools to bring change.

Job rotations help a lot to build integrative mindsets. When a person works in a department for a short or long period of time, they understand the purpose of the department and also appreciate the difficulties faced by the department. When the person moves from one department to another or one region to another through job rotation, there is a lot of scope to develop an integrative personality.

Visiting other places also helps to develop insights into the way one should work. Field visits to benchmarkable institutions or best practice institutions to emulate them help a good deal.

It has also been found that vision-sharing exercises and participative vision developing exercises also build an integrating outlook among people.

Are You Divisive or Integrative? Assess Yourself

Choose among the following 'a' or 'b' for each item

1.   Whenever I interact with people I look at their
     a. Background
     b. Qualifications
2.   Whenever I interact with people I look at their
     a. State from which he/she comes
     b. Competence
3.   In the choice of my team members I prefer to have people from
     a. All from one gender (males or females)
     b. A mix of both genders
4.   In the choice of my team members I prefer to have people from
     a. From good background
     b. With good qualifications
5.   In the choice of my team members I prefer to have people from
     a. Institutions known for their education like IIMs, IITs, RITs, etc.
     b. Hard-working people from any institutions
6.   In the choice of my team members I prefer to have people from
     a. Certain regions of the country known for their sincerity
     b. Anywhere depending on the sincerity of the person
7.   Poor performers are mostly from
     a. Lower-caste groups
     b. Anywhere
8.   Poor performers in jobs are mostly from
     a. Upper-caste groups and rich families
     b. Anywhere

9. High performers in work are from
   a. Good colleges
   b. Any college
10. In carrying out the work assigned to them employees should give preference first to
    a. Their job assignment
    b. Their departmental interests
11. In carrying out the work assigned to them employees should give preference first to
    a. Departmental goals
    b. Organizational goals
12. For political parties to be successful they should work more for their
    a. Party
    b. Country
13. MLAs and MPs should put first the interests of their
    a. Party
    b. Country
14. In carrying out the work assigned to them employees should give preference first to
    a. Company
    b. Customer
15. In carrying out the work assigned to them employees should give preference first to
    a. The instructions of the boss
    b. What is good for the company
16. MLAs and MPs should put first the interests of their
    a. Party
    b. Poor people
17. MLAs and MPs should put first the interests of their
    a. Constituency
    b. National interests

18. MLAs and MPs should put first the interests of their
    a. State
    b. Country
19. People from certain religious backgrounds are more likely
    to be terrorists
    a. Agree
    b. Disagree
20. People from certain religious backgrounds are more likely
    to promote communalism
    a. Agree
    b. Disagree
21. People from certain religious backgrounds are less likely to
    be nationalists
    a. Agree
    b. Disagree
22. People from certain parts of the country are lazier than others
    a. Agree
    b. Disagree
23. Specialist doctors should treat only their area of specialization
    rather than look at other areas
    a. Agree
    b. Disagree
24. Doctors who prescribe alternative medicine are not
    competent in their field
    a. Agree
    b. Disagree
25. Companies investing in developing CSR activities on
    their own
    a. Have a hidden agenda
    b. Are helping the nation
26. The trouble with our government is that there are too
    many departments that divide their work while people
    need an integrated look
    a. Disagree
    b. Agree

27. In doing my job I am always conscious of the larger goals of my job rather than the outcome of the specific activity
    a. Disagree
    b. Agree

28. I am always conscious of the larger interests of my country in my thoughts and actions
    a. Disagree
    b. Agree

29. In my view
    a. Corruption can never be eliminated in our country
    b. If we all put in effort it can be minimized

30. I strongly support abolishing caste-based preferences and barriers
    a. No
    b. Yes

31. I strongly support religion-based preferences for any jobs
    a. Yes
    b. No

32. I honour my commitments
    a. Rarely or never
    b. Mostly or almost always

33. I speak my heart
    a. Rarely or never
    b. Mostly or almost always

Count the number of 'b's in your responses. All 'b's tend to indicate an integrating orientation and 'a's indicates divisive tendencies. Notionally if you score above 25, you have a strong tendency to be integrative, and scores closer to or lower than 17 indicate more divisive tendencies. Discuss your results in a group, have a debate and come up with ways to make tools on integrating personalities as opposed to divisive minds.

Epilogue

After having completed the book, as I shared my thoughts with friends and fellow professionals, some of them suggested that I should have included sports persons, musicians and other professions in my study too. This book is not meant to be an exhaustive canvas to survey all professions. The professions that I have picked have been taken as illustrative rather than being an exhaustive coverage. One of the suggestions made was on film actors. My long-time friend and colleague at IIMA, Kandaswamy Bharathan, who teaches the first-ever course on the business of film industry in IIMs suggested that while film actors were effective in portraying characters, film directors played a much greater role in the industry in terms of effectiveness. Film directors like K. Balachander, Rama Naidu and others created those very films that had inspiring stories and characters which shaped and even transformed the lives of thousands of viewers in their lifetime. In addition, they created many hundreds of actors who became stars on the power of their acting performances! In a career spanning almost five decades, Balachander created more than fifty actors in Tamil and Telugu cinema including the superstars of south like Kamal Haasan, Rajinikanth, Chiranjeevi, Sridevi, Jayaprada and many others. Ramoji Rao, the founder of the Eenadu publications had a vision of creating the largest film city in the world and built Ramoji Film City in Hyderabad which attracts film-makers from all over the world. In the Hindi film industry, the late Yash Chopra was a highly effective person who created memorable films and effective actors. These super effective persons could use their talent to transform the society through meaningful films and provide benefits that lasted for a long time. These names are illustrative; there are many others who can be called as 'effective' or 'super effective' based on their contribution to the society. I have not covered film directors here. There are production houses, like the Kavithalayaa Productions, which have been symbolic in nurturing and promoting many artists.

However, when one looks at the world of music, dance and other fields, the formulations made in this book stand out clearly. In every field there are many effective people who have excelled in their given area and served others for long years; very effective people who have spread their talent and multiplied it through others; and super effective people who have made and are making lasting impact through the institutions that they have built.

In the field of dance, many great dancers—Mrinalini Sarabhai and Mallika Sarabhai who direct Darpana Academy of Performing Arts in Ahmedabad; Sonal Mansingh (Odissi) who founded the Centre for Indian Classical Dances; Protima Bedi (Odissi) who started her own dance school in Mumbai (Odissi Dance Centre); Chitra Visweswaran who established the Chidambaram Academy of Performing Arts (CAPA) for imparting professional training sessions and music therapy treatment for disabled children; Anita Ratnam (Kathakali) who authored and publishes books and magazines to promote art—stand out as super effective persons. The legendary dancer Birju Maharaj (Kathak) has popularized dance and taught at many places and continues to disseminate his knowledge and skills even at this late age. Vempati Chinna Satyam established the Kuchipudi Art Academy in Madras in 1963 and has taught over thousand students the intricate styles and techniques of Kuchipudi dance. He also founded in Vizag the Kuchipudi Kalakshetra in 1985. Raja and Radha Reddy, the world famous dance couple, established an institution for dance called Natya Tarangini in 1976 and popularized the traditional dance form of Kuchipudi among the younger generations. Dancers like Kelucharan Mahapatra (Odissi) trained and left behind a number of their disciples.

In the field of music, musicians like A.R. Rahman (K.M. Music Conservatory) and Shankar Mahadevan (Shankar Mahadevan Academy) have created music schools to develop and disseminate their talent.

In the field of sports, similar examples can be found. For instance, Pullela Gopichand established Gopichand Badminton Academy and has delivered champions from India. Prakash Padukone established a badminton academy, Prakash Padukone Badminton Academy, and trained a large number of people. Vijay Amritraj has established Britannia Amritraj Tennis Academy in Chennai and Virendra Sehwag started a cricket academy. Geet Sethi and Prakash Padukone together also promote an institution called the Olympic Gold Quest.

All these examples only support the theory with which we started. Very effective people influence and nurture many others (thousands and millions benefit from them) and super effective people take institutional forms to build talent all around which is the best capital one can give to the country and to the world at large.

Some other friends suggested that a book like this will be greatly informative to our NRI friends. I hope this will encourage many of those living in other countries and are passionate about giving back to India some of their talent, to choose institutional forms that will enable them to make a lasting impact. There are a few examples in recent times where super

effective people like Sam Pitroda have established institutions
that have left a remarkable and lasting impact on the country's
talent development. If this book inspires a few of them to
become more effective in nurturing and spreading their talent a
good purpose will be served.

Suggested Reading

Bansal, Rashmi, *I Have a Dream*, Westland and Tranquebar Press, Chennai, 2011

Bansal, Rashmi, *Stay Hungry Stay Foolish*, CIIE, IIMA, Ahmedabad, 2008

Bansal, Rashmi, *Connect the Dots*, Ekalavya Foundation, Ahmedabad, 2010

Bansal, Rashmi, *Follow Every Rainbow: The Inspiring Story of 25 Women Entrepreneurs Whose Gentle Touch Created Strong Business*, Westland, Chennai, 2013

Bhogle, Anita and Harsha Bhogle, *Winning: Learning from Sport for Managers*, Westland, Chennai, 2011

Centre for Social Initiatives and Management Publications, 'Unsung Beacons: Stories of People for Whom Humanity Matters', volumes 1 and 2, Chennai

Chary, S.N., *Business Gurus Speak*, Macmillan, New Delhi, 2002

Chengavalli, Venkat, *Manage Live and Lead: An Inspirational Guide for Managers, Students and Citizens*, Sampark (www.samparkpublishing.com), Calcutta, 2014

Chopra, Shaili, *The Leaders Look Back*, Random House, New Delhi, 2014

Church, Peter, *Added Value: The Life Stories of Indian Business Leaders*, The Lotus Collection, Roli Books Limited, 2010

Harpanahalli, Deenanath and Mamta Vengunta, *Awakening: There Is a Leader in Every One of Us*, the Atlanta Foundation, Hyderabad, 2013

Kenkare, Suresh, *The Charismatic Leader: Creating Effective New Age Leaders with Self Mastery and Global Vision*, Platinum Press, Mumbai, 2014

Kher, Anupam, *The Best Thing about You Is You*, Hay House India, New Delhi, 2012

Kidwai, Naina Lal, *30 Women in Power: Their Voices, Their Stories*, Rupa Publications, New Delhi, 2015

Nilekeni, Rohini , *The Uncommon Ground: Dialogues Between Business and Social Leaders*, Penguin Books, New Delhi, 2011

Pandit, Srinivasan, *Thought Leaders: The Source Code of Exceptional Managers and Entrepreneurs*, Tata McGraw-Hill, New Delhi, 2001

Paul, Samuel, *A Life and Its Lessons: Memoirs*, Public Affairs Centre, 2012

Pitroda, Sam, with David Chanoff, *Dreaming Big: My Journey to Connect India*, Portfolio Penguin, Gurgaon, 2015

Portfolio Penguin, *The Portfolio Book of Great Indian Business Stories: Riveting Tales of Business Leaders and Their Times*, Penguin Books, New Delhi

Pota, Vikas, *India Inc.: How India's Top Ten Entrepreneurs are Winning Globally*, Nicholas Brealey, London, 2010

Rao, T. V., *100 Managers in Action*, Tata McGraw-Hill, New Delhi, 2012

Rao, T. V., *Managers Who Make a Difference*, New Delhi, IIMA Books, Random House, 2010

Sharma, Robin, *The Leadership Wisdom*, Jaico, Mumbai, 2003

Zenger, John H. and Joseph Folkman, *The Extraordinary Leader*, Tata McGraw-Hill edition, New Delhi, 2002

Acknowledgements

The first person I would like to acknowledge is Radhika Marwah from Penguin Random House for her perseverance and encouragement from the time the idea of this book was conceptualized till the end. She was the main source of the idea and operationalization of this book. My grateful thanks to Paloma Dutta who worked very hard, even spending personal time, and meticulously edited to get this book out on time.

An important person to whom I owe a lot and without whom this book would not have been possible is my wife, Jaya, who supported me in all possible ways for several weeks, days and nights, supplying patiently, smilingly and appreciatively all the energy I needed to do this work.

Four people who helped me in collecting some of the case studies and interviewing the effective people mentioned in this book are: Debangshu Bhattacherjee, Akash Kaushik and Yash Raj, summer trainees from Xavier University, Bhubaneswar; and Nidhi Rai of Nirma University. Siddharth Saxena, Academic Associate from IIM Ahmedabad, assisted me at times to get some case leads.

I wish to thank each and every one of the fifty and more case studies whom we featured for giving their time for interviews and responding to our questionnaire. The case histories mentioned in this book are the best acknowledgements of their contribution.

The time for writing this book has come from my company TVRLS, besides my family. I thank my team members at TVRLS for all the support they have given directly by funding the summer trainees, and indirectly in many other ways.

I thank N.R. Narayana Murthy, Prof. M.R. Rao, Harsha Bhogle and K.K. Nohria for taking time to scan pre-publication chapters of this book and offering their comments.

I also thank the Penguin Random House team, including Vaishnavi Singh, for all the support they have provided to bring this book to this shape and making it available to the readers in record time.

For the 2024 edition

I am grateful to the world-renowned coach and thinker, Dr Marshall Goldsmith, for reviewing this book, and Kate Rocha, editor and project manager at Marshall Goldsmith Inc., for facilitating the same. I am deeply thankful to Satya Nadella, CEO Microsoft, for readily agreeing to comment on the book, Greg Shaw, his co-author, and Caitlin McCabe, chief of staff at Microsoft Chairman and CEO's Office for enabling the connection. I thank Dhananjay Singh, director general, National HRD Network; Akhilesh Jukareddy, founder, Street Cause; and D.N. Venkatesh, dean, Goa Institute of Management, for their inputs on effective youth and students. I once again thank Radhika Marwah and Saba Nehal from Penguin Random House India for working on this edition and incorporating various changes swiftly.

Notes

Chapter 2

1. Source: http://pib.nic.in/newsite/PrintRelease.aspx?relid=116952http://pib.nic.in/newsite/PrintRelease.aspx?relid=116952

2. Source: http://www.asianheartinstitute.org/cardiac-surgery/dr-ramakanta-panda.html

3. Source: http://www.iloveindia.com/indian-heroes/doctors.htm

4. Source: http://www.iloveindia.com/indian-heroes/doctors.html downloaded on 17 July 2015

5. (With inputs from Smitha Rao in Bangalore)
   Sources: http://timesofindia.indiatimes.com/home/sunday-times/The-super-doctors/articleshow/911822.cms downloaded on 17 July 2015. Details of Naresh Trehan downloaded from file:///C:/Users/User/Downloads/Medanta-The%20Medicity.html on 20 July 2015

6. Source: http://timesofindia.indiatimes.com/home/sunday-times/The-super-doctors/articleshow/911822.cms

7. Source: https://en.wikipedia.org/wiki/Murugappa_Channaveerappa_Modi
   downloaded on 20 July 2015

8. Source: http://orkut.google.com/c33998380-t40e00335142f2c58.html

9. Source: http://indiatoday.intoday.in/story/dr-m-c-modi-one-man-crusade-against-blindness-in-karnataka/1/329273.html

10. Sources: http://www.iammadeinindia.com/?p=1020

http://online.wsj.com/news/articles/SB12587589288
7958111?mod=slideshow_overlay_mod&mg=reno64-
wsj&url=http%3A%2F%2Fonline.wsj.com%2Farticle%2F
SB125875892887958111.html%3Fmod%3Dslideshow_overlay_mod
http://www.economist.com/node/15879359
http://www.business-standard.com/article/companies/
devi-shetty-to-leverage-frugal-engineering-for-medical-
fraternity-112082800078_1.html
http://articles.economictimes.indiatimes.com/2012-09-19/
news/33952757_1_hospital-chain-narayana-hrudayalaya-cardiac-
surgery

11. Source: http://www.outlookbusiness.com/special-edition/
    super-seven/a-mighty-heart-1111

12. Source: http://www.economist.com/node/15879359

13. Sources: http://www.mapsofindia.com/who-is-who/health-
    life-style/dr-pratap-c-reddy.html
    http://socaltelugu.com/index.php?option=com_content&tas
    k=view&id=1971&Itemid=75http://www.caclubindia.com/
    forum/-indian-business-tycoons--52260.asp
    http://www.chennaionline.com/personality/interview_with_
    pratap01.aspx

14. Source: http://www.reddysociety.com/?q=node/11

15. Sudhir Chowdhary, *Financial Express*, 19 July 2010, downloaded
    on 24 July 2015: http://archive.financialexpress.com/news/
    magic-of-medanta/648319/0

16. This was stated by Dr Trehan when he was in Patna to
    attend the joint conference of the Bihar chapter of Indian
    Cardiological Society and Eastern India Interventional
    Cardiology Conclave.

17. Extension motivation means a desire to extend one's self to serve
    others. This term, coined by Udai Pareek, denotes an internal
    state of mind that pushes one to have a high service motivation
    and an internal desire to help others.

Chapter 3

1. Source: http://www.anupamkherfoundation.org/
2. Source: http://www.actorprepares.net/
3. Source: https://in.lifestyle.yahoo.com/7-things-women-learn-kangana-ranauts-queen-003225890.html
4. Source: http://www.rediff.com/getahead/slide-show/slide-show-1-specials-10-lessons-to-learn-from-amitabh-bachchan/20121011.htm#11
5. Source: http://businessofcinema.com/bollywood_hollywood_photos/5-lessons-learnt-aamir-khans-pk/186885
6. Source: http://techstory.in/aamir-khan/
7. Source: https://en.wikipedia.org/wiki/Uday_Kiran
8. Source: https://en.wikipedia.org/wiki/Silk_Smitha
9. Source: http://www.rangashankara.org/home/rangatest/

Chapter 4

1. Khanna, Inderjit, 'Importance of Values in Civil Service, in HRD and Institution Building for Development' edited by T.V. Rao and Anil Khandelwal, New Delhi, Sage, Udai Pareek Memorial volume (forthcoming).
2. Source: http://www.arvindguptatoys.com/arvindgupta/anil-bordia-tribute.pdf
3. Page 282, 2nd Administrative Reforms Commission (ARC) Report
   rc.gov.in/10th/ARC_10thReport_Ch16.pdf
4. 2nd Administrative Reforms Commission (ARC) Report
   rc.gov.in/10th/ARC_10thReport_Ch16.pdf
5. Source: https://en.wikipedia.org/wiki/Vinod_Rai
6. Source: https://en.wikipedia.org/wiki/D._R._Mehta
7. Sources: http://www.goodnewsindia.com/Pages/content/transitions/tihar.html

http://www.kiranbedi.com/digmizoram.htm

http://www.essortment.com/all/kiranbediindia_rloe.htm

http://www.kiranbedi.com/trafficchief.htm

http://www.kiranbedi.com/narcotics.htm

http://www.kiranbedi.com/moralforce.htm

http://www.kiranbedi.com/igchandigarh.htm

http://www.blogbharti.com/kuffir/india/kiran-bedi-not-retired/

8. Source: http://www.truthlabs.org/aboutus.php

9. Source: http://articles.economictimes.indiatimes.com/2015-07-19/news/64595304_1_vyapam-entrance-exam-national-investigation-agency

10. Source: https://en.wikipedia.org/wiki/Jayaprakash_Narayan_(Lok_Satta)

11. Source: http://news.bbc.co.uk/2/hi/8550548.stm

12. Source: http://www.sunday-guardian.com/investigation/nadella-is-still-rooted-to-his-village-in-ap

13. Role efficacy is a term used to describe the strong and positive perceptions and feelings with which roles are performed effectively by the role incumbent. For a discussion of this concept see *Managers Who Make a Difference* by T.V. Rao: IIMA Books, Random House, 2010.

Chapter 5

1. Sources: http://www.thesmartceo.in/starting-up/for-a-greater-cause.html
    http://www.thesmartceo.in/starting-up/for-a-greater-cause.html

2. References downloaded as on: 25 April 2015
    http://www.amitabhshah.com/about/
    http://yourstory.com/2009/03/amitabh-shah-founder-yuva-unstoppable/
    http://www.yuvaunstoppable.org/yuva/about.php

http://www.fpa2.com/details_actualite.php?idactu=3521&lang=en
http://www.asianage.com/people/changing-world-437
http://bama.ua.edu/~rotaract/members_2001-2002.htm

Chapter 6

1. Sources: http://siteresources.worldbank.org/
   INTEMPOWERMENT/Resources/14832_Bangalore-web.pdf
   http://siteresources.worldbank.org/INTEMPOWERMENT/
   Resources/14832_Bangalore-web.pdf

2. Sources:
   Samuel Paul: A Life and Its Lessons, Public Affairs Centre, Bangalore,
   2012 http://www.thinktankinitiative.org/think-tanks/PAC
   https://en.wikipedia.org/wiki/Samuel_Paul

3. Source: www.businessweekasia.com

4. Source: http://www.sristi.org/cms/en/our_network

5. Source: http://www.iloveindia.com/indian-heroes/shanta-
   sinha.html#Kq5R3dVwhXCyFq6H.99
   down loaded on 29 July 2015

6. Source: http://www.rmaf.org.ph/newrmaf/main/awardees/
   awardee/biography/34

7. Source: https://en.wikipedia.org/wiki/Kiran_Seth

8. Sources: http://www.spicmacay.com/articles/interview-dr-
   kiran-seth
   https://www.facebook.com/DrKiranSeth/info?tab=page_info)

9. Source: *I Have a Dream* by Rashmi Bansal, Westland, Chennai,
   2011, and personal discussion with the author in July 2015

10. Source: http://www.adrindia.org/about-adr/mission-and-vision

11. Source: http://www.adrindia.org/content/adr-daksh-
    national-voters-survey-0

12. Source: http://www.isb.edu/faculty/ramachandran/Institution_
    Building.html

13. Source: https://en.wikipedia.org/wiki/M._S._Pillai

See more at: http://www.scmld.org/Leadership%20is%20not%20 just%20Knowing%20or%20Doing.html#sthash.vsr21VnV.dpuf

14. Source: http://www.scmld.org/Leadership%20is%20not%20 just%20Knowing%20or%20Doing.html

Chapter 7

1. Source: http://www.rediff.com/news/2001/may/21spec.htm

2. Comments by Anupam Hazra: http://employmentnews.gov.in/ Current_Prospects_Social_Work_India.asp

3. Sources: http://aidindia.org/main/content/view/812/399
   http://india.ashoka.org/fellow/balaji-sampath
   http://www.ahaguru.com/
   http://cerebrate.in/thekkady2010/2012/03/15/dr-balaji-sampath/
   http://www.thehindu.com/features/education/a-new-jee-avatar/article3907060.ece
   http://www.arvindguptatoys.com/arvindgupta/balaji-physics.pdf

4. Source: http://www.wise-qatar.org/rajani-paranjpe

Chapter 8

1. Pareek, Udai, *Effective Organizations: Beyond Management to Institution Building,* Oxford and IBH, New Delhi, 2002.

2. Lala, R.M. *In Search of Leadership,* Vision Books, New Delhi, 1986.

3. Pandit, Srinivas, *Thought Leaders,* Tata McGraw-Hill, New Delhi, 2001.

4. Chary, S.N., *Business Gurus Speak,* Macmillan India, New Delhi, 2002.

5. Zenger, J.H. and Joseph Folkman, *The Extraordinary Leader: Turning Good Managers into Great Leaders,* Tata McGraw-Hill, New Delhi, 2003.

6. Rao, T.V., *100 Managers in Action*, Tata McGraw-Hill, New Delhi, 2012.

7. Source: http://www.iibf.org.in/documents/RKTalwar MemoLecture2011.pdf
   downloaded on 10-8-2015

8. Source: http://www.iibf.org.in/documents/RKTalwar MemoLecture2011.pdf
   downloaded on 10-8-2015

9. Source: http://www.iibf.org.in/documents/RKTalwar MemoLecture2011.pdf

10. Source: http://alphaideas.in/2012/06/25/sbis-greatest-chairman/
    downloaded on 10 August 2015

11. Source: http://alphaideas.in/2012/06/25/sbis-greatest-chairman/
    downloaded on 10 August 2015

12. S. Parthasarathy, the author, a former managing director of SBI's Overseas Operations, in *The Hindu Businessline*, 7 May 2002. Downloaded on 10 August 2015: http://www.thehindubusinessline.com/2002/05/07/stories/2002050700040900.htm)

13. Pota, Vikas, *India Inc. How India's Top Ten Entrepreneurs Are Winning Globally*, Nicholas Brealey Publishing, 2010.

14. Pota, Vikas, *India Inc. How India's Top Ten Entrepreneurs Are Winning Globally*, Nicholas Brealey Publishing, 2010.

15. Sources: http://www.thehumanfactor.in/01082009/storyd.asp?sid=395&pageno=1
    http://www.shrmindia.org/interview-close-anil-khandelwal
    http://www.ibscdc.org/Case_Studies/MultiMedia/MMA0004.htm
    http://www.ibscdc.org/executiveinterviews/Q&A_with_Dr_Anil_K_Khandelwal_3.htm
    http://74.125.153.132/search?q=cache%3Ai1xMRgoCZaMJ%3Awww.bankingfrontiers.com%2F2007%2Fstory_0701_01.pdf+contact+details+of+anil+khandelwal+of+bank+of+baro

16. Source: https://en.wikipedia.org/wiki/Homi_J._Bhabha
17. Source: http://www.knowqout.com/science-technology/contributions-of-5-famous-indian-scientists-and-quotes/4/
18. Source: http://www.india-seminar.com/2012/638/638_in_memoriam.htm
19. Source: https://en.wikipedia.org/wiki/C._N._R._Rao
20. Source: http://timesofindia.indiatimes.com/india/CNR-Rao-gets-Japans-highest-civilian-award/articleshow/47736301.cms
21. Sources: http://www.abdulkalam.nic.in/profile.html
    http://www.abdulkalam.com/kalam/jsp/display_content.jsp?menuid=22&menuname=Dr.Kalam%F6s%20Page&linkid=130&linkname=Profile&content=896&columnno=0&starts=0&menu_image=-&myheader=My%20Mother&titlename=null
    https://knowledge.wharton.upenn.edu/article/former-president-apj-abdul-kalam-a-leader-should-know-how-to-manage-failure/
    http://content.time.com/time/world/article/0,8599,2040386,00.html
    http://timesofindia.indiatimes.com/city/chennai/Kalam-tells-students-to-follow-their-heart/articleshow/4689858.cms?referral=PM
    http://www.thehindu.com/books/books-authors/failed-in-my-dream-of-becoming-pilot-abdul-kalam-in-new-book/article5035287.ece
22. A quote from Kalam's autobiography.

Chapter 10

1. Johari Window details: See Rao, T.V., and Chawla, Nandini, Performance Management Skills workbook, Bangalore, T.V. Rao Learning Systems, 2013, p. 44. http://hsc.uwe.ac.uk/practicesupport/Default.aspx?pageid=121
2. Rao, T.V. and Pareek, Udai, *Changing Teacher Behaviour through Feedback*, Hyderabad, ICFAI Press, 2006.

3. Rao, T.V. and Charu Sharma, *100 Managers in Action*, New Delhi, Tata McGrawHill, 2012. This book presents several case studies of effective managers and their experiences with 360 Degree Feedback.

4. Goleman, Daniel, *Working with Emotional Intelligence,* Bantam Books, 1998.

5. Singh, Dalip, *Emotional Intelligence at Work*, Response Books, Sage Publications Inc, 2001.

6. Source: http://www.usb.ac.za/Common/Pdfs/usb-career-center/articles/HBR%20Managing%20Oneself.pdf
(also see *Managing Self* by Peter Drucker, *Harvard Business Review*, January 2005)

7. Rao, T.V. and Rao, Raju, *The Power of 360 Degree Feedback: The India Way for Leadership Effectiveness*, New Delhi, Sage Publications, 2014.

8. Rao, T.V. and Charu Sharma, *100 Managers in Action*, New Delhi, Tata McGrawhill, 2012.

9. Personal Effectiveness Manuals: Ahmedabad, T.V. Rao Learning Systems Pvt. Ltd.
Pareek, Udai, *Training Instruments in HRD & OD*, Second Edition, New Delhi, Tata McGraw-Hill Publishing Company Limited, 2002.

Chapter 11

1. Source: http://humanscience.wikia.com/wiki/Personal_values

2. Sources: http://www.oaj.fi/cs/oaj/The%20Values%20lying%20behind%20a%20Teacher%20s%20Professional%20Ethics
https://www.utdanningsforbundet.no/upload/1/L%C3%A6rerprof_etiske_plattform_a4_engelsk_31.10.12.pdf
http://link.springer.com/chapter/10.1007%2F978-90-481-8675-4_4#page-2

3. Source: http://www.quora.com/What-are-some-moral-values-one-can-learn-from-celebrities

4. Source: http://www.quora.com/What-are-some-moral-values-one-can-learn-from-celebrities.

5. Source: http://www.quora.com/What-are-some-moral-values-one-can-learn-from-celebrities

6. Source: http://www.scoopwhoop.com/entertainment/rajinikanth-heroism/

7. Pareek, Udai, *Effective Organizations*, New Delhi, Oxford & IBH, 2002.

8. Sources: http://www.akshayatrust.org/krishnan.php
    http://edition.cnn.com/2010/LIVING/04/01/cnnheroes.krishnan.hunger/
    http://www.oddeitycentral.com/news/narayanan-krishnan-the-selfless-hero-helping-indias-helpless.html

9. Source: *Managers Who Make a Difference*, IIMA Books, New Delhi, Random House, 2010.

10. Like this many other insensitive conversations and experiments to change such behaviour have been discussed in a report called 'Family Planning Worker Client Transactions' brought out by T.V. Rao at Indian Institute of Management, Ahmedabad, in 1975 as a part of the World Bank sponsored project in UP.

Chapter 12

1. Source: http://www.nursingtimes.net/whats-new-in-nursing/management/can-you-measure-compassion/5000543.article

2. Quoted by Helen Mooney in her article, 'Can you measure compassion', 21 April 2009, see: http://www.nursingtimes.net/whats-new-in-nursing/management/can-you-measure-compassion/5000543.article

3. Source: http://www.huffingtonpost.com/dr-fran-grace/measuring-the-immeasurabl_b_6407794.html?ir=India&adsSiteOverride=in

4. Source: https://www.academia.edu/3215500/Compassion_Measurement_Tool_-_CMT

Compassion website: http://www.compassionspace.com/. The CMT was developed by W. David Hoisington.

5. Source: https://www.academia.edu/3215500/Compassion_Measurement_Tool_-_CMT

6. See for details: https://www.cafonline.org/docs/default-source/about-us-publications/caf_wgi2014_report_1555awebfinal.pdf

7. Source: http://www.dnaindia.com/india/report-india-ranks-106th-in-list-of-145-countries-for-world-giving-index-2144238 (down loaded on 12-11-2015).

8. McClelland, David C., *Power the Inner Experience*: New York, John Wiley, 1976.

9. For a discussion on the concepts of Extension Motivation and training programmes on extension motivation see: *'HRD, OD and Institution Building: Essays In memory of Udai Pareek'* edited by T.V. Rao and Anil Khandelwal, New Delhi, Sage, 2016.

Chapter 13

1. Source: http://www.inc.com/jeff-haden/9-essential-habits-of-remarkably-effective-people.html

2. Source: http://www.inc.com/jeff-haden/9-essential-habits-of-remarkably-effective-people.html

3. Source: http://www.inc.com/jeff-haden/8-habits-of-remarkably-successful-people.html
   Things Remarkably Successful People Do.
   The most successful people in business work differently. See what they do—and why it works.

4. McClelland, David C., and D.G. Winter, *Motivating Economic Achievement*, Free Press, New York, 1969.

5. Pareek, Udai, *Training Instruments in HRD*, Taat McGrawHill, New Delhi, 2002.

6. See in *Stay Hungry Stay Foolish* by Rashmi Bansal, pp 18–27, CIIE: IIM Ahmedabad, 2008.

7. Cited above.

8. Chary, S.N., *Business Gurus Speak*, Macmillan, New Delhi, 2002. Collins, J.C. and J.I. Porras, 'Building Your Company's Vision', *Harvard Business Review*, Sep–Oct, pp 65–77.

9. Pota, Vikas, *India Inc. How India's Top Ten Entrepreneurs Are Winning Globally*, Nicholas Brealey, London, 2010.

Chapter 15

1. Pareek, Udai, *Effective Organisations: Beyond Management to Institution Building*, Oxford & IBH, New Delhi, 2002.

2. *Institution Building: Experiences, Learnings and Challenges* by Professor Kavil Ramachandran.
   This article is a modified version of the speech delivered at the N.J. Yasaswy Memorial Lecture on 8 October 2013, IFHE Campus, Hyderabad. Specially modified for the Udai Pareek Memorial volume.

3. *Nurturing Excellence: Indian Institute of Management*, edited by Vijaya Sherry Chand and T.V. Rao, Macmillan, New Delhi, 2010.

4. *Ahmedabad Management Association: Annual Report 2014–15*, AMA, Ahmedabad.

5. Source: http://www.narayanahealth.org/about-us/nh-overview

6. Source: http://www.actorprepares.net/about-us/alumnus/

7. Source: https://en.wikipedia.org/wiki/Mamidipudi_Venkata-rangaiya_Foundation

8. Source: http://mvfindia.in/impact/

9. Source: http://mvfindia.in/wp-content/uploads/2014/07/Victoria-Measles-Finished-MVF-Report.pdf

10. Source: http://www.pacindia.org/annualreports/content/35

11. Source: http://jaipurfoot.org/our_reach/index.html#.Vc2K6bKqqko

Chapter 16

1. From a paper presented at the NAOP Conference at IIT, Mumbai.

Scan QR code to access the
Penguin Random House India website